"Despite being in Marketing and Bus[iness for]
30 years and having read a plethora o[f books, I have never]
encountered a book that offers suc[h practical advice for]
navigating a rebrand in a controlled, calm and structured way. I can
easily see myself revisiting this book to re-read it. My wish for you is
that it becomes well-used, with highlighted pages and turned-over
corners by anyone serious about leveraging brand strategies to win
customer loyalty and drive growth."

Lucy Murphy, Chief Growth Officer, Linklaters LLP

"*Rebrand Right* was the perfect resource for me and my team as we
approached the first rebrand of our organization's 25-year history –
we had to get it right. Fairley and Robb have written a masterpiece that
makes you want to take notes, look back on pages and then get back
to your team feeling inspired and ready to take action. A must-read for
every marketer!"

**Kayci Evans, Head of Marketing and
Brand Partnerships, Evil Geniuses**

"Effective marketing teams need a playbook to establish a common
understanding of brand strategy, but more critically, a practical
methodology to implement the grand vision. This is the first book to
do both and will be indispensable regardless of product category or size
of organization."

Anil Gadre, Advisor and Chief Marketing Officer

"As a CEO, navigating branding can be daunting, but Sarah and
Rachel's book makes it straightforward and enjoyable. Their decades
of experience are distilled into a clear, relatable guide that's simple for
non-marketing leaders like myself yet packed with real-world examples
that have given me lots to think about. This is a must-read for anyone
looking to elevate their brand with confidence and ease."

Philip Randerson, Chief Executive Officer, HotTopics

"I found the book authentic, engaging, practical and something that I
can see myself, my team, implementing at so many different parts of
our own business, brand and marketing journey. It was so refreshing
for me to read this – you made me fall in love with the concepts of
marketing all over again! Thank you! *Rebrand Right* is a practical guide
for every marketer – doesn't matter if you are the CMO or someone who
has just started your career in marketing, this is a must-read for you! I
would encourage everyone around the leadership table, irrespective of

the letters that follow the 'C' to read this book to better understand the impact that marketing can play in the company's growth."

**Mehul Kapadia, Chief Revenue Officer,
Locus and Non-Executive Director, England Boxing**

"Professionally I've had three decades working in the world of brand management. Every now and again you need to look yourself in the mirror and this book is the perfect catalyst for that. The techniques, process, templates and ideas are proven in the cauldron of delivery, with pragmatic insights for the experienced or those starting for the first time."

**Duncan Daines, Chief Marketing Officer &
Group Head of Engagement, Gama Aviation**

"If you're looking for a definitive guide on how to help your business grow through effective brand management and strategy, then look no further."

Pete Markey, Chief Marketing Officer, Boots

"*Rebrand Right* provides a step-by-step guide to rebranding the organisation in a cohesive, holistic way, encompassing all elements of the business in support of business growth. A must for any business bookshelf!"

Amanda Jobbins, Chief Marketing Officer, Vodafone Business

"This is bite-size best practice for marketing that you will go back to again and again because it's timeless."

**Abigail Comber, Vice President Marketing
and Customer Experience, HCA Healthcare**

"If you want the definitive guide to developing and implementing a brand strategy that will deliver for your company this is it! Practical yet strategic. The perfect combination!"

Sarah Tookey, Marketing Leader

"The book may be called *Rebrand Right* but it contains what you need to define, build, and maintain a brand that resonates with your key audiences and delivers on business objectives. It smartly deflects the immediacy of the bells and whistles of fancy brand redos for a drains-up company review that equips marketing with data for informed decisions and a flexible lattice for action and results. This is one of those essential 'book buddies' you'll keep with you for a very long time."

Leo McCloskey, Chief Marketing Officer, Echodyne Corp

"Rebrands can be painful, underwhelming affairs. This book will help you avoid common pitfalls and give your rebrand the best possible chance of succeeding."
Nick Liddell, Brand Strategist, Founder of Baron Sauvage

"This book demystifies the rebranding process, offering clear, actionable advice that any business can implement to drive brand growth. A must-read for anyone serious about brand strategy."
Jack Parsons, UK's Chief Youth Officer

"This book goes beyond just exploring the theory of rebranding; it dives deep into the practical, transformative steps that can reshape how both internal and external audiences perceive and connect with your organization. It sheds light on the cognitive and emotional processes that drive brand loyalty and trust, offering invaluable insights into how rebranding can create a more powerful and resonant brand experience."
Shallu Behar-Sheehan, Chief Marketing Officer, Non-Executive Director and Trustee

"This is the book I wish I'd had earlier in my career. It's a faultless, fool proof guide to anyone considering a rebrand, brimming with obvious experience, relatable examples and practical steps to follow."
Marisa Kacary, Chief Marketing Officer, WilsonHCG

"Rachel and Sarah generously share their deep experience to make the rest of us better at brand. They show that brand is more than logos, fonts and colours – it's the people who live the brand each and every day. If you're new to brand, this book will help you to be successful on your first try. If you already do brand, it will make you better and more successful."
Mark Baker, Fractional Chief Marketing Officer

"*Rebrand Right* cuts through the jargon, hype and proprietary garbage so often used when branding is mentioned. The result is the first hands-on, practical how-to book I've come across. You really could pick this book up and use it to drive your rebrand step-to-step. It provides really good advice on how and when to work with agencies and how to brief them, and presents a powerful alternative to brand guideline documents that suffocate brands more than they enliven them."
Dom Hawes, Chief Executive Officer Selby Anderson and Host of Unicorny podcast

"If you are considering a rebrand, this book is your new north star. Rachel and Sarah have expertly distilled their vast knowledge and expertise, along with the best insights from countless industry resources, into a hands-on, step-by-step guide. (They have done all the hard work so you don't have to.) It's practical yet deeply insightful, offering a clear path through the often murky waters of brand transformation. From a client's perspective, this book is absolutely vital. It's the resource I wish I'd had during my time at VWG and one I would have eagerly shared with my peers. It educates without patronizing, arming you with the knowledge to show you've done your homework and can challenge your agencies constructively. It bridges the – often wide – gap between agency expertise and client understanding, setting the stage for more effective, aligned and ultimately successful rebranding efforts. Whether you're a seasoned marketer or new to the branding game, this book is invaluable for your professional toolkit."

Silke Anderson, Fractional Chief Marketing Officer

"When it comes to rebranding, no one is more qualified than Sarah and Rachel. Brand is often misunderstood, lost between business strategy and marketing. But successful branding is what sets an average business apart from an exceptional one. This book is your guide to getting it right! With experience in more rebrands than anyone I know, Sarah and Rachel have distilled their extensive knowledge into this invaluable playbook on mastering brand."

Alisha Lyndon, Chief Executive Officer, Momentum ITSMA

"This book is long overdue. For many years now, the world of branding has become complex, long-winded and confusing, leaving marketers with little or no confidence in what they are doing, resulting in many simply winging it. This book is the definitive guide to know when, why and how to rebrand. It's written in a way that is easy to understand and follow, leaving you chomping at the bit to get started. From a creative perspective it has challenged me to completely rethink the way I approach brand identity creation. This book is simply a must have for anyone involved in branding."

Sean Cornell, Founder and Chief Creator, Wonderment

"There's no better book to help you lean into the power of what marketing can do to help drive the growth of a business. Must read!"

Gabie Boko, Chief Marketing Officer, NetApp

*How to refresh
your brand and marketing
to grow your business*

RE-
BRAND
RIGHT

RACHEL FAIRLEY　　　　SARAH ROBB

First published in Great Britain by Practical Inspiration Publishing, 2025

© Rachel Fairley and Sarah Robb, 2025

The moral rights of the author have been asserted.

ISBN 978-1-78860-721-6 (paperback)
      978-1-78860-720-9 (hardback)
      978-1-78860-723-0 (epub)
      978-1-78860-722-3 (Kindle)

All rights reserved. This book, or any portion thereof, may not be reproduced without the express written permission of the author.

Every effort has been made to trace copyright holders and to obtain their permission for the use of copyright material. The publisher apologizes for any errors or omissions and would be grateful if notified of any corrections that should be incorporated in future reprints or editions of this book.

EU GPSR representative: LOGOS EUROPE, 9 rue Nicolas Poussin, LA ROCHELLE 17000, France Contact@logoseurope.eu

Want to bulk-buy copies of this book for your team and colleagues? We can customize the content and co-brand *Rebrand Right* to suit your business's needs.

Please email info@practicalinspiration.com for more details.

For Donovan, Kabe and Orson. Gracias a la vida.

Rachel

For Andy, Thomas, Sadie and my parents. You are my sunshine.

Sarah

Contents

Introduction xiii

PART 1: DIAGNOSE 1

1: The four factors of brand growth 3

What you will know by the end of this chapter:

- How your rebrand can drive growth
- The four factors that influence brand growth
- The things you control that contribute to those factors
- Examples of brands that made changes to those factors and turned around their growth
- How to quickly assess where your brand stands today against these factors

2: Brand diagnosis 33

What you will know by the end of this chapter:

- What to include in a brand diagnosis
- How to structure a brand diagnosis presentation
- How to sequence and run the research required
- How to approach it when you're squeezed on budget or time
- How to share the diagnosis and get buy-in to next steps

PART 2: DEFINE 57

3: Brand strategy 59

What you will know by the end of this chapter:

- What a brand strategy is
- The difference and connection between brand and business strategy
- How to get beyond the jargon and frameworks
- The questions you need to answer in a brand strategy and how to answer them
- How to present a brand strategy and get buy-in

4: Brand identity 91

What you will know by the end of this chapter:

- When brand identity change is necessary
- What makes a good brand identity
- Why you need distinctive brand assets
- What assets you can create and change
- How to work out what to do with yours
- How to brief and run a brand identity process
- Whether to test the brand identity and how
- Why to say no to guidelines – a better way to ensure your brand identity gets used in the optimal way

PART 3: DELIVER 119

5: Implementation, engagement and experience 121

What you will know by the end of this chapter:

- How to implement the brand strategy and identity
- How to get leadership engaged and spearheading the change
- How to launch well

- The core implementation team and partnerships you need
- How to make the brand how we do things, every day
- What to focus on in the employee and buyer experiences
- How to inspire everyone to use the brand identity cohesively and creatively
- How to know you've done a good job

6: Brand to demand – your marketing strategy and plan 141

What you will know by the end of this chapter:

- The eight decisions you need to take in your marketing strategy
- The eight components of an integrated marketing plan that drives brand to demand
- How to invest your budget effectively
- How to sequence and test the work
- The make-or-break elements

7: Measurement and momentum 175

What you will know by the end of the chapter:

- The three reasons to measure
- How to listen for what's changing in the market
- How to know whether your brand CRED is improving
- How to measure the impact of your rebrand and marketing plan
- How to adjust implementation plans and keep up momentum
- How to measure *your* progress

About the authors 191

Authors' acknowledgements 193

Notes 195

Index 209

Introduction

"We need to refresh our brand."
"People don't know who we are."
"We need to become one brand, one company."
"The brand isn't working. It needs to drive more growth for us. You need to fix it."

Have you heard any of these recently?

Are you wondering where to start and what it takes to rebrand successfully? Maybe you're already under pressure to make changes but you're not sure they're the right ones. Perhaps you just have a hunch that your brand isn't performing as strongly as it could and needs a rethink.

Welcome. You're in the right place. This is your guide on how to refresh your brand and marketing to drive business growth. How to rebrand right.

We're Rachel and Sarah. We've worked on rebrands for over two decades. Close to 100 of them, for some of the world's most famous global brands, promising start-ups and wonderful charities. Across the A–Z of industries, from accounting firms to zoos. But in the first decade, we didn't always feel certain that we were making the right changes to drive growth.

Like you, we read and loved the books that share the theory, principles and 'laws' of brand and marketing. We read of others' rebrand successes in glossy stories and dry case studies. But none of them told us exactly how to run a rebrand and most of them were so full of jargon they made our heads hurt. So we blindly followed agency advice – leading changes without really knowing whether they were going to make a difference.

Perhaps you feel a bit like this too? A third of all marketers rate their brand-building knowledge as average to very poor and only 21% rate it as excellent.[1] In our hundreds of conversations with marketers and consultants we know that imposter syndrome is really common, even for people in senior roles. And leading a rebrand can trigger it badly. Because rebranding is not just about doing better marketing or redoing a brand identity. It requires a holistic marketing skillset. You have to know what actually needs to change and why, then identify the right brand strategy and implement it across the whole organization, experiences and marketing. This is what rebranding means to us and this is what we cover in this book. Whether you call it reinvigorating, refreshing, revolutionizing or rejuvenating the brand, it's about making positive changes to your brand to drive business growth.

It has taken working at the world's largest brand consultancy, as marketing leaders, chief brand officers and advisors to some of the world's most valuable companies for us to work out how to do this properly. What we always wanted was a clear, step-by-step process identifying why and how to make successful changes to a brand within a business, with all its politics, idiosyncrasies and resistance to change. But we've had to figure this out ourselves – the hard way.

We hope this book will make it easier for you. It's really clear and practical. It draws on our breadth and depth of brand-building experience and the latest thought-leadership on how brands actually help businesses grow. It shares specific and practical details of how to diagnose, define and deliver your rebrand.

This requires detective work at the beginning to understand what's not working well for your brand. We've seen this diagnosis stage missed out in so many rebrands. Changes to strategy, identity, messaging, marketing and experiences are made without really knowing what problem they're trying to solve. Then you face that disappointing conversation with your chief executive officer (CEO) and chief financial officer (CFO) that the investments made "weren't worth it". Let's avoid that together.

In Part 1, 'Diagnose', we'll explain the four factors you control that underpin how brand changes drive growth (chapter 1) and how to diagnose what's really wrong with your brand and get buy-in for the changes that are needed (chapter 2).

In Part 2, 'Define', we'll talk through how to create a brand strategy that ditches the jargon and actually engages the organization (chapter 3) and how to develop a brand identity that stands out, inspires creativity and works cohesively (chapter 4).

In Part 3, 'Deliver', we explain how to engage the whole organization to improve the buyer and employee experience to align with the brand strategy (chapter 5) and how to align your marketing strategy with the brand diagnosis and strategy, driving from brand to demand to revenue (chapter 6). We finish with how to measure the impact of your changes and sustain momentum by feeding your plans and making improvements (chapter 7).

Our methodology is agnostic: business to business, business to consumer, whatever your size, markets, countries, industry or niche. You might be working on an 80-year-old brand making a category pivot. You may have a relatively new brand and you're now ready to brand 'properly' following an influx of investment. You could be in the aftermath of a merger and acquisition (M&A) maelstrom – trying to make the most of the brands you own and get a group of separate companies and people to work collaboratively. Perhaps you're experiencing a worrying sales decline, or seeing talent leave in droves. Refreshing your brand can help in all of these instances. We share stories of turnarounds throughout the book, the right shortcuts to take when time and money are limited and 30 'watch-outs' to help you avoid common mistakes.

What you won't find in this book is us telling you that you've been getting it wrong. We're not fans of 'experts' who berate marketers for not being good at their jobs. We all do the best we can with the knowledge we have. When we talk about rebranding right, we mean helping you get it right for your brand.

We want you to feel in control and fully equipped to lead this. We want you to know how to guide the organization through the changes needed to achieve the growth you're looking for. We want you to know how to get leadership buy-in on the journey and how to get the best from your agency relationships. We want you to understand what 'good' looks like and what 'realistic results' are. We want you in the boardroom confidently justifying the changes and investment needed. Because here's the thing – you should be one of the most valuable people in that room. Brands contribute on average 19.5% and in many cases well over 50% of enterprise value.[2] The impact you can have with a rebrand is huge.

So, grab a coffee and your highlighter. Get ready to rebrand right.

PART 1
DIAGNOSE

Chapter 1
The four factors of brand growth

What you will know by the end of this chapter

- How your rebrand can drive growth
- The four factors that influence brand growth
- The things you control that contribute to those factors
- Examples of brands that made changes to those factors and turned around their growth
- How to quickly assess where your brand stands today against these factors

What's the point of a rebrand? To refresh, reinvigorate, modernize, streamline and make your brand and marketing more effective, right? But that's not what you're measured on. Rebrands should lead to growth. They're instigated to help turnaround a decline or create more momentum. So, we have to start with an understanding of how brands actually impact growth.

The great news is that we know a lot about how and why brands grow, thanks to data and insight companies like Kantar; academic institutions like the Ehrenberg-Bass Institute; industry bodies such as WARC and the IPA; neuroscientists, behavioural economists and behavioural scientists; and agencies and individuals within them. Their work, plus our experience, has helped us to identify the four ways rebrands drive growth and the four factors that underpin them. This chapter takes you through them one by one.

We're going to explain this as simply as possible. Much of the great work referenced above is academic and jargon-heavy. It's hard to trawl through words like *predisposition, penetration, salience, affinity, heuristics* and *mental availability*. Throughout this book we ditch the jargon and express all of what we know in clear, simple language. It helps us and the brands we work with and we hope it will help you too.

How your rebrand can drive growth

There are four main ways that rebrands can drive growth:

1. Attracting more buyers
2. Stretching into new sources of revenue
3. Supporting price increases
4. Improving employee engagement, decision-making and cohesive working practices across the business

1. Attracting more buyers

For most brands, the biggest shifts in growth come from attracting new buyers. It's often called *improving acquisition* or *penetration*. Yes, you need to also retain loyal ones and continue to cross and upsell, but data shows this isn't enough to drive growth. You need to get more new or infrequent buyers to buy from your brand.[3]

2. Stretching into new sources of revenue

Large brands can see sales plateau. If this is the case, you may also need to 'stretch' your brand to grow. Stretching your brand can include redefining your strategy and innovating from there, expanding your range, getting more people to think of your brand across more usage occasions, becoming associated with more of the reasons why people come shopping, or undertaking Mergers and Acquisitions (M&A) activity.

3. Supporting price increases

Growth in profits can come from raising your prices. Rebranding can create higher 'perceived value'; a belief that something is worth the price being asked for. As Rory Sutherland states, "Value resides not in the thing itself, but in the minds of those who value it. You can therefore create (or destroy) value in two ways – either by changing the thing or by changing minds about what it is."[4] Rebranding can be all about changing minds to increase value. While marketers don't always get to set the price, they play a critical role in framing it.

All three of these ways to grow require you to get into the minds of your buyers. In Kantar's words it's how to "predispose more people"[5] to feel like your brand is the right choice. For Professor Byron Sharp of the Ehrenberg-Bass Institute for Marketing Science, it's "how to get a brand thought of, more often, in more buying situations".[6] To justify a price increase you'll need people to believe your brand is worth the price you're asking. And none of this can happen if no one pays attention to your brand in the first place.

The problem is that people aren't eagerly looking out for your brand. Most people don't think that much about brands and they're bombarded with options. So, what happens? Well, our brains don't slowly analyse the rational pros and cons of 30,000 brands within a supermarket and then make a choice.[7] We'd never get out of there! The human mind has shortcuts (called heuristics) that overtake our rational decision-making process.[8] The harsh reality is that we screen out most of the options and have 'go-to' brands that we grab (if we're in the supermarket), or that become our shortlist of options if we're making a bigger purchase (like buying enterprise software).

Imagine we gave you money to buy a new car. Which brand of car would you buy? We bet you came up with an answer, or at least a shortlist, almost immediately. And we bet there were at least 20 well-known car brands that weren't on the list, despite them having high-performing models in the same price bracket. In fact, research shows that even with cars – a significant, expensive purchase that you might assume people consider more than other categories – the number of brands on most people's shortlist is just two.[9]

What happens, without us realizing, is that we tap into a mental network in our minds about car brands. Neuroscience proves that brands exist in our minds as a complex network of nodes that hold pieces of information. What's in these nodes? Associations and assets. Associations are the words, thoughts and feelings people have about a brand. Assets are the multi-sensory things that help people recognize a brand: like logos, colours, shapes, taglines, music.

These networks of associations and assets are important. IPSOS research showed that, "Brands with richer and more positive mental networks provide more mental cues at the moment of choice and, as a result, have larger market shares."[10] Kantar explain, "strong and consistent" connections, "predispose more people to buy the brand more often". Brands with strong predisposition have nine times more volume share, people will pay twice the price for them and they're twice as likely to grow value share in the future than brands with weaker predisposition.[11]

So how do we build strong predisposition? Or in simpler terms: how do we make people feel our brand is the right choice? Three ways: relevance, ease and difference.

According to Kantar, in a study across 54 markets and 540 categories, relevance (what they call being 'Meaningful') and difference together determine about 60% of how predisposed people are to buy a brand.[12] The other 40% is down to how 'salient' your brand is. Salience is about making sure you're automatically thought of in a buying situation. We call it being 'easy to mind'. And this ties back to those mental networks of associations and assets again. Professor Byron Sharp in *How Brands Grow* points out, "Brand salience depends on… the quantity and quality of memory links to and from a brand."[13]

So, your job is to make people feel your brand is the right choice, by building relevant and different associations and assets in their minds, and to ensure your brand comes to mind easily when they're ready to buy.

We suspect you've heard about the importance of relevance, ease and difference before. They've been talked about for decades, though not always explained clearly. But there's one other critical thing that can make or break the success of your brand: that's being cohesive.

Cohesiveness can make or break your rebrand. You can spend weeks identifying the new associations you want to build, then hear the CEO refer to the old ones in the next all-employee meeting. You can spend thousands on a brand agency to develop the right assets but fail to engage marketing colleagues to confidently use them. You can communicate the associations you want to be known for, but not engage employees to deliver them through the buyer and employee experience. As Denise Lee Yohn states: "What separates a truly great brand from one that is merely good is whether the company is capable of a complete and thorough implementation of its brand as its business."[14]

Being cohesive is a theme you'll find in all our chapters, but it's not one you'll read about in many other brand and marketing books. That's because you only really know how important it is when you've worked on a lot of rebrands and seen some succeed and others fail. You have to consider all four factors – cohesion, relevance, ease and difference – to rebrand successfully.

No one person can drive cohesion alone – you need to engage all employees in the journey. And the great news is this can be another mechanism for growth.

4. Improving employee engagement, decision-making and cohesive working practices across the business

The reason many businesses want to refresh their brand can be nothing to do with buyers. It's to generate a sense of cohesion across disparate business units, often as a result of playing M&A 'Pacman' and failing to properly integrate new entities that have been acquired. There's a common internal communications theme we've seen across almost every large business we've worked with: "One ____"; One EY, One Siemens, One Team, One Dream… When book value trumps market capitalization (i.e. when the whole of the business is valued at less than the sum of its parts), investors can clamour to break a business apart, returning value to shareholders. Refreshing a brand can be a way to inspire and engage all employees around a common goal, stimulate more cohesion across working practices and collaboration across the business to improve performance. It can improve employee engagement, satisfaction and retention and make the whole worth more than the sum of its parts.

Your rebrand remit

Your rebrand remit as a marketer will likely sit under one or more of these four growth challenges: how to get more people to choose to buy your brand; how to know where to stretch to; how to create stronger perceived value; and/or how to improve engagement and help the business work more 'as one'.

Here's a summary of how rebrands can drive growth, what you need buyers to feel and do, and the four factors that enable this. This is our model of brand and marketing success, based on our experience and the latest brand and marketing studies, neuroscience and behavioural economics. It helps you structure your diagnosis on where things are going wrong and right for your brand and what your focus should be.

Table 1: Your rebrand remit

YOUR REBRAND REMIT			
Rebrands can drive growth by:			
Attracting more buyers	Stretching into new sources of revenue	Supporting price increases by increasing perceived value	Improving engagement and performance
Buyers need to:			
<ul><li>Feel like your brand is the right choice (be predisposed to buy you)</li><li>Think of you more often, in more buying situations</li><li>Believe you're worth the price you're asking</li><li>Notice you</li></ul>			
To achieve this, your brand needs to be:			
Cohesive	**Relevant**	**Easy**	**Different**

> **Little note:** in this book we refer to the people who already or could potentially buy from your brand as buyers, not customers, clients, consumers or target audience. We understand that buyers buy from multiple brands. They are never only our brand's customers. We cannot take their custom for granted. Calling them buyers stops us from becoming complacent. It encourages us to consider carefully what they experience compared to new buyers, for example in the pricing they are offered for repeat purchasing. For non-profits we realize that the growth challenges and audiences are slightly different. But the four factors – being cohesive, relevant, easy and different – apply just as much.

The four factors that influence brand growth and the things you control that contribute to those factors

Let's go deeper into the four factors that can ensure your rebrand achieves your growth objective. We'll explain the ways in which your brand can become more **C**ohesive, **R**elevant, **E**asy and **D**ifferent, or 'CRED' for short, and give you a quick way to assess your brand CRED at the end of the chapter.

Factor 1: Be cohesive

Here's the most important point about cohesion: a brand is not just about design, communications and marketing; it's about everyone and everything working well together – across the product, pricing, buyer and employee experience. Michael Eisner, former CEO of Disney, explains, "A brand is a living entity – and it is enriched or undermined cumulatively over time, the product of a thousand small gestures."[15] We suspect you know this, but perhaps you struggle to get the organization to embrace this. We hope to help you get over this hurdle.

When we talk about cohesiveness we mean:

- things, touchpoints, experiences and people being united and working together effectively
- your brand feeling like it has a sense of consistency over time, but allowing for appropriate flexibility to stay fresh.

Where it starts is by ensuring that a change of management does not de facto mean a change in brand. As a marketing leader, you need to remember that you're a short-term caretaker on a brand's long journey. But we've met new chief marketing officers (CMOs) who've spent only 30 minutes of their first three months in the job understanding the previous work on the brand, then the next 30 months pulling it apart and redoing the identity to make their mark. When there's no brand diagnosis, no depth of understanding of the equity within the current associations and assets or of the problem you need to solve, the brand identity is often the first casualty. So many get wilfully disregarded and redone, throwing away familiarity, trust and being easier to buy in the process. This can provoke a customer outcry and a significant decline in sales (search the cautionary tales about Tropicana, Gap and Mastercard).

Instead, take a leaf out of Boots CMO Pete Markey's playbook:

> *Often as CMOs we can come into the business and think we need to do a scorched earth strategy. I can start again. Wrong approach… What I've always done is gone, where's the brilliance? Where's the magic happening? Who's doing it and how do we get more of it? We fuse the sort of greatest hits, the best of Boots of yesteryear, but we're progressive for the future…*[16]

As a brand leader you're a guardian of something that will outlast your tenure. It's important to retain the relevant equity and familiarity in your brand associations and assets so they continue to tie together all of your marketing and experiences and help your brand be recognized.

Think how much McDonald's has changed over the years: new ways to order and pay, redesigned restaurants, new products, etc. But the brand identity still feels familiar to the point where the name is not needed on an ad because the assets are so strong we know it's McDonald's. Difference and freshness can be introduced in ways other than changing the brand identity.

But when we talk about building a cohesive brand it's about much more than identity. It's about:

- Balance. Understanding, respecting and building on long-term historical associations that are still relevant, while ensuring you understand the future priorities of the business so your brand strategy reflects a balance of familiarity and stretch.
- Not treating Marketing and HR, and brand strategy and culture, as separate and unrelated. The inside needs to deliver what's promised outside. Buyers and employees are indelibly connected. And there is no 'employer brand'! Just like there's no 'shareholder brand'. There is one brand and different people it needs to appeal to.
- Ensuring your HR policies and practices, and not just your marketing, are aligned with the brand strategy.
- Putting practices in place that get things done effectively. Not through dogmatic policing but through equipping, inspiring and galvanizing the team.
- Integrating brand marketing and demand generation campaigns and ensuring you have the right long-/short-term balance and investment.

- Making sure your executions are effective in different countries and in the latest cultural contexts.

- Understanding what sits at a brand level and what sits at a product/service level and how identity, naming and marketing should reflect this.

- Your perceived value being in line with your price.

- Not making promises you don't intend to keep. There are too many examples of brands being called out by customers, or regulators for not living up to their promises. Telling the truth and acting with integrity are a must for all brands.

We'll cover how to be cohesive in every chapter, since, as Anil Gadre, advisor and CMO identifies, "Being cohesive is the essential ingredient, like salt in a recipe."[17]

Factor 2: Be relevant

There are six different facets to being relevant: being relevant to the right people, to what they care about, to cultural and market shifts, to more need states or usage occasions, to each stage of the buyer's journey and why they come shopping. So often, a rebrand intended to stem a decline in sales doesn't need a logo change, it needs a relevance change.

Be relevant – to the right people

Remember we said that brands can grow by attracting as many new buyers as possible? And that most of them will likely be buyers of your competitors and light buyers of the category (read Professor Byron Sharp's *How Brands Grow* if you want to understand this more deeply). Maybe your rebrand problem is that you're not relevant to, or reaching enough people. Perhaps you're targeting so narrowly that you just can't reach that next stage of growth?

It certainly was the step-change for Nike. In 1988 they realized that they were limiting their growth by talking only to elite athletes. The brief that led to the infamous slogan, 'Just Do It', read:

> *We need to grow this brand beyond its purist core…. It's time to widen the access point. We need to capture a more complete spectrum of the rewards for sports and fitness.*[18]

Contrast this, as authors Greg Creed and Ken Muench do with the brand Brooks. Brooks have narrowed their buyer focus over the years to just runners. Their annual sales in 2019 were just under US$750m. Nike's at the same point? Just under US$40bn.[19]

The other people you need your brand to be relevant to are employees. We've seen so many experts advising businesses on brand without any consideration or involvement of employees beyond the leadership team they're presenting to. This is a mistake.

The associations you want to build in buyers' minds about your brand have to be understood and delivered from the inside, by the people shaping the buyer experience. Brands are built through every experience or interaction a buyer has that the brand name is attached to. The product, customer service call centres, the person at the checkout, the waiter at breakfast, the person fixing your boiler, the sales team. We'll talk about how to engage employees at every step in the process.

Besides buyers and employees there are other people who matter in building brands. It helps to identify and reach influential voices that guide buyers in your category whether that's leading wine masters, industry analysts, travel agents, pharmacists, or TikTok beauty influencers. They're not just valuable as potential promoters of your brand but also as a source of insight for your brand strategy development.

The other people who can make or break your brand's success are shareholders, investors, non-execs and, most importantly, the C-suite. The CEO and CFO in particular have to understand why what you're doing is important to their priorities so you can secure the investment you need to make a difference. You have to make this rebrand process relevant to them. We'll be addressing how to do this at different points throughout the book.

For now, know that relevance starts with people – and not just your buyers.

Be relevant – to what people care about

Brands are the bridge between what you want people to buy, join or invest money or time in, and why anyone is going to care about it. Those associations you're trying to build have to be created with this in mind. This is basic brand strategy, but it's amazing how so many organizations still get it wrong. They talk only about the company, the product, the functions and features, but not about why anyone will care. Here's a couple of quick examples so you get what we mean.

Case study: Dove

Relevance for Dove started with the belief (following conversations with women in their ad agency) that the beauty industry made women feel ugly.[20] Further research then showed that "Only 4% of women around the world consider themselves beautiful" and "6 out of 10 girls are so concerned with the way they look, that they actually opt out of participating fully in daily life, from swimming and playing sports, to visiting the doctor, going to school or even just offering their opinions."[21]

Their brand idea of 'honest/real beauty', which launched with 'The Campaign for Real Beauty' in 2004, is highly relevant to the women and girls they are targeting. It's intended to create a more positive relationship with the way they look, helping to raise their self-esteem and realize their potential. Identifying this relevant insight into what their buyer was struggling with has seen this soap brand worth US$200m in the early 1990s grow into a brand estimated to be worth nearly US$6.5bn by 2023.[22]

Case study: Nike

Nike began marketing their brand focusing heavily on the product. Each monthly ad in *Runner's World* simply introduced a new model.[23] But in 1977 there was no new model to focus on, so the brief became "write something that makes runners feel good about themselves".[24] The resulting ad showed a solitary, distant runner on a long road, with the line, 'There is no finish line.' On seeing it, runners sent letters to Nike thanking them for supporting them and used the ad as a poster on their walls at home.

From that point onwards, Nike shifted their focus from purely pushing product to putting themselves in their buyer's shoes. Nike inspired runners with their understanding of the runner's experience: emotion, grit and sweat. They defined a mission that still stands today:

> "To bring inspiration and innovation to every athlete*
> in the world.
>
> *If you have a body, you're an athlete"[25]

This shift inspired the famous line, 'Just Do It', but it started with this effort to become more relevant on an emotional level – to simply express "something that will make runners feel good about themselves."

Case study: Salesforce

Salesforce prioritized deeply understanding and connecting with their buyers from the beginning. They didn't just spend time with customers, but also queried prospects on why they didn't choose Salesforce and spent time with the larger buyers to identify the functionality they needed.[26]

In 2016 they were running an event for a particular set of buyers they'd worked closely with and wanted a name for them. Sarah Franklin, leader of their developer relations team identified them as 'Trailblazers' based on a common mindset they shared. They were people who "want to learn, to better the world, they aren't afraid to explore, they crave innovation and enjoy solving problems and also giving back".[27]

What Salesforce promise today is that "everyone who wants to innovate and deliver success with Salesforce can be a Trailblazer. Whether you're just starting your career or reskilling for a new one. Whether you're an experienced leader helping teams to deliver digital transformation or an entrepreneur building business apps."[28] They have built a powerful sense of identity and community with their buyers built on a relevant mindset, not just a relevant product.

Ensuring you've got the right answer for your brand starts by identifying what your buyers care about that they can get, feel or experience by using your brand. You need something clear and simple that you can build the brand around over the long-term.

Be relevant – to cultural and market shifts
Cultural codes are the shared meanings, expectations, values and norms that influence what buyers find relevant. These can change, both in society and in buyer expectations. Organizations can see a steady sales decline as they continue to build brand associations that are based on a set of beliefs that buyers just don't share or value as much anymore.

Case study: Taco Bell

Taco Bell turned around a precipitous decline in sales with a successful rebrand built on a better understanding of the cultural codes that were relevant to their buyers. They had been operating on an outdated belief that their buyers saw food as fuel. This served them well in the 1990s, but by 2011 their buyer research unearthed that "food wasn't just fuel anymore… a brand had to offer a memorable, shareable experience".[29] To reflect this cultural shift the CEO's motto became "From fuel to experience. He had it printed up and put on everyone's desks. In addition to being affordable, delicious, and convenient, Taco Bell would become surprising, exciting and shareable."[30] Note the words 'in addition'. This rebrand didn't throw out strong brand associations, it added more relevant ones in line with cultural shifts. With this change in focus for the brand, innovations in their product and marketing followed: the Doritos Locos Taco, the Quesalupa and campaigns like 'Live Más'. Sales increased year on year.

> ## Case Study: IBM
>
> IBM provides an example of aligning brand associations with market shifts. In 2008 the world was becoming more interconnected, data-driven and complex. IBM rebranded around the idea of 'building a smarter planet', positioning themselves as a leader in helping the world create systems that were smarter, across industries like energy, water, traffic and education. This brilliant synergy between the business changes they were making, and the brand and marketing work that helped people understand why they should care, significantly helped expand IBM's market potential and won their agency, Ogilvy, the Gold Effie.[31]

Be relevant – stretch into more need states or usage occasions

Has your growth stopped because you've reached a ceiling? Is this really your rebrand problem? Maybe it's time to stretch a little. There are different ways to stretch. The obvious one is through introducing new variants, sizes or formats to your core product or increasing the number of products or services your brand offers. Kantar have identified that Consumer Packaged Goods "brand leaders offer more choices than their closest rivals. In fact, range is almost essential to gaining dominance in a category."[32]

Another way to stretch is through M&A activity, as Duncan Daines, CMO and Group Head of Engagement at Gamma Aviation, told us:

> *In order for me to generate organic growth in market share... it could take me 15, 20 years in order to gain, I don't know, maybe 2 or 3 points of market share. If I'm lucky. At the same time, I have competitors who are trying to churn me out of my positions... It becomes more opportune to then look at M&A strategy rather than doing the hard yards of traditional organic marketing.*[33]

Stretch growth can start with a redefinition of what you are and what you do. IBM redefined their remit from an e-business technology solutions company to one focused on building a smarter planet. Baileys reframed their product from being a cream liquor drunk mainly at Christmas to an adult treat. The shift dramatically boosted its consumption occasions and increased global sales by 32% in five years. Sheila Cunningham, Baileys' Global Head of Planning, Diageo reminds us that "the brands we shepherd needn't be forever beholden to the conventions of the categories they came from. We should be confident in future-proofing our brands through finding more dynamic category contexts to play within.[34]

Watch-out #1: Know when to stretch, when to steal

One of the things that really influences whether you should stretch your range is your brand's size. Kantar's research indicates that less is more for smaller brands, as 80% of their growth will come from stealing buyers from competitors within the category, rather than extending their range of products, whereas bigger brands get only one in ten of their incremental sales in this way, so adding different products or services can be a helpful investment for growth.[35] The shorthand is: steal if you're small, stretch if you're big!

Watch-out #2: Don't assume you need a new brand

There can be a tendency internally to believe that stretching means you need a new brand rather than a new variant, but there's great efficiencies of scale that come with managing one versus multiple brands so approach this carefully. Even highly bespoke, completely different products can still sit under the same brand as long as the brand strategy is expansive enough to contain them. Amazon is a classic example. And just look at many of the luxury hotels in the Corinthia Group, Four Seasons or Rosewood collection. Different buildings, locations, restaurants, spaces, penthouses, spas, gyms, bars, yet still the same brand.

Be relevant – at each stage of the buyer's journey

You need to understand how relevant your brand is at each stage of the buyer's journey. You can do this using a 'brand funnel'. Figure 1 shows a typical example. You're gauging the movement of buyers from top of funnel (ToFu), which covers awareness, familiarity and favourability, to bottom of funnel (BoFu): consideration and intention to purchase.

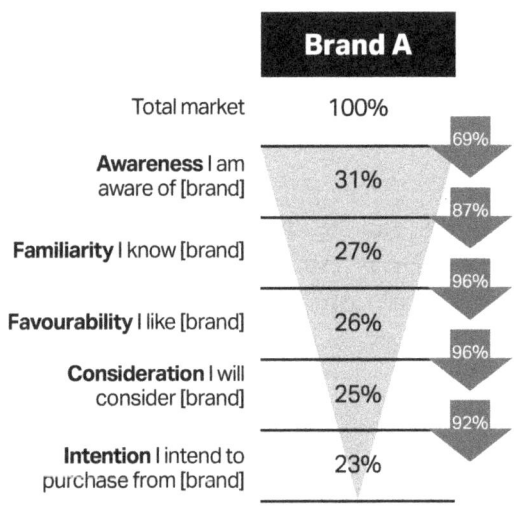

Figure 1: Brand funnel

This starts with 100% of the market and shows how many buyers convert from one stage to another (arrows on right) and what percentage of buyers are left at any given stage; it's known as a true funnel.

You get these numbers from quantitative research by asking buyers to name brands that come to mind spontaneously for the category (unpromoted or unaided awareness), before prompting them with brand names to ask if they are aware of them (aided awareness). For the brands they are aware of, you then ask them how familiar they are with these brands. For those they are familiar with you ask if they would consider them. And for those they'd consider, you ask whether they would buy from that brand within a specific timeframe (typically much longer for B2B than B2C). All of this is best understood relative to competition and category norms. What you're looking for are the 'leaks' in the funnel, where the percentages in the arrows drop considerably.

Can you see where the problems lie in Figure 1? In this example, the main 'leak' is at awareness; 69% of buyers don't know the brand's name. But there is also a leak at familiarity. Awareness, familiarity and favourability are usually built together, so we'd focus on increasing awareness and associations with buyers. The further down the funnel the leak appears, the more we'd focus on making the brand easy to buy.

There is debate on whether a buyer's journey is linear, or circular, or personal to them. People also argue that you need funnels customized for your brand. We say you have to start somewhere. Customize your funnel in year two, because it takes thought and buy-in and won't make the difference in year one. Brand funnels tell you where to focus your efforts and spend. They are invaluable in conversations with leaders to show the size and shape of the challenge ahead.

Be relevant – to why your buyer comes shopping
The final aspect of relevance is understanding the reasons your buyer comes shopping and ensuring your brand is associated with them. This is also crucial to becoming easy to mind.

Factor 3: Be easy

Be easy – to mind
Being easy to mind means automatically popping into people's minds in a buying situation. Professor Byron Sharp calls being easy to mind "mental availability".[36] It's also called 'brand salience'. We saw from Kantar research that it explains 40% of 'predisposition' – helping buyers feel that your brand is the right choice. And we know that this is key to growth.

So, how do you become easy to mind? You've got to become associated with the reasons people come shopping. These are often called usage occasions, need states or 'Category Entry Points' (CEPs).[37]

Here's an example: you're on holiday, sitting in the blazing sunshine at a beach bar. You really fancy a beer. Corona wants to be the brand that pops into your head. They've spent years building up associations and assets that link Corona to that moment and that feeling, even if you're in a sweaty bar in town rather than that idyllic beach.

Here's some other Category Entry Points and some of the brands that we associate with them:

> I want to repaint my living room. Out comes the Farrow & Ball palette.

I'm desperate for a better night's sleep. I need to get some Ambien.

I'm planning a romantic city-break. Well, everyone knows that Paris is the city of love.

I want our business to run better. SAP are known for that.

I want the best way to set up accounts for my new business. Sage are known for helping small businesses.

I want to stay where the stars do in London. Corinthia or Claridge's are the places to be.

What's important to realize is that both the number of Category Entry Points your brand is associated with and the strength of this connection are key. The fewer Category Entry Points a customer associates with a brand, the greater the likelihood of choosing another brand. And being associated with a lot of them increases the likelihood that your brand will be the one selected when a buyer switches. It's also important to prioritize being associated with the most popular ones. Research by the Ehrenberg-Bass Institute has shown this applies both to business-to-consumer (B2C) products and business-to-business (B2B) brands.[38]

We'll tell you how to work out what the ones are for your category, how to choose which ones to focus on and how to build them into your marketing. All you need to remember at this point is that Category Entry Points (CEPs) mean the reasons people come shopping and that brands are primed for growth when buyers think more often about you, in more buying situations. As Professor Jenni Romaniuk, of the Ehrenberg-Bass Institute for Marketing Science, expresses:

> *CEPs influence which brands are initially mentally available in decision-maker memory – and form the list of initial 'go to' options. Understanding CEPs helps you build useful associations between your brand and the category's core buying situations. Therefore, when a buyer enters the category, your brand has a greater chance of being mentally available, which is the first step to being bought.*[39]

Be easy – to find, navigate and buy

There's another part to being easy – being easy to find and buy. It's no good predisposing people to want your brand if they're then not able to buy it.

Maybe they can't find you online or on the shelf in the supermarket, or can't find the right product among the thousands you offer. You've got to make buying easy. It starts by being present in the right places. Kantar's data shows that "Brands that are always present attract 7 times more buyers compared to those present on just one half of buying occasions".[40]

But don't beat yourself up if you're not everywhere your buyers are. Only the top 5% of brands are in over 80% of the right places.[41] It's something all brands have to work on. There are lots of direct and indirect 'routes to market', like using influencers or working with affiliates. Gymshark is one of the most successful examples of this with their use of Gymshark athletes. In August 2020 they became only the second brand in the UK ever to achieve unicorn status with no external capital funding.[42]

Being easy to navigate can be a thornier problem to solve. This is particularly challenging for many B2B organizations, especially tech companies. We've worked with some where it took up to six months to train a new sales team on the portfolio. Even if the company could afford for sales not to be quota-bearing for half a year, it was unlikely the buyer would have that kind of time available to invest in understanding which brand, product/service was right for them.

You need to ask these questions:

- How straightforward is your portfolio for marketers and sellers to understand?
- Do your buyers and customers understand what products and services are right for them, what goes with what, and what the natural upgrade path is?
- When they visit your site, are you showing them the right things to help them answer their need?
- Are you making it easy to buy or easier not to?

Imagine everything you sell in a stock room. Are you clear on which products/services are the priority to put out on the shelf for the buyer to see? Which ones are your priorities for revenue growth? What gets to be at eye level? What will get promoted at the end of aisle? What do buyers typically buy first? What do they go on to buy? What do you want to cross-sell and upsell?

You may not be in retail, but your sales colleagues and web designers need these answers to inform the experience. If you have multiple products or services it's unlikely you can afford to promote them all equally, so prioritizing them is critical. Figuring out this aspect of being easy to navigate is often wrapped up in language like 'brand architecture' and 'brand portfolio strategy'.

The work that may be required from you is to:

1. Establish a clear role for the different parts of a brand portfolio.
2. Communicate the relationships between different parts of a brand portfolio using an appropriate naming strategy and identity assets.[43]

Be easy – to use

We once checked into a hotel where there were no reception staff. The idea was that guests fill in a form on a tablet, load up their card key and are good to go. But it didn't work, so we were left wandering the halls, looking for someone who could help us. It was late. We were tired and felt increasingly frustrated.

We've all experienced poor customer service. It's galling when you hear things like, "That's not my area" or, "We outsource that to a partner so that's not really within our control". When your siloed, messy, internal issues spill over into a negative customer experience, your brand has a problem. Your brand does not feel good and that becomes an association that you never wanted to build in people's minds.

Your experience with a brand needs to live up to what's promised and be easy to move through. This touches all aspects of an organization so you need to engage all employees in your brand strategy so they understand what's expected of them.

The strategy itself also needs to be easy to use. Do people inside your organization get it? Is it simple enough? Or is it mired in complicated jargon and shown in a multi-layered brand onion or pyramid? We'll give you a simple, proven model, talk about how to engage employees, and explain how to turn the strategy into messaging.

Be easy – to pay attention to

To build any association in our buyer's minds, we've first got to get their attention.

Generating an emotional response from creative executions really helps. We know this thanks to people like Iain McGilchrist and his extensive work on brain lateralization (the way the right brain and left brain do things differently) captured in *The Master and His Emissary* and Orlando Wood's analysis of this and its importance for brand building in *Look Out*.

There are five different types of attention. The right hemisphere of the brain is occupied with four of them. It's vigilant, alerting us to new experiences and it prioritizes what the left side of our brain, which is all about focused attention, should concentrate on. As Iain McGilchrist shares, "In almost every case, what is new must first be presented in the right hemisphere, before it can come into focus for the left... it alone can bring us something other than what we already know."[44]

So, what gets the attention of our right hemisphere? Orlando Wood explains that getting the attention of the right requires tapping into a more emotional strategy. Emotion helps to embed associations in our minds and helps predisposition.[45]

> *Emotional response plays an important role in orientating and sustaining attention.*
>
> *It also helps to place experiences firmly in long-term memory....*
>
> *Moreover, it helps us to decide for or against something in the future when the time comes – to conjure up a feeling for or against a certain course of action.*[46]

Case study: Sage

When we worked together on Sage in 2014, we conducted research with buyers to dig deeper into a more emotional territory for the brand. Beyond the functional support the tech provided, small business owners spoke most about how they wanted to feel: peace of mind and in control. Whether they used Sage or not, they believed they were a dependable provider versus the other options in the market. We evolved the brand strategy and marketing to focus on the idea of building business confidence. Wunderman Thompson's 'Boss It' campaign drove engagement and sales for Sage by brilliantly reflecting this,

> and injecting humour into the creative, celebrating the small businesses that were 'bossing it' post-pandemic. Being clear on an emotional territory the brand can own has helped Sage become an even more easy to mind and relevant choice for small business buyers.[47]

The emotional response that's appropriate for your brand is defined in your brand strategy. Sage build confidence, Cadbury focus on the spirit of generosity, Amex on reassurance – they've got your back.

Being easy to pay attention to also means you can't be boring. It sounds obvious. But around 50% of all ads generate no emotional response whatsoever. The reaction is neutrality.[48] The last thing a brand needs is to make no impact at all on the buyer!

Be easy to recognize
Finally, you need to be easy to recognize. If people don't quickly make the connection between your communication and your brand name then your marketing dollars can be wasted. According to a study of 143 TV ads by the Ehrenberg-Bass Institute, only 16% of advertising is both recalled and correctly attributed to the brand. What helps counter this is having a brand identity that is used cohesively and stands out from competition. This takes us to our fourth factor – being different.

Factor 4: Be different

For decades, brand strategy books have been using phrases like 'differentiate or die!' Recent books on strategy profess "The market doesn't reward better, it only rewards different".[49] Both are overblown statements. Differentiation alone does not make or break a brand – nothing alone does – but it is very important.

A study of customer perceptions of brand differentiation related to stock price showed that the average next-year risk-adjusted stock return for firms with increased versus decreased differentiation was 4.8%, versus –4.3%.[50] A second study analysing 872 brands' financial results between 2006–2022 across multiple categories showed that difference:

1. is the number one driver of share outperformance

2. accounts for 35% of share growth, and
3. is increasing in importance.[51]

And we've already seen from Kantar's work that it helps predispose people to buy.

So, it's important, but what does difference really mean? We know there are debates in marketing circles about the meaning of 'differentiation' and 'distinctiveness', and which one to use when. To us it's splitting hairs. Far more helpful is to understand the different ways to be different, which we'll cover here. The problem with the word is that what often springs to mind is the 1940s' idea of unique selling propositions (USPs), which is based on the outdated assumption that every brand has a genuine functional difference that is unique to them (e.g. Persil washes clothes whiter). The reality is that most do not, and functional differences are so fleeting that even if you do have one for a bit, it's unlikely to last.

So, what else can difference be about? There are four areas:

1. **Distinctiveness** – an identity that stands out from the competition based on a suite of Distinctive Brand Assets that help your brand to be recognized.

2. **Perceptual leadership** – being perceived as a brand that sets trends, innovates and leads a category and/or challenges the status quo.

3. **Relative strengths** – being perceived to be better at or more associated with something that matters to your buyers. You don't have to be the one and only.

4. **Emotive clarity** – an odd one, we know, but Kantar's research show that this also contributes to a perception of being different.[52]

Case study: Liquid Death

Liquid Death, a healthy beverage brand that began by selling water, are a great example. They have difference on so many dimensions: name and a very distinctive look and feel; emotive clarity, particularly through the use of humour; a leading responsibility platform; product size, material (a 700ml can of healthy beverages versus water in transparent plastic bottles and sugar-filled drinks in cans). They've challenged the status quo at every level of the brand building process and combined this with a highly relevant sense of purpose:

Our evil mission is to make people laugh and get more of them to drink more healthy beverages more often, all while helping to kill plastic pollution.[53]

People aren't just predisposed to buy it, they're willing to wear it! Even getting tattoos of the brand's logo. Merchandize and special collaborations often sell out, like the US$225 gold watch that netted US$145,000. Being different is a huge part of how they reached a US$1.4bn valuation in just seven years.[54]

Where they're struggling is being easy to buy. They're up against the dominance of Coca-Cola, PepsiCo and Anheuser-Busch in the traditional retail environments, so from the beginning they had to think differently about their routes to market. Their first distributors were bars, tattoo parlours and liquor stores (and their delivery transportation was occasionally a hearse). Their other challenge at the time of writing is relevance – converting their high awareness into better conversion down the funnel – getting more people aware of it to consider drinking it.[55]

Case study: Salesforce

From the beginning, Marc Benioff, Chair and CEO of Salesforce, was focused on differentiation. He calls it the most important rule in marketing. Their relative strengths at launch were ease of use, a business model of shared risk and low-risk commitment. What they added to this was a highly distinctive set of identity assets, a different way of engaging with customers in events such as Dreamforce and a strong emotive connection between employees and buyers – all classified as 'Trailblazers'. Salesforce have become one of the most highly valued B2B brands in the world, ranking high in all the three global brand valuation studies.[56]

Both founders give us cautionary tales of why difference in functional benefits is fleeting:

> *If your brand is functional benefits you don't have a brand because you can't own functional benefits. I can't own aluminium cans. So the minute Coke or someone else makes a can of water I spent all my marketing dollars to tell people why their product is great.*[57]
>
> Mike Cessario, Founder, Liquid Death

In Marc Benioff's words,

> *A brand is a company's most important asset. A company can't 'own' its facts. If the company's facts (speed, price quality) are superior to the competition, any good competitor will duplicate them, or worse, improve upon them, as soon as possible. What a company can own, however, is a personality... It goes beyond logic. It's an emotional attachment, and that's an asset that cannot be stolen by any competitor.*[58]

If you're in awe of these two brands, be reassured that it's rare for brands to be different on multiple dimensions. Kantar explain that Doritos' perceptual difference rests in a couple of things: their strong flavour; and their distinctive look and feel. TikTok are seen to be stronger than competitor brands on measures like 'shaking things up' and 'leading the way', which are both about perceptual leadership.[59]

Remember that you don't need to be 'unique'. The reality is that you just need to be perceived as relatively different: better or more associated with something that matters to your buyers. And you need to present your brand differently in order to get noticed and be easily recognized as you. This requires you to understand competitors' brand strategies and Distinctive Brand Assets, and buyers' perceptions of competitors.

The four factors your brand needs to be and what to do about it

A picture of your rebrand remit is emerging. Your job is to decide upon, and be noticed and remembered for, a relevant and different set of associations and assets in people's minds. To rebrand right you need to evolve these things carefully. You need to: identify the associations and assets that don't need to change; identify what's not working well that you should change; and identify what's missing or lacking that you need to add. You also need to make your brand easy to mind and notice. If you get those things right, your brand makes it onto people's shortlists. You then have to make it easy for people to take the action required to meet your growth objectives – to find and buy the brand.

Brand strategy, branding and marketing all play roles in this process. Brand strategy identifies the relevant and different associations we want and need to stand for. Marketing strategy is about finding ways to embed them in the right people's minds and ensuring the brand is easy to find and buy – so people take action in the way needed to grow the business. 'Branding' (creating and applying identity assets) and marketing help get the brand noticed and recognized; trigger, refresh and embed associations; and drive demand and consumption of products and services. Marketers should influence decisions on product, customer and employee experience and pricing to ensure things are cohesive – that the desired associations are delivered and pricing is in line with perceived value. But brand-building isn't just a marketer's job. Things and people need to be working together effectively, aligned across the buyer and employee experience, for the desired associations to be built. It's not just about driving buyers to take action, it's about ensuring leadership and employees take action too.

For a summary, look at Table 1 which we have included again here.

Table 1: Your rebrand remit

YOUR REBRAND REMIT			
Rebrands can drive growth by:			
Attracting more buyers	Stretching into new sources of revenue	Supporting price increases by increasing perceived value	Improving engagement and performance
Buyers need to:			
• Feel like your brand is the right choice (be predisposed to buy you) • Think of you more often, in more buying situations • Believe you're worth the price you're asking • Notice you			
To achieve this, your brand needs to be:			
Cohesive	**Relevant**	**Easy**	**Different**

Assess your brand CRED

Where does your brand stand on the four factors? Get out your red, yellow and green pens and do a quick assessment. You'll get a visual snapshot that you can compare to a deeper diagnosis that we'll share in the next chapter. Ask your team and leadership to do the same. Do you all agree on the problems and priorities?

Table 2: Cohesion assessment

C: How cohesive is your brand?	Yes (green)	Somewhat (yellow)	No (red)
1. You've got the right balance between building on past strengths and adding associations needed for the future.			
2. Colleagues are clear on the brand strategy and are using it to take decisions that shape the buyer and employee experience.			
3. Leadership is role-modelling and communicating the strategy.			
4. Brand strategy is embedded across HR policies and procedures.			
5. Identity, messaging and experiences are cohesive across touchpoints.			
6. Price reflects perceived value.			
7. Brand and demand campaigns are integrated.			
8. Long/short campaign split and investment is right for your business.			
9. Executions and media are integrated, customized and localized effectively.			
10. All branding initiatives aimed at employees and prospective recruits are aligned with the overall brand strategy.			
11. You understand what should sit at a brand level and what sits at a product/service level and how communications should reflect this to buyers.			

Table 3: Relevance Assessment

R: How relevant is your brand?	Yes (green)	Somewhat (yellow)	No (red)
1. You understand how your rebrand is relevant to the C-suite and their priorities to secure the investment you need.			
2. You know your growth remit, whether attracting new buyers, raising perceived value to raise prices, stretching or improving engagement.			
3. You're clear on the people you need to attract and reach, and what they care about.			
4. You're clear on the associations you're building and how they're meaningful to the people you're trying to reach.			
5. You understand the market and cultural shifts that are influencing buyers and employees.			
6. You know the reasons buyers come shopping, which are most common, and which you should focus on.			
7. You understand the buyers' journey from knowing your brand's name, to what it offers, liking it, considering it and intending to purchase from it, and how 'leaky' this funnel is.			
8. You understand why buyers and employees would or would not recommend your brand.			

Table 4: Ease assessment

E: How easy is your brand?	Yes (green)	Somewhat (yellow)	No (red)
1. Your brand is associated with the most important Category Entry Points.			
2. Your brand is easy to find.			
3. Your brand and products are easy to navigate – for the sales team and buyers.			

4.	Your brand is easy to buy.			
5.	Your brand is easy to use.			
6.	Your long-term brand building campaigns generate an emotional response.			
7.	Your brand is easy to notice through your use of Distinctive Brand Assets and creativity.			

Table 5: Difference assessment

D: How different is your brand?	Yes *(green)*	Somewhat *(yellow)*	No *(red)*
1. You understand competitors' brand strategies and Distinctive Brand Assets and hence what to avoid.			
2. Buyers and employees/prospective recruits play back that your brand is different from competition.			
3. You have a suite of Distinctive Brand Assets.			
4. You know what your relative strengths are versus competition (and buyers agree).			
5. You are challenging the status quo and/or leading the category in some way.			
6. Buyers associate an emotion with your brand.			

So, what's your brand CRED? Can you already identify the areas you need to focus on for your rebrand? Take our CRED quiz on www.rebrand-right.com to get your personalised score and recommendations, and compare your results to others. Please don't worry if you're staring at a lot of 'no' or 'somewhat'. If you had a 'yes' across the board, you wouldn't need to rebrand in the first place! But you do need to find out. That's why you need the next chapter: your brand diagnosis.

Chapter 2
Brand diagnosis

What you will know by the end of this chapter

- What to include in a brand diagnosis
- How to structure a brand diagnosis presentation
- How to sequence and run the research required
- How to approach it when you're squeezed on budget or time
- How to share the diagnosis and get buy-in to next steps

When we've been asked to help a business rebrand, our first question is always, "Can you share the brand diagnosis?" Cue blank look. Every time.

It's rare to meet a CEO or CMO who has ever had a data driven, holistic and comprehensive view on the health of their brand, market opportunity and where they stand on the four CRED factors. Not that they are likely to tell you this. But when presented with one, the reaction is often a wide-eyed look that says, "So this is a brand diagnosis? I've never seen anything like this before." You can look forward to that moment.

In order to identify what changes you need to make to your brand you need to put on your detective hat, set all your preconceptions to one side and diagnose what the problem really is. Exactly what changes you need to make to your brand will depend on whether you already have clear answers to any of the four CRED factors. This chapter will give you a comprehensive approach you can tailor as needed.

What you're working towards is a point in time where you present your brand diagnosis to the CEO and leadership. It's a critical point because you need to get everyone to understand and agree what needs to be done with the brand, marketing and experience to achieve the growth objectives for your business. Without it, you may embark on a subjective and unwinnable fight with any leader who wants to refresh the brand identity to make their mark. With it, you can show them a truly objective view of what needs to be done and why.

Start by structuring your brand diagnosis presentation so you can work backwards

Getting the right answers requires some research, but you need to think about it backwards. Rather than going on a fishing expedition, hoping for insights, it's best to know what 'exam questions' you need answers to. Then you can create the structure of the brand diagnosis presentation that you will complete. The five areas you need to cover are your rebrand remit (why this is needed and where growth will come from), then where you stand on the four CRED factors. It will give you the areas you need to focus investment and time on and help you make decisions on next steps.

We've found this works really well as a presentation flow.

Introduction – The rebrand remit

Begin your presentation by explaining you will structure your brand diagnosis against the four CRED factors to identify what needs to change and why.

> **Watch-out #3: Make sure leaders understand CRED**
>
> Does your leadership team understand the four CRED factors and the ways in which brand drives growth? If they don't, you may need a separate presentation based on the previous chapter to walk them through it.

Then introduce the research methodology, so they can see the sources that have informed your recommendations.

Next is the summary of your rebrand remit:

- What's the perception of the problem and opportunity? Why is a rebrand being called for?
- What's the value of the market and how is it growing, or declining? What's your current market share?
- What's your rebrand growth objective and why?
- How often are buyers in market shopping, who else do they shop from and what was their last purchase?
- What's your brand's biggest threat/brand enemy?

Part one: the story in the data of the brand's relevance

- What do buyers associate with your brand? How does this align with our current strategy?
- What are the functional and emotional benefits, motivations and feelings buyers seek? What's changing? What are the trends?
- Why do buyers come shopping? Category Entry Points in order of importance.
- Where is the brand funnel leaking – i.e. where are you losing buyers on their journey?

- What is the Net Promoter Score (NPS) and why do buyers say they would or would not recommend your brand? Why do they stop shopping from you?

- Are buyers positively amplifying your brand (looking at things like retweets, shares and sentiment measurements on social) and how does this compare to competitors?

- What is your brand's share of search (SoS)? (Calculate the ratio of searches for your brand to the total searches across your industry.)

- Write a narrative that brings the buyer to life, weaving in quotes. This is a great breathing point, a story on one slide in words you can read aloud. You can emphasize a particular problem or something surprising.

- What do employees' associate with your brand today?

- How do they describe *what we do, why we do it* and the values of the company? Does this align with what we say? How do these values align with theirs?

- What are employees' thoughts on buyer needs and motivations and how your brand is relevant?

- Would employees recommend working for the brand and why/why not? Calculate your Employee Net Promoter Score (eNPS).

- Would employees recommend the brand to buyers and why/why not? Calculate your Employee *Buyer* Net Promoter Score (ebNPS).

- What do people influencing buyers say about your brand?

End part one by answering 'Is this rebrand about increasing relevance?' Summarize the key findings that indicate why change is or is not required.

Part two: the story in the data of the brand's difference

- How different do your buyers and employees believe your brand is from the competition? (*quantitative measurement*)

- What do buyers and employees say is different about your brand compared to competitors? (*qualitative feedback*)

- What do buyers and employees say is a strength of your brand compared to competitors?
- Is your brand considered a category leader in any way?
- Is your brand challenging the status quo in any way?
- Do you have 'emotive clarity'? Are you focused on an emotional territory for your brand and do buyers associate your brand with a particular feeling or emotion?
- Does your brand come easily to mind for some Category Entry Points more than others and more than your competitors?
- Do you have any assets that have high recognition and connection to your brand? (These are your Distinctive Brand Assets. You'll show them on a four-by-four grid, which we'll explain later.)
- How do you compare to competitors on products and services, pricing, the places you're available to buy, and how you are marketing?
- What do we need to avoid in our brand strategy and identity? Show a competitor summary slide here and put the detail for each competitor in an appendix.

End part two by answering 'Is this rebrand about creating a greater sense of differentiation?' Summarize the key findings that indicate why change is or is not required.

Part three: the story in the data of the brand's ease

- Which brands are most associated with each Category Entry Point? Rank in order from most to least important, and how strongly each brand is associated with them.
- Do buyers associate your product and services with your brand? When you ask them who sells this product/service by name, do they mention your brand?
- Are your products and services easy to buy? Do buyers know what is right for them, what goes with what, and what the natural upgrade and downgrade paths are?

- Are you easy to find compared to competitors? Where are they selling and how do you compare?
- Do buyers attribute your advertising to your brand?
- Are your campaigns generating an emotional response?
- Do employees understand and remember the current brand strategy? Can they play back why the company exists and how we do things around here?
- How easy is it to understand and use your brand identity? How well is it being used?

End part three by answering 'Is this rebrand about being easier?' Summarize the key findings that indicate why change is or is not required.

Part four: the story in the data of the brand's cohesion

- Looking back, what has your brand been known for? What associations have you built in the past and walked away from? When were sales strongest and what associations were you building at the time? Do these align with what buyers are seeking and where your business is going?
- What is changing in your business model, and what does that mean for the associations you want to build and behaviours you need to encourage?
- What do leadership and employees believe should change and never change about your brand?
- How cohesive are you being across the buyer experience with your assets and associations and marketing? Show a journey that a selection of recent buyers have experienced.
- What is your long-/short-term marketing budget split?
- Do employees know and understand the business strategy and brand strategy?
- Do employees think the brand strategy reflects what's special and different about the organization and where it needs to go?

- Do employees think people are behaving and taking decisions in a way that will make the brand strategy real? Do they believe that others are role-modelling it? Do they feel they are being held accountable for executing the brand strategy? Do they feel it makes a difference to how they can progress their career in the organization?
- How cohesive is the brand across your HR and recruitment communications, policies and procedures? From recruiting, onboarding, thriving, departing?

End part four by answering 'Is this rebrand about being more cohesive?' Summarize the key findings that indicate why change is or is not required.

Summarizing findings

To help the audience follow the most important findings and to begin writing an executive summary, create the following summaries as you go through.

- Use a Red Amber Green (RAG) status to assess how your brand is performing against the CRED questions you ask at the end of every section.
- Use the Venn diagram in Figure 2 to capture the themes you hear across the research. This is key for any brand strategy work to come since it gives you the areas of relevance, difference and cohesion you can build the strategy from. Fill in each circle separately for each section as you go, then complete the Venn diagram at the end so you can see which themes cross over into more than one category, as these are powerful ones to build from.

Within the Venn diagram, 'Relevant' needs to cover rational and emotional motivations – why buyers are going to care about your brand. Within 'Different' you want to capture relative strengths, emotive clarity, and areas of perceptual leadership/challenging the status quo.

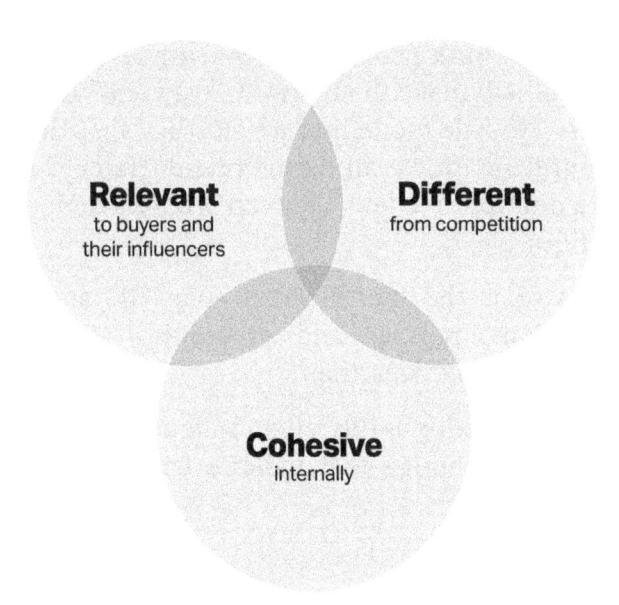

```
        Relevant                Different
      to buyers and           from competition
     their influencers


                    Cohesive
                    internally
```

Figure 2: Venn diagram – themes to build on

The 'Cohesive' part of the diagram captures themes that are strong in the internal research that you may not hear played back from buyers and influencers, like long-term historical associations with the brand and founding values. Additionally, it can capture new associations that the organization intends to support in the future (for instance, if you know all of the software is being completely redesigned to be incredibly easy and user-friendly). It's also the place to capture themes employees share about how they perceive the brand and the values of the organization.

On the same slide, to the right of the diagram, summarize what you need to avoid – the associations competitors are strongly associated with. For instance, you'd avoid talking about 'priceless' memories or moments if you were competing against Mastercard, or 'trailblazing' if you were competing against Salesforce. You can then compare this to your current brand strategy to help decide the extent of change required.

Capture your Distinctive Brand Assets compared to competitors on a slide to help you make the decision on what assets you may need to add or change and the scale of brand identity work needed.

Finish your brand diagnosis with these questions:

1. What is your brand CRED? How well is your brand performing on each factor?
2. Where do the problems really lie?
3. What needs to change to refresh the brand to drive growth?
4. What do we need to get this done (e.g. investment, leadership involvement, team structuring)?

Don't panic!

Now, you may be thinking one of three things at the moment:

1. This is all great, but how on earth do I find all this out?
2. Well, this is clearly just for those big brands that have large research budgets. We can't afford to do all this.
3. Wow – this looks like a lot of work. I think I might skip it.

Number 3 requires a deep breath. The reality is if you don't know what the problem is with your brand, how are you going to solve it? You've got to do the detective work. Once you know how to do a brand diagnosis it becomes so easy to do it again if you move to a marketing role elsewhere, or if you get a new leader who demands a brand change. You can totally do this!

Number 1 and 2? We're coming to that right now. Where to start. How to sequence it. How to do it if you've got a large budget or very little budget. We'll get into how to brief people to help you and what you should be leading on.

What you need and how to sequence it

You will need to review the relevant research and data your company already has to understand what is already known. You'll need to look at competitors to understand differentiation. For fresh insights, you will interview buyers, as well as leadership and colleagues and important influencers. You'll look at trends and buyer influencers. Then, building on that knowledge, you will get a broader view from buyers and employees through quantitative research, to give you a higher degree of confidence in your findings.

We have found the sequence in Table 6 works well.

Table 6: Research sequencing

Order	What you need to do	Timings
First	Confirm the Business Strategy. Source and review existing relevant research and data.	Month 1
Second	Work with HR on the employee research, agreeing whether you will do it yourselves or hire external researchers. Find the right researchers for everything you want to commission. Agree investment in research and inform any colleagues who need to know. Commission.	Month 1
Third	Conduct the internal qualitative interviews with leaders and movers and shakers and analyse any additional research they provide. Research competitors.	Months 2–3
Fourth	Conduct the qualitative interviews with buyers and influencers. Analyse the results. Use what you've found out from all the qualitative interviews to define the final quantitative research questions.	Months 2–3
Fifth	Run the quantitative research and the Distinctive Brand Assets quantitative research.	Months 3–4
Sixth	Analyse and write your brand diagnosis presentation.	Months 4–5

Don't panic. You don't have to do this alone. You can outsource all of it to brand strategy consultants, research firms or the team in your business who run research and insights, if you have one. You can just hand your brand diagnosis structure over and say 'I need this populated please!' You can brief your team to do the competitor audit and look at trends. You can put together a small team to work on this. You just need to be the one with the overview and the sequencing of it so you can orchestrate it into a compelling brand diagnosis in a timely way.

The schedule can feel like a long time when you look at it in months. In reality, these are aggressive, but doable, timelines. Every stage of research can have its own presentation to keep leadership engaged – the research firm should be giving you those as part of your agreement with them.

You will know the culture of your organization and leadership, the way they prefer to be kept informed, and the time pressures you're under. This work is not just about answering questions. It's also about building engagement. Amy Fuller, CMO of Accenture, revealed that she changed her view on what works while leading their rebrand. She now advises others, "Instead of focusing on speed to the answer, focus on inclusion of the process."[60]

Let's walk through each stage, exploring the ideal approach and then what to do if budget and time constraints can't stretch to every part.

First – confirm the business strategy

Make sure that you have correctly understood the business strategy. When an organization is changing sometimes the new direction is kept a little under wraps. It can be important to quietly ask the confidential questions such as, is this rebrand to help with a sale or acquisition or listing or delisting?

The three business strategy areas you want to know the answers to are as follows:

1. **What are we aiming for?** Usually you'll get a growth goal, typically expressed as a revenue ('become a US$Xbn business by [date]') or profit goal ('increase margin by X% in the next X years').

2. **Where do we play?** Which categories are we in? Which countries are we going to operate in and which of those are our priority for selling in? Who are and should be our buyers?

3. **What are we focusing on?** What is going to drive growth alongside this rebrand? Which products and services are we prioritizing or have in our roadmap as future earners? And what capabilities are we strengthening or developing to achieve that?

The business strategy informs your brand strategy which informs the marketing strategy and experience. Dig into this with your boss, the CEO and any crucial peers (strategy, sales, product, finance, marketing) so that you can be certain. Ask them to walk you through how the company is investing in making this business strategy happen. Be clear also on what you call the market you sell into, which should be what the analysts call it, because we've found that there is often disagreement about this within in a business. Understand which countries are a priority because they make, or are targeted with making, the majority of your revenue, and of all your products and services, which are the priorities. Define who the buyer is. You'll need to know this to qualify respondents to participate in the research (your research providers will ask for this) and to inform your marketing strategy.

> ### What if you don't know who the buyer is?
>
> It's rare in any rebrand that there's no knowledge of who the buyer is. Even when working with a start-up, investigations will have been done on 'product/market fit'. Potential buyers will have been identified and different versions of a product will have been iterated with them. Those early engaged buyers are often very willing to be interviewed.
>
> Your conversations with leadership will help. You'll ask who typically buys the types of products and services you sell. They can talk to you about the demographic or the right company profile and role. There may be more than one type or profile of buyer – for example, Oracle's breadth of portfolio means they sell to marketers, human resources, finance and IT buyers and procurement may also have a role.
>
> If there is truly no one you can be connected to, the reality is your competitors' buyers will be your buyers, so if in doubt, recruit buyers who are 'lookalikes' of your existing buyers or those of the competitor you want to steal share from.

Second – partner with HR and the right researchers

Partner with HR
Make friends with HR. Explain the big picture: that growth will come from making the brand more cohesive, relevant, easy and differentiated for buyers and employees, and that you're defining what rebrand means for your organization. So much of the work to turn strategy into reality will be done in partnership with them, so make every effort to begin this journey positively and collaboratively.

Talk through the questions you want to ask employees. You may be able to piggyback on a survey HR plan to run. They may already have a survey tool you can use. They may already have some insights you need from past employee engagement surveys. Share with them the sections of the brand diagnosis presentation structure you need to complete with employees' perspectives. Talk to them about how best to incorporate brand questions into future surveys once the brand strategy is confirmed. Ask them to assign people for you to work with.

Successful rebrands require Marketing and HR to be joined at the hip. Even if you're working on a product brand and not a company-wide brand, you'll still need employee input. It's critical you build a strong partnership and work together.

Find the right researchers
Ideally, you'll bring in expert researchers. Do the qualitative interviews first to really listen, probe and understand the answers to the exam questions. For the qualitative, try to hire a researcher with a behavioural science background so they can get into why people are saying what they are saying and better explore underlying motivations and emotions.

From this you can develop hypotheses to prove/disprove in the quantitative research. Look for quantitative providers that tap into relevant panels of buyers, can do back and forward translation if you need it and offer quick turnarounds (weeks from start to finish, not months).

Your brief should include your market definition, target countries, priority products and services, and who your buyers are. Give them the exam questions you want the answers to, your brand diagnosis presentation outline, and the sequence and deadline for all research to be back.

With them you will need to agree how many qualitative interviews you need and the sample size for the quantitative that will give you 95% confidence level. Get the provider(s) set up with procurement and sign off on the work you've agreed with them (it can hold up the process if you don't get on this quickly!).

Third – internal interviews, existing research and data, competitors

Interview your leaders, movers and shakers
Begin the research by interviewing leadership as well as the 'movers and shakers'; typically the next level down or rising stars within the business. If you work with founders, be sure to interview them

separately. You'd be surprised how often they disagree and one may dominate in a group setting. Book them all in for 45 minutes in the same week or two. Doing it quickly creates internal momentum ('Have you been interviewed yet? I have…') and helps you connect the dots across what you are hearing. If time is tight, do the movers and shakers in pairs. We've also had success running regular workshops with movers and shakers who we've tapped into at different moments throughout the rebrand process.

Explain that you'd like their input for a holistic, research and data driven brand diagnosis, to understand what the rebrand has to achieve for your business and to inform the brand strategy. Ask for their permission to record and transcribe the interview but commit to all quotes being anonymous. Work your way through the questions. You want to cover the CRED themes, the business strategy and listen for commonalities, differences and pain points across the interviews.

Review existing research and data

Straight after each interview, ask them to send you any data and research they have that could be useful: Net Promoter Scores (NPSs) and any related feedback, win/loss reports, research conducted with buyers and employees, press coverage, analyst reports, churn data, exit interviews, buyer feedback, advertising effectiveness, history of the brand and company, great speeches, stories of special employee or buyer experiences, inductions, buyer definitions and competitor intelligence. Add any useful insights to the brand diagnosis and keep a list of everything you review in a methodology slide in your presentation.

Fourth – buyer interviews and defining your quantitative research

Conduct the buyer qualitative interviews

You need to balance speaking to your most important existing customers and within that your biggest fans, with buyers who never or rarely buy from you. You may need to negotiate with sales for access to existing buyers. If so, do make that call yourself to the head of sales, so they feel involved from the start and will encourage their teams to give you timely access.

You want to interview your biggest brand fans because if you could get everyone to appreciate your brand as they do, you may be able to get more people to shop from you more often. As Roy Spence, author of *It's Not What You Sell, It's What You Stand For* expresses, "Your fans will let you in on your value to the world."[61] They will want to tell you in detail why they choose your brand and what they love about it. They will want to help the brand they appreciate become even stronger.

You don't just want to know the answers to the questions, you also want to explore their motivations, fears and understand what they aren't saying. We're all prone to rationalize our decision-making but as Rory Sutherland points out in Alchemy: "If you want to change people's behaviour, listening to their rational explanation for their behaviour may be misleading, because it isn't the real 'why'."[62] This is why we love working with researchers with a behavioural science background, because they have the knowledge and techniques to help go deeper.

Once the qualitative research is complete, use it to shape the final quantitative research questions, for example the list of competitors and the Category Entry Points.

Do a competitor audit

Begin your desk research of competitor brands. Be sure you're researching what buyers perceive to be competitors, not just what market share data tells you. It may be they are increasingly choosing iced tea rather than carbonated soft drinks, so don't think too narrowly about the things they are choosing between. If the business hasn't done this already, you need to compare competitor products and services to yours, the places they are available to buy, pricing and how they are marketing. Look on the most popular media used in your industry, hunt on their website, search for CMO and CEO interviews, agency rebrand case studies, and downloadable assets. Look at the questions you need to answer in the brand strategy in chapter 3, and the explanation of Distinctive Brand Assets in chapter 4, and identify competitors' answers and assets. What you need to get to is a simple summary slide of areas to avoid, to help build your differentiation. You also need an assessment of how easy your competitors are to find, buy, navigate and notice compared to your brand. Include an individual analysis for each competitor in the appendix.

> **Watch-out #4: The bigger the better recall**
>
> If any of your brand assets look similar to a brand with a bigger market share, it's likely that buyers will think of the competitor and not your brand when they see them. The bigger brands get, the better recall they get. Disappointing if you are a smaller brand but true. Look at where you stand out, for example if your brand is blue and your competitors are red, it makes sense to hold on to the blue. If you can't afford to run the Distinctive Brand Assets research recommended below, this desk review of competitor brands may give you enough guidance to take decisions from.

Fifth – quantitative research and Distinctive Brand Assets research

Quantitative buyer research
Now to test what you have learned in interviews with lots of buyers and non-buyers. A quantitative 'whole market study' gives you a balance of views from those that know your brand and those that don't and statistically significant conclusions that give you greater confidence in your decisions.

You can't run this research until you've identified some key Category Entry Points from the qualitative research. The quantitative research helps you prioritize the Category Entry Points and understand which you can be differentiated on. You should also ask respondents the brand funnel questions for your brand and competitors, so you can build the funnels out and see the story in them. You can also cover: Net Promoter Score, reasons for recommending/rejecting, associations, perceptions of differentiation, business outcomes sought and areas for improvement. All of this will need a little tailoring to your brand and category. When you look at the findings, it can help to profile the market by taking two dimensions and plotting your brand and competitors on them in a simple grid. For example, trying different combinations of two Category Entry Points from those that buyers tell you are the most important as the X and Y axis to see which brands are perceived as most associated with them (appearing in the top right of the grid). Playing with different dimensions can help you find the combination that could differentiate your brand in a way that is most relevant.

> **Watch-out #5: Manage your expectations**
>
> Please bear in mind that across all of the research, you're looking for deviation from expected. Both what's expected for the category and expected for a brand of your size/stature. This is difficult if you don't have benchmarks, which is where the bigger research companies who do this sort of research often come into their own. But more affordable DIY tools like Survey Monkey also include things like NPS benchmarking, so do what you can to understand this with the budget you have.

Quantitative employee research

Employees know your brand from the inside-out. Marrying this with the outside-in perspective will identify perceptual gaps: "We think our brand is all about this, but buyers don't." You'll find cohesion problems: "We say our brand represents these values but our employees don't feel they are in evidence, or don't understand them, or don't know them." There will be problems of ease: "We don't know/understand what the brand is all about." You'll be able to compare why buyers recommend your brand, to why employees recommend the brand to buyers, as well as prospective talent. You will have a more holistic view of your brand's four CRED factors and whether employee engagement is a problem you have to solve with the rebrand.

You don't need to run this research with all employees, just a representative sample that will give you a 95% confidence level. Your research provider will be able to tell you how many you will need, or you can use one of the many online sample size calculators. Not everyone you ask to participate will bother. Looking back at previous research with HR, you may find that completion rates are only about 20%, so you'd need to ask 5× what you need. Imagine you have 10,000 employees and are looking for a 95% confidence level with a 5% margin of error, you'd need a sample of 1,915 (383 × 5).

We find about half of all respondents take action when they get the first email, so if you get less than 50% responding at that point, don't be afraid to extend the ask to more colleagues. If you get more than you need responding don't worry (an abundance is no bad thing) and definitely don't turn people that you've asked away once you reach your required number, as that risks disengaging colleagues you will need later. When you communicate with employees about the survey, ensure you explain what is going to happen with their input and when they will hear the results. It really helps to use the same research team to author and analyse the findings from all your diagnosis research.

Distinctive Brand Assets research

You can find out whether you have any Distinctive Brand Assets by testing them. Figure 3 shows the world of assets you could investigate and is explained further in chapter 4. It is additional quantitative research, but we've found it more effective to run it separately from the buyer research to avoid questionnaire fatigue.

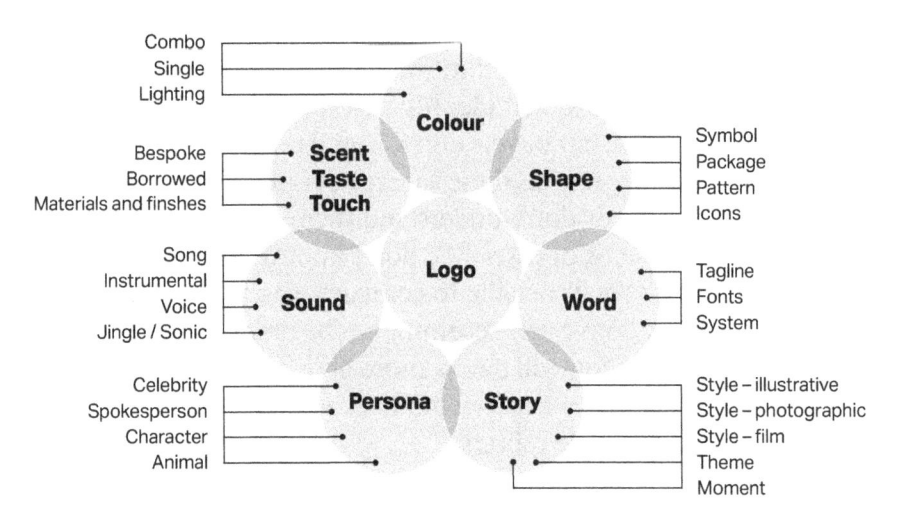

Figure 3: The world of brand identity[63]

What you want to find out is how strong your assets are on two dimensions. The first is recognition – how many buyers recognize the asset. The second is connection – how many connect the asset that's shown to your brand. This can be plotted on a two-by-two grid. Recognition on the vertical axis, connection on the horizontal. On the bottom left you'd plot the assets that people neither recognize nor connect with any brand. These might have potential for you in the future if they are just so new they haven't been seen by many buyers yet, but if you've been using them for a while it's likely that they are just so generic or bland they won't help you differentiate; consider changing. Top left are the assets that are recognized by lots of buyers but aren't being connected to your brand. These may be the weakest ones in your mix since, if you continue to use them, they may work against you, triggering another brand in the buyer's mind; consider changing. Bottom right have potential. Not many people recognize the asset yet, but those that do connect it to your brand; consider keeping and building. Top right is what you're aiming for. Assets that are recognized by a lot of buyers and attributed to you; keep building these. This approach was inspired by the brilliant thinking of Professor Jenni Romaniuk in her book *Building Distinctive Brand Assets*.[64]

From your competitor brand identity audits, pick an example of each type of asset to test, as this will give you a comparison to judge yours against. You will need to strip out the brand name from any logo. Map findings into your two-by-two grid and add into your brand diagnosis presentation.

If your assets aren't distinctive and they are not fit for purpose, then you will need some degree of brand identity change. More in chapter 4. For now, just know that you need to build this into your brand diagnosis.

How to approach a brand diagnosis when you're squeezed on budget or time

Some research is almost always better than no research and there are different ways to get to the answers. Take identifying Category Entry Points. You'll read in some places that you need a sample of 3000+ people and in others that you can do it with 60 interviews.[65] Neither is right nor wrong – they're just different ways to get the information you're seeking with different confidence levels in the answers. Start somewhere within the budget you have.

The easiest way to save money is to not default to a full-service research agency, but instead to look at options such as do-it-yourself vendors, or agencies that are more panel-providers versus analysis-focused. If your budget is very small, do as much of it as you can yourself. You still want to find out the answers to the questions. Do the qualitative interviews with buyers yourself (aim for 20), or ask a colleague or brand strategist to do it. Get the list of who to talk to from your sales colleagues. Use your network of friends, family and colleagues to connect you to potential buyers. Or reach out in relevant social media communities and ask. You can always offer an incentive, like a gift card or charity donation.

If both speed and budget are the issue, keep an eye on the progress of synthetic research, where buyers are generated by AI and asked questions. It is cheap and fast, with some users reporting a decent match to human research findings.[66] It can be useful for understanding what is average in the category (from Category Entry Points to perceptions of brands) or for brainstorming issues to explore in research. ChatGPT can also be used: paste profiles of your buyers from LinkedIn into ChatGPT and ask them questions.

Do understand the data biases that are informing the intelligence, as the sex and gender data gap may mean the answers are based on the average "*default male*" who may not be your buyer.[67] And at time of writing, you can't expect the surprises and oddities found in human research that can inspire really different ideas, or the speech or physical expressions of real people. Michael Mace, VP of the Center for Human Insight, explains why this matters: "The quirkiness, diversity of answers, and variety in phrasing that you get from human interviews feed your intuition. In contrast, the synthetic participants feel averaged out, like a stone sculpture that's been sandblasted until you can only see its basic outline."[68]

Also consider providers that turn research around quickly through a platform that enables you to give questions and tasks to real people who are members of an online panel. Using their computers or smartphones, they record themselves doing tasks and answering your questions. You receive a transcript and video of their responses, plus an AI-generated summary of the results. Results can come in just hours.

You can run your own employee survey using an online form or pay for better survey functionality and the ability to add different languages. HR can help with communications and fielding of the research.

Look for pre-written reports on trends, your audience and cultural and market shifts. At the time of writing, leading cultural strategists like Amy Daroukakis collate all the global trends reports in one place: in 2024 there were 115 reports in the free resource she pulls together.[69] Kantar Marketplace and YouGov provide a lot of free data for the US and UK markets in particular.

You could ask the brand strategy consultant, who you may need to work with in the next stage, to run the research for you. Check out their credentials, as they need to be able to design and run all the qualitative interviews, and design and run the quantitative research using online tools. They can also use a panel provider to provide pre-vetted buyers to talk to. Even if you are running all the research with research partners, having a brand strategist working on this from the beginning can help hone the questions and get them engaged before writing the brand strategy if it needs to be changed.

If you can't afford to run Distinctive Brand Asset research, there are other things you can do. When working on Gatorade's packaging redesign at Landor in 2002, we ran a few focus groups. We started the groups by asking consumers to draw the Gatorade bottle from memory. It was clear that the lightning bolt was one of the most associated signals with the brand and it's been retained in all redesigns since.

Critically assess your identity versus your competitors'. Does your brand look too much like another, bigger brand? If so, it's likely buyers attribute your marketing to it. Your identity probably isn't working hard enough for you. Search for your brand online and see how you show up. Act like a buyer, follow

> recent buyers' journeys to see how easy and cohesive they really are. Then do it for competitors.
>
> Will this be as perfect as working with a brand research market leader with decades of benchmarks and data scientists who know exactly how to ask every question? No. But will it get you actionable insights if you can't afford to invest six figures on your research? Yes, absolutely.
>
> And there's always the middle ground. The disruptors. Seek out independent researchers who have worked at the bigger research organizations and are now challenging them. They often have a great network of specialists and knowledge of the best way to design and field the questions, but don't charge the overheads of the large research agencies.
>
> A robust brand diagnosis will help you ask for more budget next year, as you will be able to demonstrate how useful research and data is in informing the strategic choices.
>
> Just don't absolve yourself from finding out as much as you can about your brand CRED just because you don't have a big budget to work with. Do the best you can.

Sixth – how to do the analysis

You have the structure of your presentation. You know what exam questions you need the answers to. Work through it step by step.

Ask the research agency to populate your presentation flow with the relevant insights from the relevant studies, rather than only writing up their findings in a different construct. Talk to them about how they will visualize each finding (pie chart, bar chart, etc.) to ensure it's really straightforward to understand the story the data is telling.

Make sure when they do the analysis they cut the data by the different qualifying questions. For example, does country or seniority or length of tenure make a difference to the answers? And look for 'people who said X were more likely to say Y'. Where they find statistically significant differences that offer angles on your buyers, simply add another slide into your presentation that has that specific view after the one that looks at that audience as a whole.

With open-ended responses, the researchers should group answers into positive, negative and neutral, and categories and sub-categories of topics, and produce word clouds. Sprinkle longer quotes from the qualitative research to bring the data insights to life throughout.

In a bar chart, rank the Category Entry Points from most to least important for buyers. Then show how well each brand was associated with each Category Entry Point in the buyer's minds. You'll be able to see whether your brand is associated with the most relevant reasons buyers come shopping and if it is more differentiated for any. It's typical to see market leaders highly associated with most of them. The Category Entry Points will help you get a sense of how the market works and which areas of it to target in a simple but useful market segmentation.

Once the researchers have done this work, spend a half day (yes, really) going through it all with them, discussing what the research and data is telling you. As you add the headlines and commentary remember it needs to read like a story as you click through. Imagine you aren't there to present it to critical stakeholders, even though you will be! Remember, you are bringing your knowledge of the market and your business, and they are bringing their knowledge of research and specifically your research. You not only need to understand it and be able to re-articulate it, but you also need to listen hard for clues on your brand CRED. Which is why it rarely works to commission the research and wait for them to come back to you with a 'ta dah!' one-hour presentation.

Yes, we know a brand diagnosis is a substantial endeavour. Yes, your team should make time to work on it. Yes, you do need to be involved. Yes, we promise it's worth it! (If this still feels overwhelming, you can find more help and resources on Rebrand-right.com).

Sharing the diagnosis and getting buy-in to next steps

Present this brand diagnosis to the CEO, the leadership, your finance, marketing and corporate strategy colleagues, and the colleagues you interviewed. If you can, do it in groups. But take the time to make sure they have all seen it. This is your data and research driven, holistic view on the health of your brand. It is your assessment of how you stack up on being cohesive, relevant, easy and different and the market opportunity.

The diagnosis findings will provoke a conversation on the degree of change needed and the ability to deliver this change. You'll need to discuss how this will affect business as usual, what financial and human resources are required, working team structures, budget allocations, timing, etc. You need to be prepared to explain what the following stages will look like and the asks of the leadership team (the following chapters will help). If there's a Project Management Office (PMO) they need to be involved at this point.

You've properly diagnosed the challenges and opportunities for brand growth and you've defined what rebrand means for your business. Amazing work! Onwards!

PART 2
DEFINE

Chapter 3
Brand strategy

What you will know by the end of this chapter

- What a brand strategy is
- The difference and connection between brand and business strategy
- How to get beyond the jargon and frameworks
- The questions you need to answer in a brand strategy and how to answer them
- How to present a brand strategy and get buy-in

Your brand diagnosis has told you that you have a problem with one or more of cohesion, relevance, ease or differentiation. You've looked at your current brand strategy and you know it's not working hard enough on some or all of these factors. It's time for a change. This chapter will tell you how to structure and change your brand strategy. To do that, first we've got to get grounded in what a good brand strategy looks like.

What is brand strategy?

Brand and *strategy*. Two nebulous words and lots of potential confusion. Stick them together and it's double trouble. You'll hear lots of terminology being thrown around and lots of 'experts' arguing for their proprietary approach. The debates usually revolve around three things people can't agree on:

1. **The framework or model for the strategy.** This is where you'll hear that you need a *brand pyramid, key, onion, ladder, prism, passport, conviction springboard*...

2. **The labels for each bit of the model.** Words like *vision, purpose, mission, essence, promise, positioning, USP, value proposition, truth, driver, signature, discriminator, idea, beliefs, values, personality, attributes, archetype, principles, pillars, philosophy, spirit, style*...

3. **How brand strategy intersects with business and marketing strategy.**

If these confuse you, then fear not!

The first thing to understand is that a strategy of any sort is just about making choices for the future. And these choices need to all make sense as a whole: they need to be cohesive. A. G. Lafley and Roger L. Martin describe it as "an integrated set of choices that uniquely positions the firm in its industry so as to create sustainable advantage and superior value relative to competition".[70]

At the simplest level, when you consider business strategy, brand strategy and marketing strategy, it's ensuring that the choices you make on each are clear and integrated. They all need to build on and support each other to increase the value of your business. The business strategy informs the brand strategy (and eventually vice versa) and both then inform the marketing strategy.

When it comes to brand and marketing strategy, people argue where things fit – particularly the definition of customer persona or target audience. Let's address this straight away. Growth comes from targeting as much of the market as possible. Brand strategy has to be created with the broadest audience and long-term growth in mind. Your marketing budget will require you to target a little more tightly in order to use that budget most efficiently. So, segmenting buyers to focus investment fits in marketing strategy.

What's the difference between brand strategy and business strategy?

Typically, you're working with a set of choices that have already been taken and labelled 'business strategy'. The three big ones are:

1. **What are we aiming for?** This is a decision that's been taken on a particular goal or ambition. Roger Martin and A. G. Lafley call this a "winning aspiration". Most often it's called a vision. It's often expressed as a revenue or profit goal – like, 'become a $5bn business by [date]'. Or it uses a growth metric – like 'increase sales by 25% in the next five years.' Or it's expressed more vaguely as an intent to win, lead or be the best in the market.

2. **Where do we play?** Choices on where to play have also been taken. Which categories are we in? Which products are we making or which services are we offering? Which countries are we going to operate in? Which markets? Over time your rebrand should be influencing these choices – particularly when it comes to product and service development. But typically, when you're tasked to rebrand, you're working with decisions that have already been taken.

3. **What are we focusing on?** You'll also be working with choices on future 'growth pillars/big bets/strategic priorities'. These are typically big themes broken down into capabilities that need to be strengthened or developed. This is often where you'll find requests to strengthen brand and marketing and improve the customer or employee experience. For instance, at the time of writing McDonald's have three areas under their 'Accelerating the Arches' strategic plan: 'Maximise our marketing'; 'Commit to the Core'; 'Double Down on Delivery, Drive Thru and Restaurant Development'.[71]

How does brand strategy connect to business strategy?

Just like business strategy, brand strategy is about choices. Now it's making choices to help bridge the gap between the business strategy and the people who will make or break its success: the buyers and employees. Because what's missing in the business strategy is *why people are going to care*. You have this growth ambition, but buyers don't care that you want to reach $5bn in a decade. Perhaps, more surprisingly, neither do employees. As Oliver Bäte, CEO of the world's largest insurance company and one of the world's most valuable brands, Allianz, states, "Nobody gets galvanised by, 'I need to double net profit.' Sorry, even my top team doesn't. So the question is, what can you rally people behind?"[72]

Brand strategy identifies the relevant and different associations you want to build in people's minds and reflect in your working practices to attract buyers to what you're selling, and rally employees around what you're doing.

To do this successfully, you've got to make the brand strategy easy to understand and cohesive. And here's where you can learn from the business strategy. How do leaders make that easy to understand? By framing it through a set of questions the organization needs to answer. You need to apply the same logic to brand strategy.

How to get beyond the jargon and frameworks

Your brand strategy project will become so much easier if you focus on the questions you need to answer, then label them whatever you want. We've used this tried-and-tested approach across the A to Z of industries, for businesses of different sizes and stages of development. It originated from Sarah's six-month study of the brand strategies of the 181 world's most valuable brands. This proved to us that there is no consistency in the labels used, but there is great consistency in the questions they all answer.

But what about brand promises, prisms, ideals, drivers, purpose, principles…?

Here's the secret. All of this terminology has only come about because agencies, academics and independent strategists are trying to differentiate themselves from their competition. It's hard for agencies to be remembered for strategy in pitch situations so they often try to create a proprietary framework. We've been there on the agency side. And we've also seen the puzzled looks from the C-suite of a huge pharmaceutical company when we were trying to push our agency's 'verbal brand driver'. The more complicated and jargon-filled the framework, the harder it's going to be for you to engage the leadership team and the rest of the organization. The more your brand strategy sounds like 'BS' (the common acronym for bullshit!), the harder it will be for you to sell it. But there is a way forward. Just focus on the questions you need to answer and you'll have a no-BS brand strategy framework.

The questions you need to answer in a brand strategy

- What do we do?
- Why do we exist?
- Who are we and how do we do things?
- How do we look, feel and sound?

Here are different examples so you can immediately see what we mean and how the questions are universally applicable. All of the words in these examples are the language used by the organizations mentioned, or from the agencies who have helped create the brands. It's not just what we think they might say.

Table 7: SAP's brand strategy[73]

What we do (vision, the role we seek to play in the world)	*Why we exist* (purpose)
We bring out the best in every business	To help the world run better and improve people's lives
How we look, feel and sound	*Who we are and how we do things* (how we run)
Open. Open is our compass for inclusive design, reminding us to embrace a global viewpoint and value diversity.	*Stay curious.* We never stop pushing boundaries of what our solutions can do for people and for the world.
Expressive. Expressive is our heartbeat, emphasizing the importance of human connection and empathy in our designs.	*Tell it like it is.* We build trust by being honest, authentic, professional, and constructive. We openly exchange ideas and perspectives.

Modern. Modern is our pulse, keeping us in sync with the dynamic, evolving world and current cultural trends. *Confident.* Confident is our backbone, infusing our designs with boldness and purpose to reflect our brand's heritage of trustworthiness and reliability.	*Keep promises.* We work as one team to constantly earn our customers' trust, delivering the best outcome in the simplest way possible. *Build bridges.* We put egos aside and work as a team towards a common vision. The competition is outside, not inside. *Embrace differences.* We are a diverse and global team. All of us have unique skills and experiences that create value for our customers.

Table 8: McDonald's brand strategy[74]

What we do (mission)	**Why we exist** (purpose)
Make delicious feel-good moments easy for everyone	To feed and foster communities
How we look, feel and sound (personality)	**Who we are and how we do things** (values)
Light-hearted Playful Welcoming Dependable Unpretentious	*Serve.* We put our customers and people first *Inclusion.* We open our doors to everyone *Integrity.* We do the right thing *Community.* We are good neighbors *Family.* We get better together

Table 9: eto's brand strategy[75]

What we do (positioning)	**Why we exist** (purpose)
We preserve wine beautifully so you can enjoy wine on your time	To bring more pleasure and less waste to wine-lovers the world over

How we look, feel and sound (personality)	Who we are and how we do things (values)
Elegant. Pleasingly ingenious, simple and stylish. *Contemporary.* In tune with modern lifestyles. *Considered.* Deeply thought-through, evidenced in lack of the superfluous. *Less is more.* Reduce to perfect. Pure, simple, minimal – but by no means basic.	We are people who: *Design without compromise* - Equal excellence in form, function, and aesthetics - Obsessive and relentless attention to detail - Genuine, distinctive innovation - Working only with companies that care for their workers and the environmental impact of their operations. *Design for longevity* - Timeless and long-lasting – in both quality and aesthetics - Made from 'good' material - Protecting the environment *Design for joy* - Always focused on how it feels, and how it enriches people's lives - Beautifully made, beautifully performing, beautiful to look at - Enhancing life's moments of pleasure

You may not have heard about eto yet. It was one of Kickstarter's most successful product campaigns in the UK, reaching its initial funding target in just 32 hours and gaining almost 20,000 backers in total. Before launching, Sarah worked with eto on their brand strategy. Since launch, eto has been selected as one of '12 Brands of Tomorrow' by Walpole, the official body for British luxury products, won a Red Dot design award, and is stocked in premium retailers and wineries worldwide.

Table 10: Corinthia's brand strategy[76]

What we do (positioning)	**Why we exist** (purpose)
Grand boutique	To uplift the lives of every one of our guests, colleagues and communities. We strive for this in every interaction, every decision we take, and every concept we create.
How we look, feel and sound (personality)	**Who we are and how we do things** (spirit)
Our style of is hospitality is Properly Inventive. Our personality is Quirky Cultivated Curious	With heart, head and hands. *Heart.* We welcome everyone who walks through our doors with empathy and kindness. We respect and embrace diversity of thought and identity and approach every day with confidence and optimism, hoping to inspire this spirit in others too. *Head.* Corinthia was born from an entrepreneurial spirit and this ambition, determination and creativity is what continues to drive us forward. We seize opportunities and embrace change to learn, grow and improve. *Hands.* We are proud of our individual skills, flair and attention to detail and we celebrate colleague's achievements and passion for excellence. It's our unwavering family spirit, team collaboration and communication that is key to our success.

You'll see that we've put the labels on where they are apparent. Some use vision or mission where others use positioning. Some say values where others say spirit. You'll see other brands describe their *why* as their purpose and their *who* as principles. Label the answers to the questions whatever you want. Be led by natural language used by the CEO or founders since you need them to talk about the brand strategy, a lot. If they've asked you for a mission, or a north star, use that as your label for 'why we exist'. If they've talked for 50 years about the spirit of the company, just like Alfred Pisani, the founder and chairman of Corinthia, had done, don't tell them they need to start talking about values now. Just help them articulate it so everyone understands *who we are and how we do things* around here. As McKinsey's study of the world's leading CEOs showed:

Communications and HR professionals, academics and we as consultants can argue all we want about the nuances of each term, but the fact remains that the best CEOs don't worry much about the distinctions – what matters for them is to have a clear and simply articulated North Star for the company that redefines success, influences decisions, and inspires people to act in desired way.[77]

How to answer your questions

Here's what you need to complete. We'd recommend you tackle it in the order shown.

Table 11: The no 'BS' brand strategy framework

The question	How to write the answer	The most common names for this
What do we do?	A short phrase that builds on what's relevant and different about your brand that's of value to your buyers: *We* [insert]	Positioning
Why do we exist?	A short phrase that identifies why we all come to work every day: *We are here to* [insert]	Purpose or mission
Who are we and how we do things?	Short sentences or phrases explaining what we value and how we want people to act to live up to this *[three ways you can write this – see below]*	Values, behaviours, beliefs or principles
How do we we look, feel and sound?	A list of 4–6 attributes to help guide your brand identity, voice and expression	Brand personality, or brand attributes

1. Defining *what we do*

Start with the connection between *what we do* and *why* we do it. Don't treat these as separate intellectual exercises and don't, regardless of what you might hear, just start with why. To answer both of these questions you can play with a laddering technique that takes your work from the brand diagnosis and creates options for the answers to these first two questions. And you need to have a particular mantra in mind while you do it: *'for the people we care about'*. You are not trying to write some insular story about what your products do on a functional level and how they work. You're identifying what your brand does that's relevant and sufficiently differentiated for the people you care about, buyers first and foremost.

Go back into the brand diagnosis and pull out your Venn diagram. Immediately you'll see you have some concepts to work with in the areas of relevance, difference and cohesion. You also know what to avoid through your competitor analysis. All of this has come from knowledge of the product, the market, the buyers, your culture, capabilities and competitors. You don't need to post-rationalize why these concepts are good ones to work with – you've done all this in the brand diagnosis.

What you might be missing is a sense of the emotional territory you can occupy. If you've got a great researcher they will have done this digging for you. They will have read between the lines, prompted well and asked the right questions to get at, not just what buyers say, but how they feel. But if it's just you, you may need to go back into the qualitative transcripts. Take the time to read them all. Capture quotes and ideas that reflect a more emotional place. Don't think too hard at first: just cull and pull these clips into a shorter document. Then read it and go for a walk. Immerse yourself in everything you've found out, then take time out to ponder. It's vital to allow for thinking time between brand diagnosis and brand strategy.

You may, at this point, get a breakthrough idea. Your answers to the strategy can come from more lateral, creative thinking or a more linear approach. A useful linear approach is laddering.

We call them 'So what?' ladders. You start at the bottom with the things you identified in your Venn diagram. Then you ask 'So what?' at each stage as you move up the ladder.

Here's some examples across different sizes of business and types of business.

Figure 4 shows one for Pampers.

Brand strategy

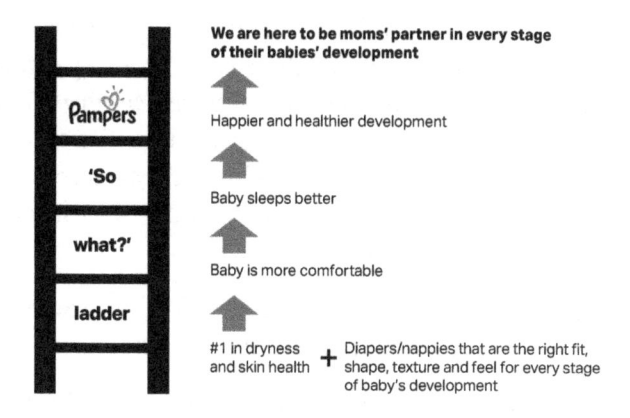

Pampers ladder:
- We are here to be moms' partner in every stage of their babies' development
- Happier and healthier development
- Baby sleeps better
- Baby is more comfortable
- #1 in dryness and skin health + Diapers/nappies that are the right fit, shape, texture and feel for every stage of baby's development

Figure 4: Pampers 'So what?' brand ladder[78]

Figure 5 shows what one might look like for Cisco.

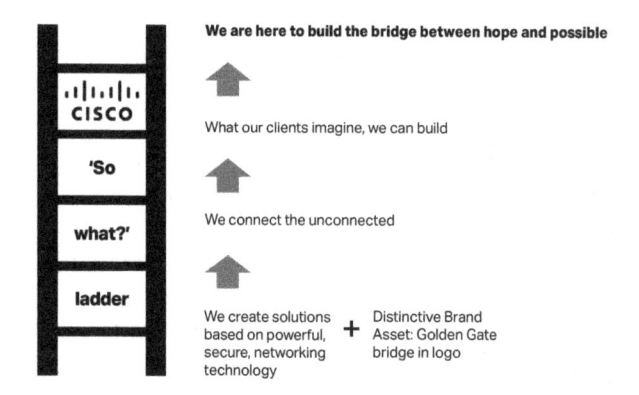

Cisco ladder:
- We are here to build the bridge between hope and possible
- What our clients imagine, we can build
- We connect the unconnected
- We create solutions based on powerful, secure, networking technology + Distinctive Brand Asset: Golden Gate bridge in logo

Figure 5: Cisco 'So what?' brand ladder[79]

Figure 6 shows what one might look like for Apple.

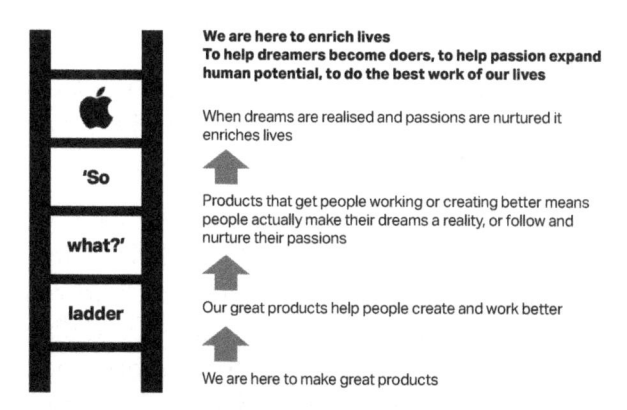

Apple ladder:
- We are here to enrich lives. To help dreamers become doers, to help passion expand human potential, to do the best work of our lives
- When dreams are realised and passions are nurtured it enriches lives
- Products that get people working or creating better means people actually make their dreams a reality, or follow and nurture their passions
- Our great products help people create and work better
- We are here to make great products

Figure 6: Apple 'So what?' brand ladder[80]

69

Figure 7 shows a final example for a family-owned jewellery brand Sarah worked with in California, called Holly Yashi. Co-founder and creative director Holly Hosterman already had a very clear sense of why she had started the business: "to inspire and excite women around the world".[81] But marketing was struggling to get across a clear and compelling idea of what the brand was about. The brand diagnosis unearthed some themes to build upon:

- Holly Yashi's hallmark use of Niobium: using innovative techniques to expose its colourful, chameleon-like magic.
- Niobium is a lightweight but hard-wearing metal: their jewellery is a treat to receive, but robust enough to be worn by customers daily.
- Colourful, handcrafted jewellery.
- Fun, friendly, lighthearted team.

Figure 7 shows the ladder we explored for Holly Yashi.

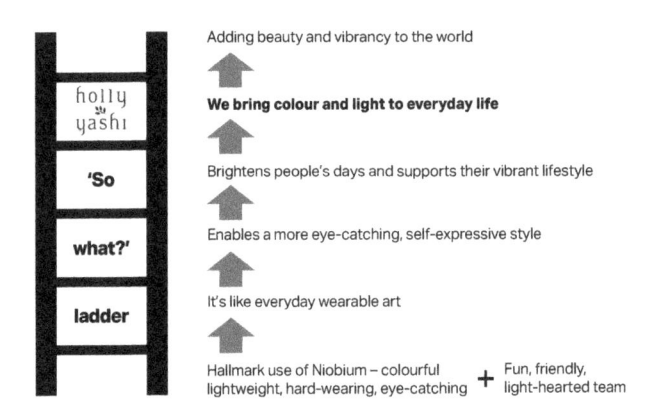

Figure 7: Holly Yashi 'So what?' brand ladder[82]

Note that we didn't choose the highest rung on the ladder. We felt it was much more powerful to ground the brand in the differentiation that came from both the product and the people.

Experiment with different starting points from your Venn diagram. Also consider how your 'brand enemy' was defined in the research. How are you challenging them? How does this help your buyers? A successful strategy for many challenger brands is to define their brand as the antithesis of the status quo that the category leader represents. Ask: how does that help people? And how does that make them feel? Engage the leadership team in this exercise too. A great thing to do following the brand diagnosis presentation is to explain what questions you need to answer in the brand strategy, then introduce this laddering technique and ask them to individually have a go. Collect their individual responses and report back the ideas that were shown at different parts of the ladder when you present options. It will give you more stimulus, engage them in the process and show them that it's not necessarily an easy thing to do.

Keep it simple

Make sure that your answer to *what you do* is simple. Not 20 relative strengths and six emotional areas. One of each. Because here's the challenging thing about all the advice on how to build a brand today. On the one hand you need to build associations with as many Category Entry Points as possible. The more you're associated with, the greater share you'll build.

On the other, you need to be crystal clear on just a couple of associations your brand stands for in order to stand for anything. As Steve Jobs said, introducing the 'Think Different' campaign to employees in 1997: "This is a very complicated world. It's a very noisy world. And we're not going to get a chance to get people to remember much about us. No company is. And so we have to be really clear on what we want them to know about us."[83]

You need this simplicity to help guide your long-term brand building campaigns which should represent around 60% of your marketing efforts. And you know from chapter 1 that this needs to trigger an emotional response, so some sort of emotional territory needs to be in there. We'd argue that most of the world's most valuable brands have at the core of their brands a more rational differentiator that taps into the relative strengths of the product, service experience or organization and a more emotional, universal need state – whether they call this out explicitly as their core or not.[84]

Nike	Innovation and inspiration
Dove	Real beauty and self esteem
Cadbury	Glass and a half of milk – spirit of generosity
Amex	World's best customer experience – got your back
Cisco	Connectivity and possibility
Southwest Airlines	Heart for service and freedom

Coke (until 2023)   Refreshment and happiness
Coke (since 2023)   The real magic of humanity
Salesforce   Customer success and a community of trailblazers

If you're really struggling with defining an emotional area for your brand it can be helpful to look laterally to other categories for inspiration. On studying 181 brands across all the global valuation studies we found that there were 26 big themes that brands clustered under. They included things like helping people thrive, empowering people, making the everyday a bit brighter/better, dream fulfilment, better health, happiness, bringing joy/pleasure, excitement, connection, making you feel smarter and enabling discovery.

Case study: Cadbury

Cadbury had been focused on the emotional area of joy for a decade, but had lost two million customers in the process. Research showed that 'joy' was very generic for the category and not distinctive for Cadbury. The VCCP agency and client team went back into the 200-year archives and rediscovered the emotional roots of the brand – the Spirit of Generosity. This stemmed from the values of the Cadbury family and their actions over the years, such as establishing their 'factory in a garden' in the 1880s to make chocolate while providing a safe and healthy environment for their employees to live and work.[85] It's also rooted in their generous 'glass and a half of milk' in every pound of chocolate – both a product difference and a distinctive brand asset. This spirit of generosity became a powerful springboard for breakthrough creative. When exploring how to express it VCCP also identified a different look, feel and sound for the brand versus the rest of the category. Where other brands are loud and brash, Cadbury are quiet, thoughtful and humble.

In the UK alone the brand went from decline to a 13% increase in revenue by 2019, and saw a growth of 30–35% on all important buyer research measures like most loved brand, brand that has goodness at its heart, brand I understand the most.[86] Clare Hutchinson, Chief Strategy Officer, VCCP London enthuses:

"When you have that simplicity and that clarity and that focus, then I think everyone can get behind it. And… it creates a great springboard for amazing creativity in all sorts of ways."[87]

Watch-out #6: Defining what business you are in

We just need to flag something here. There's this funny grey area that sits between business strategy and brand strategy and that's about defining what business you are in. Usually this is obvious and doesn't need to be considered as part of your rebrand. Cadbury make confectionary. Coca-Cola, beverages. But sometimes reconsidering this is critical to help to turn-around a brand to drive growth.

If you're a big brand, whose rebrand has been instigated because your growth is stagnating or declining it might be that your definition of the business you are in is too narrow for growth, or simply out of synch with the way your buyers shop the category.

Consider Gatorade who, despite being 'the most trusted brand' in the US$8bn 'hydration' market, were experiencing double-digit volume declines. Through their work with Prophet they identified there were seven other athlete need states they could serve beyond hydration.[88] Reframing the business they were in from 'hydration' to 'sports fuel' inspired the launch of new products and helped them achieve 15% growth in year 1 and over US$3bn in franchise revenue increases.

Starting with a bolder frame of reference from the get-go – the ambition to be 'Earth's most customer-centric company' – has enabled Amazon to stretch into multiple categories.[89] Jeff Bezos explains how AWS sits comfortably alongside Amazon retail because, "They share a distinctive organizational culture that cares deeply about and acts with conviction on a small number of principles. I'm talking about customer obsession rather than competitor obsession, eagerness to invent and pioneer, willingness to fail, the patience to think long-term, and the taking of professional pride in operational excellence."[90] Doing this can help new entrants in long-established categories leapfrog established players. For example, from the beginning Casper defined themselves as a 'sleep company' not a mattress company.[91]

Hewlett Packard Enterprise could have said they offered enterprise technology servers, storage, compute, networking, software and services. Instead, they defined themselves as the 'edge-to-cloud company' because it made sense to buyers, could encompass all their products, services and innovation and was differentiated from competitors.[92]

We know that writing this might feel like a no-brainer. "We just make bubble teas"; "We create face recognition software". But take the time to make sure you are articulating this as powerfully as possible. We've found it interesting how nuanced and debated the decision on what business you are in can be. If you can't agree *what you are*, it will be very difficult to agree the other parts.

Make sure that the answer is expansive enough to allow for planned growth and innovation. Then look at how competitors describe what they are from the brand diagnosis. Is there a category descriptor that you just have to use to help people understand what you offer, or is there a way of making your brand and business more relevant, differentiated and future proof?

2. Defining *why we exist*

Let's address the elephant in the room. Purpose. *Purpose* is a word that means *why we exist* and hence should be the perfect label for this question you have to answer. But it has been somewhat hijacked as a means of talking about an organization's 'social purpose' or the good they are doing in the world.

The big problem with the idea of purpose and the way in which many companies have adopted it, is that it has become completely disconnected with the role of a business – which fundamentally is to drive revenue and profit. This has been exacerbated by organizations such as the IPA (the Institute of Practitioners in Advertising) who defined purpose as, "The reason a commercial brand exists beyond maximising profit to produce other meaningful forms of positive impact for individuals, societies, or the environment. It communicates both an organising principle for action in the brand's present and an aspiration for its future."[93]

Unless you're a non-profit, your purpose, the reason you exist, needs to include ways to continue to serve buyers to make profit. Any 'organising principle for present and future action' must have applicability to better customer experiences, employee experiences and product innovation strategies that generate revenue. It must be grounded in the products and services that are how the business makes money – it must build from the bottom of the ladder.

Fortunately, there are still plenty of good examples from some of the world's most valuable and fast-growing brands to counter the lost-the-plot examples you might see. Take Microsoft, who define the reason they exist as, 'To empower every person and every organization on the planet to achieve more.'[94]

They call this their mission – they could just have easily called it their purpose. It's their answer to *why they exist*. This statement works for buyers, employees, and as a driver of other meaningful forms of positive impact. It is rooted in what they do and can drive product innovation just as much as it can drive ESG and employee initiatives, such as Satya Nadella's focus on growth mindset.

Here are some further examples of how the world's most valuable brands express why they exist, that are grounded in their products and services' relative strengths.

'Why we exist'

Meta	To give people the power to build community and bring the world closer together.[95]
Intel	To create world-changing technology that improves the life of every person on the planet.[96]

Accenture	To deliver on the promise of technology and human ingenuity.[97]
TikTok	To inspire creativity and bring joy.[98]
The Walt Disney Company	To entertain, inform and inspire people around the globe through the power of unparalleled storytelling, reflecting the iconic brands, creative minds and innovative technologies that make ours the world's premier entertainment company.[99]
WWF	To build a future in which people live in harmony with nature.[100]
TESLA	To accelerate the world's transition to sustainable energy.[101]
Liquid Death	To make people laugh and get more of them to drink more healthy beverages more often, all while helping to kill plastic pollution.[102]

When answering your *why*, make sure you are not overstating the role of your brand in the world. Just stay grounded and, as Nick Asbury suggests, show some humility: "Purpose asks you to start with why, define your higher societal mission, then lead the global conversation. Humility asks you to take it down a notch. Correctly defined [humility] is not about self-deprecation or falsely talking yourself down: it's etymologically related to the idea of being grounded and in touch with reality."[103]

That's why we recommend you build your strategy from the bottom of the ladder – starting with *what* – not *why* – because the bottom grounds you.

Watch-out #7: Differentiating your *why* gets harder as you stretch

As organizations scale and diversify into different products and services the answer to *why* has to get broader. Consider EY's answer – that they "exist to build a better working world".[104] Then take a look at IBM's refreshed purpose: "IBM is the catalyst that makes the world work better".[105] Then look at SAP's answer: "To help the world run better and improve people's lives".[106] Not so different, right?!

You've got to remember that ideas aren't ring-fenced within categories. We're all exposed to different brands from different categories all day long. The best talent may well be comparing your *why* to others outside your category: graduates looking at entry jobs at SAP, IBM and EY, for instance. If you have a generic definition of why you exist, that other big spending brands share, then you either need to revisit it, or other things in your brand strategy have to work harder for you. *What you do, who you say you are and how you do things, how you look, feel and sound* and your brand identity and the Distinctive Brand Assets they are based upon can all contribute. As can your creativity: how you express your *what* and *why* in a way that grabs attention and helps you stand apart. It's why you might need to dig into the archives again. IBM spent a lot of time and money in the past on concepts like 'progress', associations with the work 'Think' and 'building a smarter planet'. Perhaps it's time for them to go back to move forward.

You may be thinking, "Well, if these answer to *why* can be so similar, maybe we don't need a *why* at all."

You do. But not so much as a driver of marketing. It's most important as a driver of internal motivation and innovation. Answering *why* you exist is another definition of business success that's a lot more motivating to people than a financial goal. It's that thing you can rally all employees behind. Larry Fink, the CEO of Blackrock, believes "[It's] not a mere tagline or marketing campaign; it is a company's fundamental reason for being – what it does every day to create value for its stakeholders… not the sole pursuit of profits but the animating force for achieving them."[107]

Survey results show that more than 90% of companies with a well-defined purpose deliver growth and profits at or above the industry average.[108] A strong sense of purpose has been shown to give employees more meaning in their day-to-day work, help employees feel more professionally and personally fulfilled and improve transformation and innovation efforts.

> ## The power of purpose
>
> 1. Mercer's Global Talent Trends Study of over 7,600 business executives, HR leaders and employees found employees crave a sense of purpose. The study showed employees feel more professionally and personally fulfilled when their company has a strong sense of purpose.[109]
>
> 2. McKinsey put some stats against this: 89% of employees at all levels say that they want purpose in their lives. 70% said that their sense of purpose is largely defined by work.[110]
>
> 3. In a pwc study with 1,500+ employees and 500 business leaders in over 39 industries, 83% of employees said having a sense of purpose gives them meaning in their day-to-day work.[111]
>
> 4. In a 2015 HBR study, 84% of executives agreed that their business transformation efforts will have greater success if integrated with purpose, and 84% agreed that an organization that has shared purpose will be more successful in transformation efforts.[112]
>
> 5. Deloitte Insights 2020 Global Marketing Trends Report also found that purpose-driven companies report 30% higher levels of innovation.[113]
>
> 6. A Harvard Business Review/EY study reported that purpose-driven companies benefitted from greater global expansion (66% compared with 48%), more product launches (56% compared with 33%) and success in major transformation efforts (52% compared with 16%).[114]

It also helps you adapt, stretch and grow. Nick Liddell explains: "The benefit of having a statement of ambition for your organization is that it gives you an ability to adapt to change by defining yourself in terms that aren't limited to what you happen to sell at any point in time."[115]

So, work hard on describing *what you do* and *why you do it*. Call it your *why*, a mission, a purpose, a north star or your monkey's uncle. The label doesn't matter. Answering it does.

3. Defining *who we are and how we do things*

Once you've got options for *what we do* and *why we do it*, you need to look at *who we are and how we do things*. Typically called values and behaviours, these are important because they help people within an organization understand what's expected of them to help the organization achieve their *why* and *what*. Both your *why* and your *who* are key to employee engagement: an IBM study showed that 80% of employees feel more engaged when their work is consistent with the core values and mission of their organization.[116]

By integrating the definition of *who you are and how you do things* into your overall brand strategy, you're building a cohesive brand – helping to ensure that what you say outside is delivered from the inside. You might say, "Oh, well – we've got values already. HR did them 10 years ago." Now is the time to revisit them. Are they relevant to what employees and buyers told you in the research? Are they differentiated? Various studies have shown that overusing common values may do more harm than good.

For instance, a Booz Allen Hamilton study across 365 companies and 30 countries showed that 90% of organizations mention 'integrity', 76% 'trust' and 'teamwork', 69% 'honesty' and 'openness', 68% 'accountability', 60% 'innovative'/'entrepreneurial'.[117] If your values read like this: 'integrity, respect, innovative, customer-focused, collaborative, open and accountable' you've got to try a bit harder.

Why does this matter? In the words of Patrick Lencioni in *Harvard Business Review*:

> Most values statements are bland, toothless, or just plain dishonest. And far from being harmless, as some executives assume, they're often highly destructive. Empty values statements create cynical and dispirited employees, alienate customers, and undermine managerial credibility.[118]

Yes – you have to answer *who we are and how we do things* simply. But you also have to do it without defaulting to meaningless, generic words that will inspire no engagement or action.

So, how do you do this well? Go back to your brand diagnosis. You know what's relevant and cohesive: you know the founding values of the organization; you know where the business wants to go and what leadership and employees believe needs to change; you've asked about buyers' and employees' values and you know what sort of values employees and buyers associate with you today. You also have a list of how your competitors answer this question, and what organizations in general say (see earlier) so you can focus on differentiation. Pull all this together from your brand diagnosis, use your answer to *why* and *what* as your guidepost, then you're ready to write.

There are three ways these are typically written. We recommend the second approach, but none of these are right or wrong – go with what works best for your organization. Bear in mind that a simple way to get attention internally and signal that a big change is required is to write them in a different way to how they've been expressed before.

The first and simplest way of pulling this together is to start by identifying a handful of attributes – single words that describe what you value (that support your *why* and *what*) – then expanding on how you need to behave and take decisions in order to live up to them. You'd write the statements in this way: "We value [insert attributes] so we do these things: [short sentences explaining the behaviours or actions people need to take]."

BMW have five of these: "openness, responsibility, transparency, trust and appreciation".[119] Starbucks use: "craft, courage, results, belonging, and joy".[120] They expand each one out into more behavioural guidance.

Under "openness" BMW explain: "We are excited by change and open to new opportunities. We learn from our mistakes in order to create our future. We take our colleagues' ideas seriously, because every little impulse can turn into something great." Under "belonging" Starbucks say: "We actively listen and connect with warmth and transparency. We recognize and appreciate every person for who they are. We treat each other with dignity and care." The positive side to this approach is that single words are easier to remember. But they also tend to be more generic and they're quite passive.

The second approach is to use commands rather than attributes, then explain how you act on those commands: "We want people to [insert short phrase] so we do these things: [short sentences explaining the behaviours or actions people need to take]."

Airbnb ask employees to, "Champion the Mission. Be a Host. Embrace the Adventure. Be a Cereal Entrepreneur."[121] Cereal is not a typo. They sold cereal in their early days to generate much-needed revenue. It's a great entrepreneurial story that they have deliberately built into their values. Meta include things like: "Move fast, Focus on long-term impact, Build awesome things, Live in the future."[122] Again, they expand each one out to help employees understand the sort of behaviours that sit underneath. You can dig into this detail on their websites.

The third way is to frame your answer around beliefs: We believe [in] [insert statement] so we do these things: [short sentences explaining the behaviours or actions people need to take]."

Google's founders wrote beliefs like: "It's best to do one thing really, really well"; "Fast is better than slow"; "You don't need to be at your desk to need an answer"; and the most quoted and controversial, "You can make money without doing evil."[123] Many political parties, charitable organizations or religious organizations also express founding beliefs rather than values.

Watch-out #8: Rebrands usually require stretch goals

Because rebrands are about change, it's likely that answers to your *who* need to have one foot in the reality of today and one in the stretch of tomorrow. If they only reflect how the company has always been they may not inspire the changes in behaviour required to help the business turnaround a decline and grow in the future. If they're too ambitious, they may never become authentic and will lack credibility from the start.

Carefully consider how to combine the authenticity of your culture, with the values employees care about, and what buyers need and value. The best definitions guide how people behave

> and take decisions so that employees, prospective employees, buyers and prospective buyers experience the company as a cohesive whole, regardless of where they are in the buyer or employee journey or who they're talking to. You want people to feel, "That is so [your brand]", like they say "That's so Apple" or, "Yes, well, it is Claridge's after all!"

Don't feel overwhelmed by the options. You will know which approach feels right based on your brand diagnosis and the culture you're working within. Work hard to make them different, authentic and memorable. Toyota use automotive phrases within theirs (like "Drive Curiosity") and tell people to exercise "Genchi Genbutsu" ("go and see for yourself").[124] Cisco frame theirs around six give-and-take phrases (e.g. "give your best, take accountability, give something of yourself, take a bold step").[125] Go back to stories and phrases that reflect the heritage of the company. Consider using language that taps into those stories. Look up the stories behind these examples to help: IBM's "Treasure wild ducks", IKEA's "Småland"; Nike: "Remember the man". Yes, this is harder to translate when you're dealing in different languages, but the successful brands here haven't shied away from that.

When you get to the final draft – particularly when you're putting this onto your 'about' and careers page – ask a copywriter to give you different articulations of the core ideas that also inject your personality and brand voice – how you want to look, feel and sound.

How many should you have?
There is no rule. Most companies write between three and seven.[126] The fewer the better in our view: three to five max. And don't waste one on a theme like integrity – isn't that already in your code of conduct and an expectation of all brands? Fight back against anything generic, throwing everything into the mix or dumbing it down so much that it loses differentiation and impact.

4. Defining *how we look, feel and sound*

Identifying *how we look, feel and sound* is the last question you have to answer. It informs your brand expression: your brand identity, language, creative executions and all your communications. It guides anyone you partner with, or brief internally, who is responsible for bringing your brand to life across the buyer and employee experiences. It acts as criteria for decision making on what is on or off-brand. At this point in the process, you need to get to a handful of words that can guide this.

McDonald's have five words they use: light-hearted, playful, welcoming, dependable and unpretentious. When you think about their ads, the copy they use such as "Great tasting coffee. Simple", the welcome board game they created for new employees or their happy meals – they all emanate from this guidance.

Three words guide how Apple look, feel and sound: *simplicity, creativity, humanity*. They call these their three lenses. According to Tor Myhren, VP of Marketing Communications at Apple: "If a product is not made up of these things, it's not Apple."[127]

When Landor refreshed Accenture's identity in 2017 they used six traits: "bring the ENERGY, every shade of VIBRANT, fortune favors the BOLD, always DIMENSIONAL, FRESH is more, be OPTIMISTIC."[128]

Coca-Cola Zero's personality and character is different from Coca-Cola's and Diet Coke's. Answering this question helps to differentiate varietals from one another in a portfolio; making it easier for buyers to navigate.

Just as in all other aspects of the brand strategy, you need to beware of falling into the safe, generic, category conventions. Remember the importance of difference. Clear M&C Saatchi created a 'Brand Desire' survey to explore how brands can break through the indifference barrier.[129] Over the years, it gathered the thoughts of 22,000 people across six countries on more than 500 brands spanning 23 different categories. Across all the categories, the most desirable brands in the study were typically those with the most distinct personalities: they scored very highly on some image attributes but also scored very poorly on others. In comparison, the least-desirable brands were those with less distinct personalities: they tended to have less 'spiky' profiles, with less pronounced peaks, as well as less pronounced troughs. The more character your brand exhibits, the more likely people are to desire it.

And if your product is not different, then your personality and brand identity become even more critical. So, be wary of using generic ways of classifying brand personality (like brand archetypes!) as a way of getting to yours. We tend to humanize brands, and brands, like humans, need to have a nuanced and distinct personality to help to break through the noise.

> **Watch-out #9: Be prepared to revise your thinking**
>
> Answering *how we look, feel and sound* is critical as a lead into brand identity and all other creative execution. Sometimes, particularly when you're working on a new brand identity, seeing creative options and having those critical conversations with designers on the right path to pursue, can give you different options for the words you should use. Be prepared to write the words in italics in your framework and to change or add a couple before you agree that the brand strategy is final. In Michael Johnson's *Branding in Five and A Half Steps*, this is the half step. He asks that you let the narrative blur a little between the strategy and the creative stages. Because differentiation is such a potent factor, you've got to try and allow some space for acceptance of an idea that "technically, falls just outside of the brief but is so unusual and exciting that you might… slightly rewrite some of the verbal ideas."[130]
>
> Get sign off on *why we exist, what we do, who we are* and *how we do things* with the leadership team and agreement of the need to lock-in the answer to *how we look, feel and sound* once you've actually explored how the brand strategy you've defined so far translates into creative work.

What happens when you're working on a brand, product or service that sits underneath a company brand?

If you're working on an entity that is part of a larger brand (e.g. Dove as part of Unilever, Cadbury as part of Mondelez, Microsoft Dynamics 365 as part of Microsoft, tax within pwc), you'll likely already have answers to *why the company you work for exists* and *who we are and how we do things*. For example, Mondelez have defined *why* they exist as to "empower people to snack right."[131] They've also defined *who they are* and *how they do things* in a set of three values: "We love our consumers and our brands. We grow every day. We do what's right. Always."[132]

When Cadbury refreshed their brand in 2017, they needed to answer the other two questions. They had to identify what they do that is really relevant and different, and how they should look, feel and sound. Cadbury is a brand – they are trying to build a set of associations and assets around the Cadbury name – so they needed both these questions answered.

Microsoft Dynamics 365 is a different sort of entity. Dynamics 365 is a product name connected to the Microsoft brand. It's capabilities support the overall *why* for Microsoft. It needs to build on the familiar Microsoft assets and not create a new identity, but still do the work to answer how Microsoft Dynamics 365 is relevant to the buyers of enterprise resource planning (ERP) and customer relationship management (CRM) applications, and different in the market they are competing in. Their answer to *what we do* is to help buyers become more agile businesses due to their more intelligent and integrated applications.

For the tax service line within pwc, the same principle applies – they need to answer how their offerings are relevant and different for the chief financial officers (CFOs) and CEOs who buy tax technology and services. Sometimes this is called *value proposition development*, sometimes it's just called *messaging*. But it's not 'brand strategy' – there's only one brand name here, and that's pwc. Again, forget the label, just do the work answering how your entity is relevant and different for your buyers in your market and against your competitive set.

You can use parts of the brand diagnosis methodology to help you do this. Buyer qualitative interviews and buyer quantitative will help understand Category Entry Points at the product level, and employee interviews with the service line leaders and movers and shakers will also give you answers to how your product is relevant and different. You can also use the laddering exercise to get to clarity on *what you do* for those buyers. But you shouldn't be briefing agencies to create a new identity once you've answered the question. The only time this should be considered is when a new entity is not viewed as credible coming from the company brand. In these instances, sometimes you need to create a bit of perceptual distance until this new capability becomes more integrated and understood. You can do this with identity assets that feel part of the bigger brand but are ring-fenced for the new entity. You can do it, as Deloitte Digital did, by creating some physical distance too – opening a new office space and even allowing for a different dress code. But be aware that the more distance you create, the harder it becomes to act as one and add the efficiencies and positive associations the new thing should bring to the company brand.

Watch-out #10: Don't outsource the responsibility

It's tempting to think that you should just hire an agency to get on with this stage of work. But you've got to understand that many agencies come with some brand strategy bias, usually driven by the thing that they make most money from as a business. Ad agencies will use the language of brand strategy to describe a campaign idea. Design agencies will talk to you about brand strategy but they're often most focused on concepts to inspire the brand identity development. Rarely will any of them consider things like values and behaviours in the mix. We've seen this too many times in pitches and we've often been brought in to either simplify or add to brand strategy work that agencies have authored.

So, take control. Even if you do outsource a lot of the work, be involved in the process. Be clear that the deliverable you want is the answers to the questions. Don't get strong-armed into the agency's jargon-filled framework. They're simply trying to differentiate themselves from other agencies with these frameworks but the inevitable jargon will make it hard for you to sell this into your business. Give them the language you know is going to resonate internally. Again, stay deeply involved in the process. Read the research. Understand and generate your own answers to the questions. Consider hiring an experienced, independent brand strategist who isn't attached to any agency

> – they're less likely to be focused on any creative deliverable and more likely to be able to immerse themselves fully and exclusively in your brand, and your brand only, for the time you need them. This may also help you save some money.

How to present the brand strategy and get buy-in

Part of the challenge with brand strategy is getting the C-suite on board and a decision taken. It starts with your interviews in the brand diagnosis phase. You'll be asking for their ideas and thoughts and engaging them in the process. You may need to run an interim workshop between those interviews and writing brand strategy options if there is substantial disagreement or if the leadership team are keen to be heavily involved in the strategy creation. When you present options for the strategy, you have to walk the tightrope of sharing ideas that you know might push them outside their comfort zone, in order to differentiate the brand, and presenting those ideas in ways that feel self-evident. However you got to the brand strategy from the diagnosis, through linear laddering or lateral leaps of thinking and inspiration – you have to write the story in a logical way, working backwards from your suggestions and not forwards from the research. The journey should be clear. As Rory Sutherland, Vice Chairman at Ogilvy and co-founder of their behavioural science practice, explains:

> *Although you may think that people instinctively want to make the best possible decision, there is a stronger force that animates business decision-making: the desire not to get blamed or fired. The best insurance against blame is to use conventional logic in every decision.*[133]

This is not a repeat of the brand diagnosis, so only pull the relevant summary slides and insights that support your conclusions. Start the presentation with the business strategy and your rebrand remit. Identify the relevant challenges you face. Share the model explaining the four questions approach and then the completed Venn diagram. Then move straight into your options. Show how they link back to the insights in the Venn diagram, reference only relevant research findings, and show

how they compare to competitors. Retrofit ladders if you didn't get to the ideas that way. You might think that sounds like 'cheating', but, as Rory Sutherland explains:

> *I used to feel bad about presenting ideas as though they were the product of pure inductive logic, until I realised that, in reality, everything in life works this way. Business. Evolution by natural selection. Even science. Even mathematicians, it seems, accept that the process of discovery is not the same as the process of justification.*[134]

You don't need to present the strategy in a table like we have. We usually take inspiration from our clients and create something that feels like them. For instance, for Claridge's we used a triangle with the *why* at the top, followed by the *what*, then the *who* and *how* in alignment underneath. But for The Berkeley, we used hexagons, and for Corinthia, circles. Why? Because these were very prominent motifs across the properties and part of their brand identity assets. Just like the labels, be led by what feels most authentic to the organization. Just keep it simple and on one page.

How many brand strategy options should you share? It depends on whether you think one of the options you've got is the best choice. It depends on whether there was great alignment in the leadership conversations or great debate. Sometimes we've presented three possible brand strategies. If we are sure of the *why* and *what*, we might only offer options on the *who*. You'll know what feels right.

Take time in the meeting to push on implications. "If we say this is our brand strategy, what does this mean we'll need to stop, start and continue doing?" You can't hash this out fully in one meeting; these questions are ones you'll need to be constantly asking and answering as a business going forward. But you do need to ensure the leadership team realize that this strategy is a filter for decision-making, that they will be expected to be role-modelling it and that they will be judging the next steps in the process against it.

There will be a glorious moment when you get agreement to the decisions in the strategy, but in the next breath the CEO will be asking you what's next. Be ready for this. The next chapters will help.

Final thoughts on brand strategy

With your four brand strategy questions answered, you've identified the relevant and different associations you want to build you brand around over the long term. And you have a simple and cohesive way of showing your business and brand strategy in one framework, on one page.

Table 12: Business strategy and brand strategy table

The question	How to write the answer	The most common names for this
What are we aiming for	Articulated in the business strategy.	Vision
Where do we play		Playing field, targets
What are we focusing on		Strategic priorities, pillars, big bets
Why do we exist?	A short phrase that identifies why we all come to work every day.	Purpose, mission
What do we do?	A short phrase that encapsulates what's relevant and different about you that's of value to your buyers. Typically includes a more rational differentiator that taps into the relative strengths of the product, service experience or organization, and a more emotional, universal need state.	Positioning
Who are we and how do we do things?	3–5 short 'commands', each with a longer explanation, explaining what we value/believe and how we want people to act to live up to this.	Values, beliefs, principles and behaviours
How do we look, feel and sound?	A list of 4–6 attributes.	Brand personality or attributes

This strategy enables you to move into other areas of change you've identified, with a clear direction and filter for all the work to come: brand identity, brand engagement, marketing strategy, driving brand to demand, and measurement.

> **Watch-out #11: Simultaneous workstreams**
>
> The work in the following three chapters needs to happen simultaneously. Read it step-by-step but plan them out as three different workstreams that begin once your brand strategy has been agreed. You may not need to change all of these things, but we'd still recommend you read each, since it's likely you'll see something that you may not have considered that can improve your brand CRED.

Chapter 4
Brand identity

What you will know by the end of this chapter

- When brand identity change is necessary
- What makes a good brand identity
- Why you need distinctive brand assets
- What assets you can create and change
- How to work out what to do with yours
- How to brief and run a brand identity process
- Whether to test the brand identity and how
- Why to say no to guidelines – a better way to ensure your brand identity gets used in the optimal way

Changing a brand identity can be exciting. It visibly shows you've had an impact and gets the attention of the whole organization. It's seen as the natural and inevitable thing to do in a rebrand. But it's not necessarily the best step at all.

Changing a brand identity takes effort and investment. Start doing the calculations. Think about all of the places your brand identity lives. Not to mention the design, guidelines and training costs.

But more significantly it can also *lose* you money by causing great damage to your brand. How? You've heard the phrase "familiarity breeds contempt." When it comes to brand identity, it's the opposite: "familiarity breeds trust."

When people are familiar with something, they prefer it and pay more attention to it. This phenomenon is referred to as the *Mere Exposure Effect*. Identified in the 1960s by social psychologist Robert Zajonc, he found that the greater the exposure individuals had to specific stimuli, the more they developed a favourable inclination towards these stimuli, considering them as truth.

Professor Jenni Romaniuk has shown that ignoring the importance of familiarity by scrapping the old and introducing the new can "influence past memories, and change or weaken the links to a brand". The opposite of this, keeping your brand identity familiar, "means every new exposure builds on the past and the Distinctive Asset links strengthen in memory, making it easier for the people you want to influence to identify the brand in any situation."[135]

So, the headline here is: keeping a brand identity familiar can ensure you are noticed more quickly, preferred over others, trusted and easier to buy.

That's a significant list of pluses right there. And it's why you see so many of the world's best brands only doing careful tweaks over the years. Coca-Cola's logo is still close to their original from 1887; BMW's logo is so close to the one registered in 1917; McDonald's golden arches stem back to 1961; Starbucks' siren (a two-tailed mermaid) first appeared in 1971. They tweak to keep the brand fresh and contemporary; they don't wait until it appears to need a radical overhaul.

So, the first question you need to be asking is not, "Who should we get to redo our brand identity?" but rather, "Do we need to change our brand identity at all?"

When brand identity change is necessary

There are a few good reasons for brands to change their brand identity, and your brand diagnosis will have given you clarity on the right approach for your business. Your brand identity can help you become more cohesive, relevant, different and easy to find, notice and use. It's a powerful way to tap into people's unconscious motivations, shape perceptions and signal higher perceived value.

New identities are often needed when companies separate or merge. When Hewlett Packard was split into separate businesses, Hewlett Packard Enterprise and HP, there was no choice but to create a new brand identity for one of the businesses, otherwise buyers would think they remained parts of the same company.

Occasionally a brand's reputation is so tarnished that a complete redesign is needed to communicate a significant break from the past. Like when Marlboro's parent company, Phillip Morris Companies Inc., underwent a major corporate rebranding in 2001, working with brand agency Landor. This transformation included the adoption of the name Altria Group alongside a change in the company's identity. The intent was to distance the group from its tobacco activities to insulate other brands they owned, like Kraft, against negative associations.

Creating completely new identities is easier to deal with – use the strategy; create distinctiveness. But that's not what we're talking about in this book. Rebrands require a more sensitive understanding of the range of change that's necessary in the brand identity. You need to attract more buyers without alienating current ones in the process. Here's some examples ranging from radical changes to identity tweaks to help you assess the degree of change required for your brand.

Changing to improve brand CRED

If a brand identity is outdated or not functioning for the business or in the places it needs to live, this is a valid reason for change. Sometimes this change is radical; more often it's about building on equity but tweaking elements to be more functional.

We have worked on many B2B rebrands triggered by dysfunctional brand identities. They often share a common story. Each part of the business had latched on to a particular colour within the palette as their own, so the brand looked very different in different places. The main colours had become dated and weren't distinctive enough against competitors' more modern, but similarly hued, palettes. The logo types were old fashioned. The identities weren't fit-for-purpose online, as they didn't have any flexible elements other than colour. There were hand-drawn logos that were noticeably wonky when seen digitally. Customers had noticed, pointing out that the marketing was messy compared to competitors. Ouch.

Once we had defined the brand strategy, the designers came up with a system that modernized the brand and introduced more cohesion and differentiation. Updated identities were used alongside the existing logo at first to help with familiarity. The logos were modernized a couple of years later once buyers had become familiar with the new identity assets.

Changing to become more cohesive and relevant

Burger King's first rebrand for over two decades was a careful homage to the heritage in their logo design while adding more relevance and difference. It reflected a deliberate strategic shift to make the brand feel less synthetic and artificial and more real, 'craveable' and tasty. They created a bespoke typeface, Flame Sans, to evoke the natural, organic shapes of food, and added a warmer, more natural colour palette. Rapha Abreu, Vice President, Global Head of Design at Restaurant Brands International, explained: "We felt that our brand personality, attributes (how we want to look, feel and sound), and all the work we've done around food quality should be better reflected in our visual brand identity. The result from JKR perfectly signals our confidence in our future, while remaining true to what our guests love about us."[136]

Once we'd identified the core of Corinthia's brand strategy – the idea of uplifting lives – it became evident the beige and grey colour palette and dark photography needed updating. Corinthia introduced a honey yellow into the palette, a bespoke handwritten font and an illustrative style that introduced more quirkiness and lightness in line with their strategy. Icons were introduced for the three headers under *who we are and how we do things* to act as quick reminders and signals for colleagues in their internal communications and training. They retained the logo for familiarity.

Sage, the business software company, had a logo that was dull green that looked muddy in a digital format and a font that was hard to read. Working with Studio Blackburn we updated the colour to be a vibrant, positive green that exuded confidence, to reflect the core of the brand strategy, as well as making the word mark more legible.[137]

The trick is to evolve without discarding the level of familiarity that gets you noticed more quickly, makes you easier to buy and gives buyers comfort that you can still be trusted. Because if customers aren't comfortable with the change, they'll let you know. GAP's new logo in 2010 only lasted a few days after people complained in their thousands on Facebook and Twitter.[138] Some 14,000 parody versions were created on a 'Make your own Gap Logo' website. The year before, Tropicana did a complete about-face on their new redesign after sales decreased 19%, or roughly US$33 million, in the two months after the new identity hit the shelves.[139]

You might still be thinking: our brand is really in decline. Isn't a complete brand identity change the best way to get people to reconsider us?

Consider Old Spice. A brand previously associated with your grandpa's bathroom cabinet became relevant to young men and their partners again. There were changes to packaging and product naming, but the fundamental brand identity assets stayed in place. The logo, the ship and wordmark, and core colour palette of red and cream were retained. In fact the ship was reintroduced, respecting the brand's history and in turn ensuring older customers maintained familiarity and trust in the brand. Word and story elements, such as scent names, tone of voice, an illustrative style and a celebrity spokesperson, were introduced and brought to life in an award-winning campaign from Wieden+Kennedy. It used humour to trigger that important emotional response (search for 'The Man Your Man Could Smell Like'). Following these brand changes, Old Spice saw double-digit annual sales growth for several years in a row. The brand's US market share increased from 3% to 6%, with total sales revenue rising from US$280 million in 2009 to over US1 billion by 2017.[140]

What P&G, the company behind Old Spice, understood really well was what needed to be retained, what needed to be added and what needed to change. They had a holistic sense of all the elements in a brand identity that they could work with and used them to great effect.

Let's get into how you can understand that for your brand.

What makes a good brand identity

When you think of a brand identity, what comes to mind? The first three things are likely to be: logos, colours and fonts. And yes – these are some of the things you need within a brand identity. But there's a whole world of other elements that come into play, as shown in Figure 3.

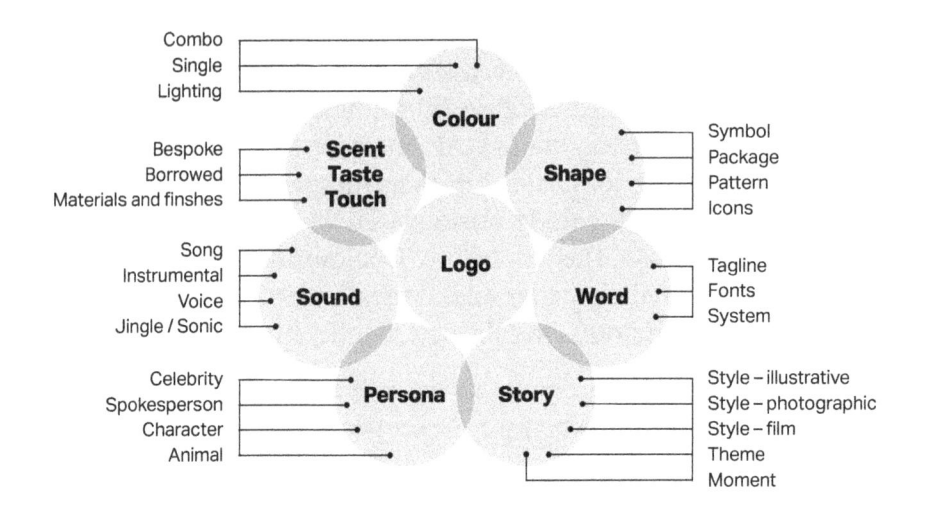

```
                    Colour
Combo   ┌─────────────────────┐
Single  ├────┐                │
Lighting├──┐ │      ┌─────────┤  Symbol
          │ │      │         ├──  Package
Bespoke ──┤ Scent  │ Shape   ├──  Pattern
Borrowed──┤ Taste  │         ├──  Icons
Materials─┤ Touch  │         │
and finishes
                  Logo
Song     ┌───┐          ┌──── Tagline
Instrumental─┤ Sound   Word ├── Fonts
Voice    ───┤          ────┤  System
Jingle/Sonic┘

Celebrity    ┌─ Persona  Story ─┐  Style – illustrative
Spokesperson ┤                  ├  Style – photographic
Character    ┤                  ├  Style – film
Animal       └──────────────────┤  Theme
                                └─ Moment
```

Figure 3: The world of brand identity[141]

You'll see there are lots of sensory assets a brand can use to express their identity, get noticed and reinforce their difference and relevance. But what do you actually *need*?

It's not about going around the model to create every one of these things. You want quality and cohesiveness, not quantity. Quality means creating a handful of Distinctive Brand Assets: things in your identity toolkit that are recognizably different from your competition. They should work well in combination, to give you the flexibility to create all the things you need to build a different, cohesive brand.

Why you need Distinctive Brand Assets

It all comes back to the four CRED factors: they help you achieve *cohesion*, *relevance*, *ease* and *difference*. Here's our build on what Professor Jenni Romaniuk points out in *Building Distinctive Brand Assets*, they:

1. Help you to stand out and get noticed. You've got to stand out to be noticed, right?

2. Help you spring to mind more easily. When used consistently they build on our quicker recognition of things that are familiar. A Kantar study found brands with the strongest assets are on average 52% more 'salient' than their rivals – in other words, they are much more likely to spring to mind when consumers are shopping

within the category.¹⁴² You might also hear Distinctive Brand Assets referred to as fluent devices, a term coined by the agency System1 – "because the biggest thing they can do for advertising and brand-building is harness and build Fluency for a brand. Fluency is all about speed of processing... it's one of the three main heuristics that drives System 1 [our automatic] decision-making."¹⁴³

3. Let people know it's you and not another brand.
4. Trigger, refresh and add brand associations in people's minds.
5. Give the brand more pathways to retrieval in people's minds by engaging different senses.
6. Help connect all of your branded experiences and communications so everything feels cohesive and each exposure builds on the next. Studies show that presenting brands consistently across all platforms can increase revenues by up to 23%.¹⁴⁴
7. Increase the effectiveness of your creative. Ipsos selected 2,015 pieces of video creative and cross-referenced creative effectiveness with the presence or not of brand assets. Their research showed that "high performing creative showed brand assets on average +34% more often than low performing".¹⁴⁵

Here are some examples of the different asset areas you can explore with examples of brands that have created Distinctive Brand Assets in each.

What assets you can create and change

1. Colour

Distinctive Brand Assets can be one colour, or colours in combination. Along with your competitive audit, your brand strategy, particularly the answer to *how you want your brand to look, feel and sound* should help guide you on what colour(s) to choose.

For instance, here's a description of a brand for you from the designer Nick Mills and his work with Wieden+Kennedy. What colours would you pick?

THIS IS F1®: A SPORT THAT'S ALL ABOUT EDGE.

*The edge of chaos. The edge of danger. Even the edge of death. Guts. Passion. Glory.*¹⁴⁶

Pastel pink? A soft mint green? Of course not!

When Wieden+Kennedy worked on the Formula 1 rebrand they chose:

F1 Hot Red | Represents the heat, power and passion of Formula 1

F1 Carbon Black | A steely blue tint. A cooling counterpoint to the heat of our red

F1 Warm White | Our neutral colour that allows our red and black to pop

F1 Pure White | Used as a highlight where required.[147]

Sometimes you can be distinctive with one colour; Tiffany's duck-egg blue, Cadbury's purple, UPS' pullman brown. Amazon claim theirs is 'cardboard'![148] But this is rare. Notwithstanding many brands' legal battles to try and protect theirs, colours are hard to own in the broader context of all the brands we see every day.

Colours in combination can be more distinctive than just thinking about one on its own. Nick Liddell has found that:

The importance of juxtaposition to colour perception means that you've got a much better chance of creating uniqueness through your colour palette if rather than trying to "own" a single colour, you instead try to establish a unique combination of colours. For this reason, the colour palettes of brands like TikTok, Wimbledon and Instagram tend to perform better in research.[149]

Watch-out #12: Don't get too deep into colour theory

There's lots written about colour theory, but unless you are creating a brand identity yourself, with no prior knowledge, it's a waste of time to read all about it. Any good designer knows this already and understands when it's appropriate to break away from the theory.

Watch-out #13: Colour and culture

Don't get too involved in colours and their meanings in other countries. Yes, when we went to Japan to launch a brand identity they asked if they could have it in red instead. No, was the answer. Different countries, departments and sectors picking different colours from the palette had caused the problem of creating an unfamiliar, inconsistent and disparate brand in the first place.

Watch-out #14: Don't follow category colour conventions

Remind decision makers that difference is crucial. Don't get stuck in category conventions or be submissive to the subjective opinion of the CEO who has worn a blue tie every day for the last 25 years. Should 'hot coral' work in banking? It does for Monzo.

2. Shape: symbol, package, monogram, pattern, icons

When you read these brand names, what shapes come to mind?

- Mastercard
- Nike
- Viagra
- McDonald's

Circles, swooshes, diamonds, arches. All shapes strongly associated with these brands.

The two circles in Mastercard's logo are so well-recognized that they dropped the name Mastercard from the logo in 2019. Should you do this with your brand? No! Not unless your assets are as well-known and distinctive as these ones and you've done the research to prove it. Mastercard conducted nearly two years of research to prove that more than 80% of people could identify its wordless logo before dropping the name.[150] It is the wrong move for almost every brand on the planet. The only two brands that the Ehrenburg-Bass Institute have identified as having visual assets that work equally or harder than the brand name are McDonald's and KFC.

Shapes can come from the product or packaging: think Coke's bottle and Doritos and Toblerone's triangles. The brief for the Coca-Cola bottle had difference at its heart: to create a "bottle so distinct that you would recognise it by feel or lying broken on the ground".[151]

Patterns can be part of your assets and are often explored by luxury brands – think Burberry's check or the use of monograms as patterns, like Louis Vuitton. In B2B it can really help to have textures, patterns or icons as an alternative to photography for when you're communicating more technical ideas, but it's very hard to get these things to become uniquely associated with your brand and not others.

3. Words: taglines, fonts, systems

Slogans and taglines are difficult things to become associated with. As marketing strategies evolve most brands use a campaign line or tagline unattached to their logo so it can change as campaigns change. But if you're in it for the long haul they can become distinctive. Consider 'Just Do It'; 'Beanz Meanz Heinz'; 'Finger Lickin' Good'; 'Have a Break Have a KitKat'; 'I'm Lovin' It.' Weetabix and its agency Bartle Bogle Hegarty described the breakfast cereal brand's revival of an abandoned strapline, 'Have you had your Weetabix?', as akin to discovering "a Rembrandt in the attic".[152] Neuro testing showed it was key to their ads' emotional impact and helped to deliver £4.5 million in additional revenue in a declining category.

Fonts are hard to own. You might recognize Disney's, based on Walt's personal signature, or Google's variation of the Catull typeface or Lego's bubble letters. These work better because they are bespoke or adapted fonts that are more unique but they are costly to commission. You will also need a system font or two that everyone can use and has access to as standard.

Sometimes brands use a system of words, or nomenclature, to help them feel more distinctive. Consider IKEA's naming system where each product is named after Swedish locations, people or other relevant Swedish words. Even though the Twitter brand became X in 2023, words like *tweet* (an official word in Oxford English Dictionary since 2013), *retweet*, *Twitterstorm*, *tweetstorm* are still associated with the brand. Apple use 'i', Air, Mac and Pro in different combinations, often on the same product line (iPadPro, iPadAir). It's not necessarily the neatest and clearest system, but these suffixes and prefixes help us identify a product name as coming from Apple and build a sense of cohesiveness across their portfolio.

4. Logos, brandmarks, wordmarks, monograms, favicons

Logos often use a combination of assets: a proprietary font/wordmark, a colour or two, a shape/image and often a sound. Images or shapes within a logo have a lot of potential strength: Amazon's smile, Target's bullseye, Adidas' stripes, Nike's swoosh.

Typically, the advice is to keep logos and wordmarks simple for legibility reasons when in a smaller size like a favicon (a favourite icon, shortened to *favicon*, it is the small browser icon you need for your website), but this doesn't always apply and can work against differentiation. Instead, what you need are different adaptations for different uses. Simplifying to the smallest common denominator can quickly look generic. In 2023, Burberry bucked this trend by reintroducing a very detailed, 122-year-old, equestrian knight motif in their logo alongside a return to a serif font for the name treatment. Looking at your category conventions and figuring which ones to break can be a great starting point for any brand.

We don't need to spend pages here telling you your logo is important. Do be wary of changing it, as we said earlier. Remember that the world's best brands tweak very carefully.

5. Story: themes, moments, style (illustrative, photographic, film), provenance

Distinctive Brand Assets can be elements used consistently in storytelling across different mediums. This can incorporate a theme (the Skittles rainbow, Hermes' equestrian) or a moment (Asda's tapping the back pocket, The OREO dunk, the Heinz slow descent down the Ketchup bottle). As part of their work that turned around a decline in the brand, ad agency Rethink and Heinz took this product moment and tilted the label on the bottle – showing the perfect angle for pouring (36.978 degrees, if you want to know). Playing up the product moment on the packaging stopped people in their tracks to look again at the bottle in the store aisles – a hard thing to do with a brand so well-recognized.[153]

A film or illustrative style can also help brands stand apart. Consider Red Bull's cartoon style that has been used for more than 30 years, or the illustrative style of brands like Headspace, Minor Figures and Duolingo. Photography that is unique to your brand helps you look more cohesive and recognizably you, but it's rare it can stand apart as a Distinctive Brand Asset and it can be expensive to create.

Provenance can be a key component of your brand identity – think back to IKEA's association with Sweden. Volvo also lean on their Swedish roots (despite being owned by a Chinese company), using Swedish accented voiceovers on radio and little flags in the upholstery of their cars. Whereas Minis are distinctly British in feel, despite being exported to multiple countries.

6. Persona: spokesperson, celebrity, character, animal

Characters are often scoffed at ("not for an industry as serious as ours…"), but don't dismiss them too quickly. Take a look at Salesforce before you tell us they don't work for B2B. They have characters at the centre of their brand identity, which has given them cut through in a conservative sector. Characters can be effective because they add personality and faces into the mix. We are hard-wired to notice faces – we even have a specific part of the brain, the fusiform face area that lights up when we see one. Some of the world's most powerful brand assets are characters: Tony The Tiger, Colonel Sanders, Duolingo's Duo. According to WARC, when frozen food company Birds Eye brought back its well-loved Captain Birdseye character it resulted in a media ROI increase of 24%.[154]

Animals in particular have been shown in research to be highly associated with emotion and attention – both of which we need for our brands to grow. This works whether they're real like the Andrex puppy and Lloyd's black horses or animated like Compare the Market's meerkats, Lek Trek the chicken from Brazil, or Geico's gecko.[155]

Spokespeople – whether celebrities, influencers or founders – can also become assets for your brand. Our eyes are drawn to faces we recognize, and we instinctively believe a face or voice we're familiar with. You just need to make sure that the buyer remembers the brand, not just the spokesperson and hope that their personal behaviour continues to reflect the values of your brand and doesn't damage it by association.

7. Sound: sonic, song, instrumental, tone of voice

An Ipsos study showed that sonic branding dramatically increases your odds of having strong "branded attention".[156] It's powerful in leaving memories and triggering the brand name. Sonic branding covers everything from 5 second start up noises (Apple, Netflix's Ta Dum) to longer soundtracks associated with the brand.

McDonald's tagline, 'I'm Lovin' It', is usually accompanied by a five-note sequence (ta da da da da – you can hear it just reading it, right?) from a song they commissioned from Pharrell Williams, sung by Justin Timberlake. Intel's sonic is recognized widely by business and consumer tech buyers. Hewlett Packard Enterprise has multiple versions of the same sonic melody, driving recall while fitting the mood of the communication. The Airtel signature tune by A. R. Rahman became the most downloaded ringtone on the planet. Any British Airways frequent flyer will recognize 'The Flower Duet' by Léo Delibes from the opera *Lakmé* that they play on their planes.

Tone of voice, or brand voice, refers to the spirit that runs through your brand language and it's another tool in your arsenal. It gives buyers a sense of your brand personality and how you are to work with. It's another way we humanize brands and is a key tool to give to copywriters, particularly if you have lots of them writing for you.

Brand voice specialist, Emily Penny, says:

> *Just as with design, it's about expressing exactly the right personality to connect with your audience, and there are many options. Think of it as a relationship: do you want to be seen as sisterly, teacherly, or that rebellious friend? Brand voice work focuses on exactly how to use words to deliver that through signature phrases, word choices, rhythm, and other linguistic devices.*[157]

It's not just for quirky food brands like Oatly and Innocent. If you compare Duolingo, *The Economist*, Pret, Nike and MailChimp, you'll find a range of clear and distinct voices. *The Economist*, for example, focuses on: Clarity, Everyday speech, Brevity, Wit, Illumination and Agitation.[158]

8. Scent, taste and touch

Our sense of smell, closely tied to memory, can evoke powerful recollections, like the nostalgic aroma of Crayola crayons from childhood. Numerous hotel brands we've collaborated with craft bespoke, distinct scents. Claridge's differs from The Connaught, which differs from The Berkeley. Despite all being under Maybourne's ownership, each brand pursues their own olfactory brand identity.

Car manufacturers have been at the forefront of scent engineering, since the late 1990s. That lovely 'new car smell'? Now largely manufactured. McDonald's in the Netherlands have started pumping their French fries smell from yellow and red outdoor billboards, strategically placed within 200 metres of their restaurants. "People could look away, but couldn't smell away."[159]

Taste is rarely controlled by marketers, but you can inadvertently influence it through other assets. In Alchemy, Rory Sutherland recounts how rounding the corners of Cadbury's chocolate prompted buyers to complain that the taste had changed. Turns out smoother shapes taste sweeter.[160] And how adding some copy calling out 'now lower-fat' on some biscuits led to plummeting sales, despite the new product testing just as well as the previous version in blind taste testing.[161] Words, shape and colours can influence other sensory expectations.

Touch is another area often owned more by research and development (R&D) than marketing, but materials and finishes add another dimension to engaging our senses in a brand. Whether paper stock, soft furnishings in offices, taps in hotel bathrooms, they're all potential signals of values and quality.

Brand identity is usually thought to be visual first, verbal second, but thinking of all the senses that can be engaged will give you a richer set of assets to use across the experiences you create.

How to work out what to do with yours

Let's move into how to create your assets and inspire people to use them.

You have defined the brand strategy so you have direction. You've researched your brand assets for how distinctive they are. You've assessed your competitors and identified the category conventions and assets to avoid. You understand whether your current identity is working easily and cohesively or causing problems inside and out. This will give you a clear rationale on what degree of change is necessary in your brand identity and what you need to add, evolve or change. Now can you crack on with hiring a design agency and see what they come back with?

Not quite. Before you do this, there are some decisions you have to take. And this all starts by having the end in mind.

Watch-out #15: The soul-sucking role guidelines play

The usual approach to developing a brand identity is to develop a set of cohesive assets and apply them to tactics (e.g. a web page, an ad, an event stand) by designing mock layouts and finally to define the rules in very lengthy guidelines.

There are lots of challenges with this approach.

1. Brand guidelines contain page upon page of dos and don'ts for designers and copywriters to adhere to. No one ever reads them; they just look up the right section and follow the prescription without 'getting it' and wait to see if they are corrected.

2. Even when brand guidelines talk about fixed and flexible assets, there are usually many fixed assets that you're told have to be used in a specific way. With rules like, 'the logo must always be bottom right' rather than where it's most appropriate for that tactic. For example, the logo being the last thing you see when you read an ad (bottom), versus being easy to spot across a crowded room of exhibition stands (top).

3. Guidelines like this take a long time to create and that in itself requires substantial investment.

4. Guidelines de-skill the experts using them by asking them to paint by numbers and stifle the creativity needed to get fresh cut-through in a noisy market. (If you issue a detailed set of instructions for how people should go about their work, the best they can ever do is to deliver what you expect.)

5. You have to define what good looks like before you've actually made any real tactics and seen how the brand identity works in execution. This one-size-fits-all approach, written in isolation of reality, makes it difficult to get the execution right in each local market.

6. Guidelines very quickly come to feel like a straitjacket. People always want to 'rebel', to do it differently and better, to contribute their creativity. We often hear: "Break the guidelines" and "They're only *guide*lines; we can ignore them."

7. Guidelines force marketing to become the brand police. Nobody wants that role, so you delegate it down and then you wonder why your up-and-coming marketing star has quit.

Guidelines stifle brands and people. Brands need to breathe; to adapt to the topic and context, to be responsive. People using the brand need to apply their creativity to be adaptive and responsive, and to instinctively know what is on and off brand. To drive recall and cut through the noise, you have to be cohesive and fresh.

What you want is for it to all feel right and complementary – to be cohesive rather than consistent. How a website works is different to a digital product user experience. It's not about the logo being in same place, or the navigation being identical. It's not about being matchy-matchy. It's about showing up in the right way for the situation. Making the tactic in the best way for the channel, message, audience, and call to action but still feeling familiar and being recognized as 'you'.

> Brands need to be nurtured, not embalmed or policed. We've found that there is a much better way to do it: ingredients and recipes.

Ingredients and recipes, not rules and guidelines

Think of your brand assets as ingredients you cook recipes with.

If you have the right ingredients, you can make many different recipes. With some foundational ingredients like eggs, butter, sugar and flour you can make cakes, or pancakes, or biscuits or pastry. Then sprinkle in ingredients like cocoa powder, vanilla essence or fruit and you can make a wide variety of tasty food that is all recognizably baking, but gives you many different dishes. To make these dishes you just need the recipes, which give you different ways of combining some or all of the ingredients.

When you apply this to brand identity, you identify some of the ingredients as *always* used in every recipe, your Distinctive Brand Assets, and some as *optional*. Your logo, the main brand colour or a shape could be always ingredients, whereas sonic, photography, graphics and the other colours in the palette could be optional. You define the ingredients (always and optional), but not how they have to be used.

Then, working with your creative team, take a variety of tactics the company has used before, and update them to show how the ingredients can be combined.

You know you have to use the *always* ingredients, but by selecting from the *optional* ones, and trying out different ways to apply them, you will begin to create recipes which can be applied in different ways.

Your focus should be on how to use a recipe in the tactic you're working on to help the audience best consume the information and recall what they saw, heard or experienced. Make as many recipes as your ingredients inspire. Then taking each tactic find different ways to use each recipe to check they actually work, to show people that they will have to decide how to get it just right in execution and give them some starting points.

Let us give you an example. One company has this as its ingredients and recipes.

Table 13: Brand identity ingredients example

Ingredients to *always* use…

| Logo | Brand colour | Font | Call to action, in a lozenge shape, in brand colour, with icon from the logo | Graphic shape |

… which can be combined with these *optional* assets.

White or black type	White or brand colour background	Contextual layered photography	Ident
Brand colour type	Colour gradient blocks	Portrait on colour photography	Film opening style 1 or 2
Texture in type	Texture in background	Linear storytelling in photography	Film closing style 1 or 2
Colour gradient in type			Sonic and animated logo
Kinetic (moving) type			Graphic shape bug on all moving images

Combining the *always* with the *optional* ingredients has created recipes such as these:

- **Recipe 1:** *Always* + black type + white background + contextual layered photography
- **Recipe 2:** *Always* + green type + white background + contextual layered photography
- **Recipe 3:** *Always* + texture in type + white background + contextual layered photography
- **Recipe 4:** *Always* + colour gradient in type + white background + contextual layered photography
- **Recipe 5:** *Always* + kinetic in type + white background + contextual layered photography
- **Recipes 6–10:** take recipes 1–5 swapping contextual layered photography for portrait on colour photography

- **Recipes 11–15:** take recipes 1 to 5 swapping portrait on colour photography for linear storytelling photography
- **Recipes 16–30:** take recipes 1 to 15 + colour gradient block
- **Recipes 31–45:** take recipes 1 to 15 + texture in background
- **Recipes 46–60:** take recipes 1 to 15 swapping white background for brand colour background

… and many other recipe combinations.

When applying the recipe to the tactic, you have to think about how it will be experienced. What do you want people to know, feel or do as a result of the interaction? How will you use the tactic to communicate? How does the audience expect it to be experienced and is it best to zig where others zag or follow the norms? How do you combine all the ingredients in the best way in that situation?

You could apply recipe one to a four-part digital ad where different frames focus on different parts of the recipe: frame 1) text on white; frame 2) photo of a human; 3) text on white; 4) logo with CTA. On an event stand, though, you might have a huge logo at the top for buyers scanning a crowded hall, with a big text message that can be read from afar and smaller photography which will be like a wallpaper backdrop to the humans standing in front of it. Same ingredients. Same recipe. Different tactics. Different execution. Both on-brand!

Think of the people using the ingredients and recipes as expert chefs, who know instinctively which recipe to use and how to make it exactly right for the situation and leave a lasting and memorable impression. Assume the best of their intentions and talent, not the worst.

So, how do you do this?

Develop your ingredients

In the brand diagnosis stage you will have assessed the brand identity assets you have and whether they are distinctive. Now you need to decide what ingredients you will retain, evolve, add or remove.

Start with what you know. From the Distinctive Brand Assets research, what do you have that is already a distinctive asset and what has potential? What ingredients do you think you need to add? Are you missing a photography style? Would a sonic identity help in the tactics you often create? Do you need to animate the logo? What do your competitors do? Use your brand diagnosis to help you and then write a creative brief.

You will want to discuss this with the creative director who leads creative development, but you need to have a point of view going into that conversation. Don't be prescriptive on the areas you're not sure about. If you're not sure a pattern would help, don't prevent it being considered. Let the creative team explore what they can add to your assets – just don't let them destroy ones that research showed were already strongly recognized and connected to your brand and ask them to explore the ones that had potential in their mix of options.

Find the right creative partner

You'll need a strong creative partner to work with. The theory of Distinctive Brand Assets is all well and good, but you can't just throw a cat on an ad and expect success. The reality is that it's in the creativity of combinations where it all starts to hang together. Nick Liddell explains:

> *Distinctive brand assets work like a signature at the end of a letter. If you don't sign the letter, then people are left to guess who wrote it. And there's a strong possibility they will guess wrong. But it's absurd to suggest that this means a signature is the most important part of writing a letter. The signature draws its power from the quality of the content that precedes it. And this is also true of brands. Distinctive brand assets draw their power from the creativity and impact of the brand experiences that they accompany.*[162]

Whether you choose to work with in-house talent, freelancers or agencies, explain the approach of ingredients and recipes. They have to be willing to partner with you on this. This means giving up on the expectation of fees from guidelines. The right people will jump at this as it gives them the opportunity to work alongside you longer term, developing and testing recipes, learning what works in execution, inspiring and encouraging those using it, and keeping it cohesive and fresh.

Brief them well and establish ways of working. When we build a team of experts we sometimes run weekly or fortnightly sprints with a Friday afternoon review. In the reviews, ideas and work in progress are shared and discussed constructively (a 'crit' in agency-speak), direction given, decisions made and plans hatched for the next wave of creative exploration. You can add or subtract members of the team depending on what you are covering on each call. What works brilliantly is having different disciplines hearing how others are thinking: sonic being informed by how the animation style is being defined, for example.

Respect your creative partners' way of working. Do not pressure them to show their first round of work too quickly. If they want three weeks and you want two – give them the three. This is not the place to squeeze on time. This is a critically important, long-term investment. They need time to create, consider, mull, run internal crits before they will be ready to share their thinking.

As you develop the ingredients, ensure they're brought to life as illustrative examples in three to four tactics: e.g. digital ad, event stand, a brochure, a web page. With cohesive application to a set of tactics, you can focus on the ingredients and how they can be combined in recipes, and how easy they are to use well.

Make sure you're able to articulate why the recipe has been applied that way. What is the hierarchy of information? How are you ensuring that it's easy to scan and that the takeaway and call to action work? Make sure the visuals and words don't compete (is there too much in the recipe?).

> **Watch-out #16: Stay on the right side of the law**
>
> Talk to your legal team regularly during this process to make sure you aren't infringing copyright or trademarks and are protecting yours. Seek specialist advice when needed.

How to get buy-in: act holistically, not politically

It can be tricky engaging critical stakeholders and getting agreement on what to adopt. The CEO, the CMO (if that isn't you) and the chief sales officers (CSOs) are usually the most critical. They may have personal preferences which they bring to the conversation. It is helpful to summarize what a good brand identity is and does. It is really important to consistently present the brand strategy, relevant parts of the brand diagnosis like the competitor audit and then the brand identity, using the diagnosis and strategy to agree clear criteria to judge the options against.

Politely sort feedback into subjective and objective and focus conversations on the objective. Constructively work with your leaders on what input you're looking for at each stage. This will help you listen and take on board feedback that can make the work better as well as engage them on the journey of getting this right, rather than getting what they prefer (typically blue!). Testing can help inform these conversations – more on that shortly.

In each conversation think about where the leader is coming from. You will be asked for logos or colours or shapes for departments or initiatives. Resist making sub-brands for anything internal, as no matter how many product brands you have in your portfolio, everyone works for the same business. You want to encourage cohesion and belonging to the collective. Identity can be a great unifier and unification needs to be actively encouraged. We remember working with Lloyds TSB *years* after the two banks were merged and still hearing people answering the phone as 'TSB' or 'Lloyds'.

Make it inclusive, accessible and sustainable

If your business works in multiple countries, you will need to think through transcreation. Transcreation is about expressing the same idea and message but in a way that is right for that market.

There are some obvious examples, like how the layout changes when the language reads left to right, or right to left, or top to bottom. Or whether the font you've selected can be used for all the languages you need; can you use it for French, Japanese, and Arabic, for example? You will also need to think about photography as some cultures are more modest in dress than others and people often prefer to see people like them, since it makes them feel they are the right fit as buyers and employees. We often work with a photography producer to build a collection of original and bought images that are right globally and locally.

You need to check that the ingredients you've developed aren't perceived to have different meanings in different cultures (and you're ok with that if they do). When you say the words aloud – the slogan, product name, URL – does it sound like something else in that language? You need to know what people see when they look at the brand identity in development. You can run simple checks with local colleagues to ask them what they see and think of for each ingredient and recipe so you can take informed decisions. Making sure they can be used in each country successfully is critical. The good news is the ingredients and recipes approach helps marketers get it on-brand and right for their culture.

Being inclusive also means putting accessibility at the forefront of your design process. Ensure you and your design partner understand design accessibility principles and always aim for a triple A rating. There are many free software tools that can help you check for issues.

At the point of writing, little has been said on how to create climate-conscious brand identities. But when the Design Council refreshed their brand identity, they enlisted the help of the Digital Lead at the UK Government Digital Service, Mia Allers, to try to set some principles to keep the carbon impact of their branding to a minimum. Here are the five they came up with:

1. Minimize the number of colours in your palette. White is the most emitting digital colour as it's made up of a combination of many others. Darker colours have been shown to use less energy on modern OLED screens and red pixels use less energy than blue or green pixels.
2. Provide options for printing in a single ink.
3. Reduce the number and size of images. "Images are one of the biggest contributors to carbon emissions on most websites and the larger the file, the larger the impact. Considering even a small reduction in image size through cropping can be beneficial for the amount of ink, materials and energy used to print or display images."
4. Limit fonts.
5. Use pattern to reduce block colour printing.[163]

Keep an eye out for more advice like this. Sustainability has to be central to everyone's way of working.

Should you test the brand identity?

There isn't a right answer to this question. In our work with brands, we've sometimes tested and sometimes not.

Testing the brand identity can be useful because it may inform your decision making and help you with internal buy in. But before you decide to test the brand identity, be mindful that testing will not tell you whether it's right or wrong. It may tell you if the brand identity is liked or not. Testing also won't tell you what people will do behaviourally when it's executed in real life. So, what you want to know from testing is whether it effectively expresses your brand strategy to the buyer and whether it's distinctive or if other brands come to mind when they see it.

If you test in quantitative research, you will need to test the illustrative tactical examples of the recipes in action, rather than the ingredients one by one. Try testing tactics with and without the logo on, as existing perceptions of the brand can sway responses. Beforehand, pinpoint the specific parts of the brand strategy that you want the identity to communicate and show a message card with these on. Then show the different examples and ask whether the visuals capture all these aspects on a five-point scale (strongly agree, agree, neither agree nor disagree, disagree, strongly disagree). Ask a question on how different they perceive this identity to be from other category brands, and in general. You can then ask two open ended questions about what they liked and didn't like about the creative. Ask them if any other companies came to mind when they saw the visuals and why. If you have multiple versions of the brand identity you want to test, then repeat for each option. End by asking them which option they prefer. Do make sure you cover your priority countries, so you understand the cultural nuances.

If you want to test in qualitative, for example with some of your loyal 'fan' buyers or with lookalike prospective buyers, then you can do the above but frame it as a conversation with visual prompts. You can do the qualitative research yourself, or use a behavioural researcher. Look for experts who have done this many times before for high-performing brands. If you do it yourself, don't 'lead' the witness by sharing your opinion. If you have different options rotate them in order to prevent order bias.

You can also test the sonic assets, if you have options you are trying to choose between. Find a specialist agency to do the testing. They can compare it to research performance data on other sonic assets they have tested and assess it for relevance to your strategy, appeal and recall. They can also test the performance of your animated logo with the sonic to see if they perform better combined, which they should!

Be prepared that in all this research different options will perform well on different attributes. It's rare the research will give you a definitive answer – it will be an informed choice you're making. Once you've decided, author a presentation to brief others on the brand identity.

Watch-out #17: What may go wrong?

You may find that some agencies don't want to work on an ingredients and recipes approach. We've met about 50 agencies over the years and can think of at least a handful who would not agree to it. We can also think of many who embrace and thrive on the approach.

Subjective opinions may derail you. You will need allies to help navigate your way, so look to the leader's right-hand marketers or Chief of Staff to help on this journey. Research can be invaluable to bring the voice of the buyer into the room and help the conversation be more objective.

C-suites are often risk averse, and there can be a lot of love for the 'safe' colour blue. Show the work in comparison with competitors and remind the stakeholders you need to cut through by being different (use the stats from chapter 1 to help).

Many colleagues will want to throw out the old and make everything new. Resist getting rid of anything that is working hard for you. Evolution not revolution. You may need to find another way for them to feel they've been bold through a tactical execution, like a new internal campaign, refreshed office décor or event look and feel. Bring the recipes to life for them in a bold way. Don't make your mark by changing the mark.

> **Shortcuts if time or money is limited**
>
> ▶ Use freelancers rather than agencies (the best freelance designers often started agency-side).
>
> ▶ You could do it yourself if you have creative talent. But this is an area we'd urge you to invest in. Think how long great brands keep their Distinctive Brand Assets. Longer than your CEO's lifespan, never mind tenure.
>
> ▶ Ask a designer for just three core assets: ones you know will help you be most distinctive in your field and you develop the rest.
>
> ▶ Ask designers to develop recipe templates in a software you're comfortable using.
>
> ▶ Research font combinations and colour palettes. There are lots of examples out there on pairings and groups that work well together.
>
> ▶ Hire university talent to develop your sonic. Consider music production students.
>
> ▶ Test with fan customers, rather than paying for research.

Where do you put all of the stuff?

Digital storage is best. No more printouts of hundreds of pages of pdf guidelines! There's a lot of providers out there, and the best have machine learning and artificial intelligence built in. Keep an eye on how the market is progressing.

Final thoughts on brand identity

The most successful brand identity changes are ones that show careful consideration of the right degree of refreshment. In order to understand how far you need to go, use your brand diagnosis and brand strategy to guide you.

Ensure you have a set of Distinctive Brand Assets that work well in combination and give you the flexibility and cohesiveness you need across all your tactics. Because if customers don't notice or recognize you, you've no chance of getting across any other associations or messages about your brand.

Whether you need to evolve, add or remove assets, the best way to make them work hard for your business is through an 'ingredients and recipe' approach. This ensures things are cohesive but doesn't stifle creativity. Get your agency or independent freelancer's commitment to this before you sign on the dotted line.

Don't fall into the trap of getting bored with your brand identity. You are not the audience. They are not paying the same attention to it as you are, day in and day out. As Professor Jenni Romaniuk points out: "The big shiny thing gets the attention, but much of an effective Distinctive Asset's strategy is rooted in the quiet, behind-the-scenes discipline of persisting on a path of consistent, excellent execution."[164]

So, create yours wisely and use them prominently and cohesively. All the time. For a long time. This creates familiarity that gets you more noticed, breeds trust and helps your brand come to mind easily in a buying situation. This is key for growth.

PART 3
DELIVER

Chapter 5
Implementation, engagement and experience

What you will know by the end of this chapter

- How to implement the brand strategy and identity
- How to get leadership engaged and spearheading the change
- How to launch well
- The core implementation team and partnerships you need
- How to make the brand how we do things, every day
- What to focus on in the employee and buyer experiences
- How to inspire everyone to use the brand identity cohesively and creatively
- How to know you've done a good job

We know that a relevant and different brand strategy and identity have the power to grow your business. What stops them from having this impact is a failure to embed them cohesively across the business.

There's a chasm between the triumphant approval of the brand strategy and the reality of making it how you do business. The harsh truth is that only one in three strategies (of any sort) are successfully implemented.[165] The shift from theory to reality is hard. Why is this? According to McKinsey "the reasons for failure are rooted in the reality that change is rarely an intellectual problem, it's an emotional one".[166]

Rebranding means change and change can cause discomfort. Larry Ellison, CEO of Oracle, says: "It has been my experience that people reflexively resist change. Change requires people to rethink the way they work and the way they are organized."[167] Our experience is that it either comes down to cultural inertia with everyone nodding and smiling before getting back to business-as-usual, or being overwhelmed by the scale of what needs to be done. Even a tweak to a brand identity takes careful implementation, by many colleagues, but a new brand strategy requires organization-wide change management. Often, it isn't until you begin talking through the implications of the brand strategy that people realize this isn't a cosmetic exercise, but one that influences decision making across the business. Leo McCloskey, CMO at Echodyne Corp points out: "A rebrand must engage the body politic of the company, and most especially the senior teams, and help it nudge, shift, or shove itself into new directions. It's not the logo that's changing; it's the company."[168]

This is where you come in, by recognizing and designing for this.

Please don't feel daunted. You're not going to even try to do it all. You're not going to map all the touchpoints, in all the journeys, for buyers, employees, suppliers, partners, resellers, influencers, analysts and shareholders. You're not going to fix everything that isn't perfect. You're not going to control everything that is implemented. This is not what will make the difference.

To really get the turnaround you're looking for, your colleagues are the answer. How they take decisions and behave will drive the experience your brand offers. Success comes from galvanizing everyone else, not doing it all yourself.

Just like the brand diagnosis chapter, we're working to the most difficult case scenario here: a large, global company with lots of hierarchy, business units and people to engage. You can tailor our recommendations down to the size and scale of your company.

Your implementation objectives

There is a reason you decided to rebrand and you've diagnosed your brand CRED so some of your objectives will be unique to your situation, but there are three that apply to all successful rebrands:

1. Colleagues understand the headlines from the brand diagnosis, brand strategy and brand identity, expectations of them and how to use the strategy to guide how they behave and take decisions in their role.

2. Colleagues are engaged to find ways to make it easy for people (buyers, suppliers, employees, partners) to move confidently from one stage in their journey to another, by fixing the issues and making on-brand improvements and creating remarkable moments that help differentiate the brand and draw attention to it.

3. Brand and marketing are cohesive, driving brand to demand.

Practically, this means you have to focus on:

- getting the leadership engaged and spearheading the change
- setting up and leading implementation
- launching well
- educating and engaging colleagues
- creating remarkable moments
- rewarding and recognizing on-brand impact.

Let's walk through the why and how for each.

Getting the leadership engaged and spearheading the change

Leaders need to do four things in particular to help ensure your rebrand has the impact on growth they're looking for:

1. Communicate and engage on-brand repeatedly and consistently
2. Role model the values and behaviours
3. Implement changes in formal mechanisms - structure, processes, systems and incentives – to support the brand strategy
4. Reinforce the brand strategy with the right people decisions.

The CEO is the only one who can set expectations with leaders that making the brand strategy reality starts and ends with them. Lou Gerstner, ex-chairman and CEO of IBM agrees that "if the CEO isn't living and preaching the culture and isn't doing it consistently, then it just doesn't happen".[169] Ask the CEO (or rather, politely insist) that they invite their direct reports to a half day rebrand session. Pre-brief each of them individually beforehand to warm them up, unless your CEO prefers to speak to everyone at once.

Now is the time to make a master briefing presentation that reiterates the key points of the brand diagnosis and brand strategy, as well as some of the implications, so that you have a brand briefing you can reuse.

Present this in the pre-briefing and the briefing. Yes, it will be a repeat, but hearing it twice, first on their own, then together, gives them a chance to take it all in as you begin to foster a sense of mutual accountability.

Chair a deep discussion on the implications of the brand strategy that is framed around what to start, stop, continue. What changes do they perceive need to be made to reinforce and strengthen the brand strategy? What would demonstrate they are serious about following through? Which areas will they personally commit to driving the change in? You're not looking for definitive answers at this stage; rather, you're giving them time to consider what the strategy means for them and to think about the actions they will need to take. As Duncan Daines reinforces: "The one thing I have learnt over the years is that success is measured by how well stakeholders understand the arguments not how well the argument is articulated."[170]

Then host an open conversation on which areas of the brand strategy they each feel are hardest for them to role-model and secure a specific commitment from each of them on what they will get started with.

Ask them to physically sign the brand strategy, as a symbolic moment of committing to what it promises which you will display at HQ and on your intranet. Talk through how the brand is connected to the growth metrics the business values, and the metrics that you'll be tracking over the long term. Agree a deadline for implementation and explain the next steps.

The call to action leaving the meeting is for them to invite their direct reports to a two-hour session, for a confidential pre-launch briefing, within the next two weeks or so. It's key to keep up momentum. Add to the master briefing presentation a photo of the brand strategy signed by them all and put their commitments in the implications section.

Setting up and leading implementation

You need a cross-departmental team to mastermind implementation. Seek out the programme management office (PMO), if you have one, to drive systematic Management of Change (MoC) through the organization, or work with whomever usually drives change. It's often the chief operating officer (COO) with project managers in smaller businesses. They have the remit, expertise and tools to drive effective change deeply and consistently over time. With your implementation team, plan as much of the implementation as possible through business-as-usual (BAU).

> **Watch-out #18: Don't try to swim against the tide**
>
> Don't try to implement by swimming against the organization. Leverage business-as-usual, the annual planning processes and the natural refresh cycles. Make a note of the business cycle as that is the spine for your timeline. Tap into work that is already underway that can be adjusted.

Unless you have to legally rebrand overnight (big bang, big budget), embrace transition over an agreed time period. The length of it will depend on how large and complex your organization is and the nature of the changes you need to make.

When HP split in one of the largest corporate separations in history, it was necessarily to launch the HPE brand as a big bang.[171] But when it made its products and services easier to buy and sell by consolidating from 29 brands to six, implementation was over three years. "When we introduce new products, or change the value proposition of existing products, we will apply the new brand architecture and naming strategy. When existing products reach end of life, we will retire that brand name," explained CMO Jim Jackson.[172]

Declare a start date from which everything new is made on-brand and a deadline for completion. Prioritize being cohesive and easy, by changing things that go together, together. For example, company LinkedIn page, website careers page, job description, offer letter and on boarding materials. Be pragmatic, update as much as possible at renewal (liveries, stationary, signage) and encourage colleagues to take the opportunity to spring clean; to reduce, finish, stop, rather than to find and replace.

This approach makes use of business-as-usual budget in the P&L where the changes are occurring over several years, reducing the need for incremental investment in rebranding.

Working with the PMO as implementation lead, you will need communications, human resources, marketing, finance, product, information technology (IT), sales, operations and facilities leads who can coordinate within their departments. Bring them in and nurture those relationships, as they can be great enablers or blockers of progress.

You are a conductor of this orchestra. Your time invested in helping everyone do this themselves is what matters. Act like a mentor, encouraging your mentees to think differently and provide direction, support and reassurance.

Make sure you brief them as you did the leadership, so they understand and can explain, defend, advocate and use the brand strategy as a criteria for decision making. Help them to get their heads around what you need to do together, so they can work out their role. Focus everyone on achieving SMART objectives: Specific, Measurable, Achievable, Relevant and Time-bound. With the implementation lead, make sure everyone has a view of what the next phase looks like, with enough time to coordinate and plan. Write a RACI to define roles and responsibilities: Responsible (doing the work), Accountable (in charge), Consulted (asked for input) and Informed (kept updated). Meet regularly. Make yourself available to answer questions. Report at least quarterly to the CEO and C-suite on progress and keep them accountable for making implementation happen.

The broader leadership

Now co-run, with each member of the C-suite/departmental/business unit leads and their direct reports, a confidential pre-launch briefing – in essence, one for each department. By the end of this you will have pre-briefed the whole leadership (the top two layers) and are ready to launch to everyone.

You are running the same session you did with the C-suite, but without the pre-briefing. This means you will need to allow more time for them to ask questions after the presentation and before moving into the discussions. Start with an intro from the C-suite leader and ask them to share what was discussed at the C-suite meeting and the commitments they made. Finish in the same way, with the attendees physically signing the brand strategy and making commitments.

The call to action before leaving each meeting is for the C-suite departmental leader to appoint their departmental implementation leader to work into your core implementation team. Make sure they are senior and have clout!

Crucial partnerships

There are many crucial partnerships needed to implement a rebrand. Find and create allies so that they become your ambassadors and enablers.

Stay close to finance. They will work with you to size your market segmentation. They'll cost and budget the implementation. You'll work on evaluating promotions, setting the right pricing and price elasticity. In the annual planning they can direct leaders to ensure implementation is part of their plan and budget for the year ahead. Together you will calculate the financial impact of the rebrand.

Brand and Product need to be in symbiosis. Work together to review the products and services roadmap to make sure that what you bring to market is in line with the brand strategy. You will also need to plan how to get the products and services on-brand. When you get into driving brand to demand, marketing must make sure it doesn't get out in front of its skis (as some marketers have described it to us) by marketing too far in advance of what can be delivered or over-promising. This will impact the credibility of your brand with buyers, who may then choose to buy elsewhere.

Developing seamless brand-to-demand marketing requires building strong relationships with all the marketing leaders, bringing them in early, and keeping them informed and engaged. With product marketing, there will be work to do on prioritization of products and services, defining use cases, authoring messaging and making tactics. With digital you'll be aligning the website, social channels and likely working on ads with them. With specialist marketers, in areas like field, event or communications, you will need to join forces to create and execute the marketing plan.

It helps sales and business development to know what the buyer has experienced before they join the conversation so they can confidently continue it. They can help you understand why buyers are choosing or not choosing the brand, and listen out for new Category Entry Points. Make sure that this information is shared with you. On account-based marketing efforts marketing, sales and customer service will be working very closely together.

You need to keep partners who sell your products and services informed and find out what it will take to displace other brands they sell. Engage with them to understand how to make this happen and build it into your plan.

With customer service, a flow of insights from their interactions on which parts of the experience are cause for concern and why buyers are leaving is invaluable. Working with them to make sure their interactions deliver the desire experience and message is really important.

IT, operations and facilities will need to make sure everyone is enabled to deliver the desired experiences. This will cover lots of areas. For example, the Martech stack, a new website information architecture and user experience (both usually run by marketing, enabled by IT) and signage (which needs to be updated by facilities). Make sure suppliers are engaged and know what the impact is on them.

You'll need a close working relationship with human resources. Together you can create a brand funnel for employees, define the journeys and evolve the employee experience, as well as driving brand to demand for recruitment. Start by having a conversation about there being only one brand before masterminding the launch together and then aligning all the policies and processes.

Launching well

Time to bring everyone in. Every rebrand needs a launch, a marker symbolizing the before and after.

Organizations will have different contexts at launch. The 'burning platform' may be an ambition to lead or stand out, get further investment or a fear of trouble ahead. Some may have a new business strategy and brand strategy to launch. Some may be pulling new teams together after M&A. Some trying to shift a toxic culture. Your context and organization's footprint will influence the best approach.

It works well to launch mid-financial year, so that you can actively engage colleagues in the brand strategy before they go into planning for the next year. This way there can be no budget or planning excuses for not being able to implement.

Watch-out #19: Make launch a remarkable moment

You could skip all that leadership engagement and go straight to launch, catching everyone unaware. Or how about a quick virtual launch, in a town hall? Or even worse, an on-demand recording, before getting back to business-as-usual? Your CEO doesn't speak, but... drumroll please... you show a glossy film that is all about the visual changes to the brand. Job done! No, not in the slightest.

If you launch a brand strategy in this way, your colleagues will struggle to understand what on earth is going on, may feel it is superficial, and that it has nothing to do with them. Employees need to know how critical they are in making the strategy

> reality and this needs to be done in person as a meaningful moment. As Chip and Dan Heath raise in *The Power of Moments*, you may get push back on this. "Reasonable voices" will want it to happen online because it is cheaper and easier. But, they argue, "Remote contact is perfectly suitable for day-to-day communication and collaboration. But a big moment needs to be shared in person... The presence of others turns abstract ideas into social reality."[173]

To get it right, your in-real-life launch (or launches) will be led by your CEO (or local leader). It doesn't have to be a glamorous or expensive moment, but it does need to be noticed. Just like we need to get buyers' attention to embed associations in their minds, this needs to be a remarkable moment for your colleagues that they pay attention to and remember.

The timing of launch is often debated. The reality is you can't get too far into implementation without everybody's help, so it's usually best to get launched as soon as the leadership are briefed and your core implementation team is set up.

Explain the brand diagnosis so everyone understands why this is necessary. Make sure employees hear their input was instrumental. Talk through the business and brand strategy. Get leaders to stand up, own the strategy and start the process of helping employees understand expectations and how it will affect their role. Give everyone a sense of what it will mean to operationalize the change. By explaining some of the implications, from the perspective of buyers and employees, it will begin to become real.

Here's a couple of examples of how we've seen it done well.

The Berkeley five-star hotel in London launched their brand strategy in back-to-back sessions for all their employees. The leadership took different parts of the presentation to show their alignment and involvement. Guests, partners (such as their resident Michelin-starred chef) and employees, appeared in a film talking about the ideas within the strategy. There were moments of surprise that had a big impact. Attendees were welcomed with drinks and snacks inspired by their answers to *how we look, feel and sound*. While a guest on screen described how much it meant to them when a staff member arranged for a bespoke Polish sweet pancake to be made during their stay, a team of waiters delivered the dessert to every audience member.

One & Only, another luxury hotel group, worked with Within People to launch their new brand strategy with simultaneous events around the world for all 9,000+ colleagues. They took a 'train-the-trainer' approach where the HR teams in each resort were equipped to launch in a way that reflected their location. Their work won the 2019 CIPD Award for Best Employee Engagement Initiative.

Accenture launched a series of virtual events to engage their 540,000 people. There is a point where in-person becomes difficult! This began with a three-hour immersion session for their 8,000 managing partners which included panels, discussions and videos. This was followed two weeks later by a shorter 75-minute dynamic presentation to the entire organization. Then their major markets ran their own events, tailored to their regions.[174]

However you do it, at the end of the launch everyone needs to have understood the brand diagnosis, brand strategy and initial expectations of them. This unlocks being able to engage them in how to use the brand strategy to make choices on how to behave and take decisions in their role. They need to leave the room inspired, proud, able to remember some of it in their own words and excited for what's next.

The call to action for everyone will be to get involved in making the strategy a reality. Ask them to come open-minded to a working session their team leader will be running soon, and let them know it will be embedded across HR policies and procedures, including an upcoming reward and recognition programme.

You need to brief industry analysts to ensure their support. You can do this once you've launched internally, or before launch under embargo. We've done it both ways successfully. Communicate to customers, partners and suppliers once you've equipped your colleagues who work with them to know what to say, and how to answer frequently asked questions.

Educating and engaging colleagues to drive action

Now you need to more deeply engage every person on the brand so they can begin to adjust what they do and how they do it to align with the new direction.

There are two parts to this:

1. **Implementing the brand strategy:** fixing and innovating to make the buyer and employee experience more cohesive, relevant, easier and different.

2. **Implementing the brand identity** and inspiring everyone to use it cohesively and creatively.

Implementing the brand strategy

The typical advice you'll hear at this point is to map all the touchpoints end-to-end for both the buyer/customer experience and employee/people experience before working out which ones are critical and what to do differently. Mapping, systematizing, putting process in place for everything, aligning the journeys and fixing all the problems might feel like the right thing to do, but it's easy to do a lot of work, without making much useful impact. It can take months and you risk losing momentum.

Don't get overwhelmed with the enormity of experiences people have with your brand, or how intertwined the experiences are, or whether their journey is a funnel, linear path or loop. For buyers and customers, NYU professor Scott Galloway suggests thinking about the experience as a simple loop. He shows this in a clock divided into thirds: *pre-purchase*, *purchase*, *post-purchase* (looping back to pre-purchase).[175] We'd add *repurchase*. The colleague/recruitment stages are more linear: *recruiting*, *onboarding*, *thriving*, *departing*. To start, keep it simple.

Your colleagues in every team need to work out what to stop, start and continue. The aim is:

- **Fix hygiene experiences.** Like your opening hours on your website being accurate; support calls being answered promptly.

- **Fix antithesis experiences.** Like your brand being about simplicity but your product taking ages to set up or a dull on-boarding experience for new recruits.

- **Make cohesion or ease improvements.** Could be simplifying your web forms from 12 fields to three. Or enabling buyers to sign up to be notified when a product is restocked who aren't currently able to do so.
- **Create remarkable moments.** More to come on this.

How to get colleague-level implementation to happen

Every team leader needs to be a confident ambassador for the brand strategy. Put together a workshop for team leaders to run with their teams, complete with a loose script. Take a train the trainer approach, running it with them before asking them to practise on each other and then run it with their teams. "We learn more effectively when we teach someone else about the topic we've just explored," explains David Robson. "Across the brain, our neurons appear to be processing the material more deeply, which results in longer-lasting memories."[176] They will become better at explaining it and more confident. This works brilliantly done in person, but is doable online with break-out groups. It's great when people sign up for slots that connect them with colleagues from other departments, as it creates new networks and experiences thanks to the rebrand.

Brief again on the brand diagnosis and brand strategy, however repetitive that feels to you. With the brand strategy as a filter, ask them to think about the work their team does and what they can stop, start and continue to improve the experience. Who will do the work? What is the SMART objective and what is the RACI? Let them know that the best work will be recognized in your awards programme. On your intranet, have a place where team leaders can declare their SMART objectives and what they are doing. Ask internal communications to share stories of their thinking and achievements.

Here are some starter ideas for what might need attention which your colleagues will add to.

For your employee experience:

- **Recruitment:** your recruitment ads, the company description on your careers page, 'about' page, and LinkedIn pages, how recruiters and hiring managers describe the company and brand, your hiring criteria.

- **Onboarding:** the first day, making sure induction enthuses new recruits and educates them on how to behave and take decisions on-brand, ensuring any briefing or core documents, ike a Code of Conduct, reflect the brand strategy.
- **Thriving:** the competencies for each role being right for the brand strategy, how employees are assessed for promotion, the weighting put on delivering on the brand strategy and role-modelling it in appraisals, how you manage behaviour that isn't *who we are* and *how we do things* in appraisals, reward and recognition initiatives, making sure colleagues are exposed to your advertising so they can see what buyers see.
- **Departing:** saying thank you, alumni program, learning from exit interviews how to improve the experience.

> ### Watch-out #20: Align policies in year one
>
> Update HR policies and procedures in the first year. Employees will believe the commitment to the brand strategy is genuine when they see the impact it's going to have on what they're expected to do in their job and how they are rewarded and promoted.

For the buyer and customer experience:
- **Pre-purchase:** easy to find what is right for them, what goes with what, what the natural upgrade paths are, being relevant, different, cohesive and engaging in the places buyers are consuming media.
- **Purchase:** marketing products that are actually available or will be soon, easy and engaging to buy.
- **Post-purchase:** easy to make the most of the purchase, easy to help themselves and get help, easy to upgrade and ensuring the experience is cohesive with the pre-purchase messages.
- **Repurchase:** rewarded for loyalty, easy to repurchase.

Creating remarkable moments

While fixing and improving is the work of everyone, you need creativity to make what Chip Heath and Dan Heath describe as "peak moments". These are short experiences, cohesive with your brand strategy, that have a disproportionate impact on what people remember and tell other people about. In short, moments people will find remarkable and will remark upon. These moments of "elevation" can have a significant impact on revenue.[177] Forrester research across 16 industries shows that while most organizations spend about 80% of their time fixing problems, you'll earn about nine times more revenue if you "elevate the positives" rather than focus on the negatives.[178]

What can these moments be? They should be very tailored to your brand and can be for buyers or employees. For example:

- Salesforce staged an 'End of Software' protest in front of rival Siebel Systems.

- Innocent started putting little knitted hats on their smoothies, giving 25p to Age UK for every behatted bottle sold.[179]

- Taco Bell opened a one-off hotel, which sold out in 2 minutes.[180]

- Pizza Hut in Taiwan creates limited edition 'flash offers' of pizza with delectable ingredients like 'stinky tofu' or bubble tea.[181]

- The W hotel have a 'whenever/whatever' service that promises to get you anything you want (as long as it's legal).

- Barbie created a real-life Dreamhouse in Malibu, rentable on Airbnb.

- For many years, Jeff Bezos insisted that desks at Amazon "were built by buying cheap doors from Home Depot and nailing legs to them", to remind everyone that "we look for every opportunity to save money so we can deliver the best products for the lowest cost."[182]

- The Saturday morning Walmart meetings start and end with the Wal-Mart cheer.

- One&Only employees put their hands on their heart when they greet a guest.

- One of Zappos' core values is 'create fun and little weirdness.' One of their interview questions is, "On a scale of 1–10, how weird are you?"[183]

All so different but all intended to create a remarkable moment.

Remarkable moments can be one-off or regular initiatives or rituals. Ben Horowitz argues that "powerful cultures are built around shocking rules", the almost daily rituals and practices that are memorable or so "bizarre", they make the culture tangible and unignorable.[184] These rituals act as a beacon in the employee experience and create a sense of belonging. They reinforce the brand strategy. They stimulate conversations. What can be tricky, of course, is if the everyday culture of the business is the antithesis, making the rituals seem vacuous and insubstantial.

These moments have to be created and this is a challenge. As the Heaths point out, most executives play defence rather than offence. First, you have to get the juicy creative ideas to flow. Second, making them happen will likely require cross-departmental effort. You are going to need the sponsorship of the CEO to break down the silos and create the momentum to execute. Bring together creative strategic thinkers, from both inside and outside, to address one opportunity in the buyer experience or employee experience or a particular business opportunity at a time. Tackle one a month, or one a quarter. Create a group of movers and shakers who have it built into their job role and renumeration. Just be sure to prioritize it.

Rewarding and recognizing on-brand impact

One of the simplest rituals to implement internally is a means of recognizing and rewarding people who do things that move the business forward with the brand strategy.

We can always do more to recognize and appreciate colleagues. Over 80% of supervisors claim they frequently express appreciation to their subordinates, while less than 20% of employees report that their supervisors express appreciation more than occasionally.[185] McKinsey research on 'The Great Attrition' among 6,000+ global employers and employees showed that the top three reasons for quitting were not compensation, work–life balance or poor physical and emotional health, as employers predicted, but rather that employees didn't feel valued by their organizations (54%) or their managers (52%), or because they didn't feel a sense of belonging at work (51%).[186]

Annual awards that recognize and reward the people who have made the fixes, improvements and remarkable moments are invaluable. Draw on your brand strategy to create award categories and criteria for judging. Make sure only entries that can demonstrate impact are considered. Put together a judging team from across the business, with a mix of skills and experience, to shortlist the top three for each category. Ask the C-suite to judge the final contenders and select one as the ultimate winner.

Launch the awards, or re-launch if you already have a programme, as soon after the brand strategy is launched as possible and as all the engagement gets under way, giving people up to a year to make a difference before submitting applications. Celebrate the awards at your annual leadership meeting and all company meeting. Make it a remarkable moment internally. Creating trophies, certificates, storytelling films, posters, and showcasing award winners on recruitment ads and your recruitment pages can all help with employee engagement. Remember that this is another way to drive business growth.

For the everyday, find a way for colleagues to recognize others for their work to make the brand strategy real. There are different ways to do this, so look at what you have that you can adapt or consider what is most practical to introduce. There is an exceptional hotel we've worked with where employees nominate colleagues for their contribution on beautiful postcards put in internal post boxes, with the most outstanding nominee each week receiving champagne. One accounting firm encourages colleagues to nominate others to receive vouchers to spend in retail stores. We have spent time with a tech company who has a section of their intranet dedicated to colleagues saying thank you to other colleagues for their contribution to a specific aspect of the brand strategy. You can choose to display this appreciation publicly, so that others can put their thanks in the thread, or share it more privately, notifying just them and their manager.

> **Watch-out #21: Failing the values litmus test**
>
> To show that your CEO and leadership are really committed to the brand strategy, they will need to consistently enforce the implications. Nowhere is this tested more than when it comes to aligning hiring and firing decisions with your answers to *who we are* and *how we do things*.
>
> Exceptions are made, often for what appears to be good reason. An old favourite we hear all the time is: "We can't disrupt our top talent." Organizational psychologist and professor Bob Sutton identifies that "leaders get the behavior they display and tolerate". Marketing and culture advisor, Hilton Barbour, concurs: "Your culture is defined by the worst behaviour tolerated by management."[187] As Denise Lee Yohn tells us, "The hiring and firing decisions you and your fellow leaders make may be the ultimate litmus tests for the strength of leadership commitment to cultivating your desired culture."[188]

Implementing the brand identity to inspire everyone to use it cohesively and creatively

When implementing the brand identity, the two biggest problems you need to cater for are control and flexibility. You need your brand identity to be used properly, so everything is cohesive. You need flexibility to stay fresh with the identity across multiple media, tactics and countries.

Questions will be abundant as soon as the brand identity is available to be used, which may overwhelm you and your team: "How do I create a graph?"; "Which colour can my product own?"; "What music should we use on our films?"; "Can my department have a logo?"; "Can this initiative have a cool name and different look and feel?"; "How do I differentiate between one event and another at the same venue?"; "How do I differentiate between tactics for one audience and another?" and on, and on, and on…

This requires strong guidance and training. You don't need a complete set of brand rules that must be obeyed and policed. Those responsible for identity implementation need to be released from lengthy guidelines, unthinking consistency and expecting the brand police to oversee them. Instead, build their confidence.

Your job is to train people and their agencies to instinctively know what is now on- and off-brand. Make the training compulsory for anyone using the identity – the HR Lead can help with that.

Brief on the brand diagnosis and brand strategy (yes – again!). Teach them about the brand identity's ingredients and how to make recipes. Show them some of the examples of tactical executions you've made. Use quizzes to help them develop their eye for what is on and off brand. Include quiz questions that disarm their expectations, like always having to put the logo in same place.

Help everyone get it. Make it fun. Not only will they 'get' what is on-brand instinctively, they are more likely to surpass any expectations you have of how brilliantly the brand can show up. Encourage coherence and creativity that works, rather than obedience.

Put the ingredients, recipes, dos and don'ts, execution examples, on demand training, quizzes and frequently asked questions online in your digital asset management tool. Make it mandatory that everyone uploads what they are publishing. Make it possible to search all the assets by campaign, by tactic, by recipe, by type of buyer, by types of products and services, or by stages in the funnel, so colleagues can look at all the touchpoints for an event, or see all direct mail, or everything made in that recipe. As real executions are made, use them as the examples to bring to life each recipe, replacing the illustrative ones you provided at the beginning. This celebrates the savvy creativity of those executing the brand, demonstrating what works in market.

Those who repeatedly execute on-brand can be fast-tracked to do their own brand approvals. Run spot checks on their work instead and course correct with training. Use their work to reinforce for others that they too can push creativity to its most effective in a way that is on-brand. Your goal is to get everyone to fast track status. Then you can move to offering advice up front, rather than investing lots of time in approvals.

Set up an open group on your company's collaboration software and add everyone who has been trained. Put someone in charge of answering questions, directing people to what they need. Every month, review what came out of questions, training, and uploaded examples into your asset management system, and add more guidance to help people get it right more often. It's a positive, reinforcing feedback loop.

Do this, rather than investing time, money and effort in comprehensive brand guidelines and brand policing.

How do you know you've done a good job?

- ✓ Your brand identity is both cohesive and fresh.
- ✓ The tactics in a journey look and sound cohesive.
- ✓ Everyone using the brand is able to get it right or almost right first time.
- ✓ People can critique each other's work as on/off-brand with confidence.
- ✓ New recipes emerge from the people using the ingredients.
- ✓ There is a wonderful collection of impactful real-life examples of recipes used in execution.
- ✓ Teams executing the identity feedback what works and doesn't and that becomes guidance that directs future tactics.
- ✓ The next time you run Distinctive Brand Asset research you find that those assets are becoming more recognized and connected to your brand.

Final thoughts on implementation

You set out to help colleagues understand the brand, the expectations of them, and how to use the brand strategy to make choices. You've galvanized everyone in the organization to find ways to make the buyer and employee experience easier and more relevant. You're creating remarkable moments that differentiate your brand and get attention. You haven't wasted time and energy trying to map or control everything. You're part of a team that is implementing together cohesively across the business.

The chapter started with three core objectives and we've covered the first two. Let's work through the third, driving from brand to demand to revenue, before we explore assessing the impact of your rebrand.

Chapter 6
Brand to demand – your marketing strategy and plan

What you will know by the end of this chapter:

- The eight decisions you need to take in your marketing strategy
- The eight components of an integrated marketing plan that drives brand to demand
- How to invest your budget effectively
- How to sequence and test the work
- The make-or-break elements

Now that implementation is underway, your colleagues are beginning to make on-brand choices because they understand the brand diagnosis, brand strategy and expectations of them. Work is happening to fix (hygiene and antithesis) and improve parts of the experience and you're creating remarkable moments. Let's turn to marketing. How do you make your brand and marketing cohesive to drive from the brand into demand for what you sell?

Your business strategy informed your brand strategy, now both will inform your marketing strategy. Marketing's job is to grow future revenue by making your brand easy to mind and easy to buy. We call this brand to demand. Demand is sometimes called performance, growth, or activation marketing.

There are decisions you need to take to define your marketing strategy:

1. Who the buyer is and how much of the market you are targeting.
2. Which Category Entry Points you are prioritizing.
3. Why a buyer would choose you.
4. The priority products and services you wish to sell.
5. The right pricing.
6. Where you will be easy to buy – your place priorities.
7. Your SMART goal to focus everyone on what success looks like.
8. Your budget.

Then you can write your marketing plan:

1. Structure your marketing plan into programmes.
2. Define journeys by Category Entry Points, use cases and types of products and services.
3. Create messaging that ladders.
4. Identify tactics that are integrated to work together.
5. Create tactics made to requirements.
6. Invest in creative that gets attention.
7. Define a media strategy that maximizes reach and frequency.
8. Measure to understand how it's working – covered in chapter 7.

The decisions you need to take in your marketing strategy

Marketing strategies #1, who the buyer is and how much of the market you are targeting; and #2, which Category Entry Points you are prioritizing

We'll consider the first two points together.

You know that to grow your market share, you need to reach new buyers, 'light' buyers (those who rarely buy from you) and existing buyers to drive new purchases, repeat purchases, cross-sell and upsell. But the first point to bear in mind is that buyers aren't all in market all the time. Purchases can be made irregularly, seasonally, occasionally. Professor John Dawes of the Ehrenberg-Bass Institute has explained that, at any time, 95% of customers are not in market shopping.[189] In a recession demand can drop as low as 1% of B2B buyers actively purchasing big ticket items.[190]

So, marketers often debate whether we should woo the mass market of buyers or target a segment. It comes down to a choice about reach and frequency. You want to reach the greatest number of buyers, who are the best fit for what you sell, with enough frequency. You only have so much budget, so you will need to prioritize. To do this, it is helpful to see the market in a segmentation.

You can do this in a simple table. Down the left column, put the different types of buyer you defined in your brand diagnosis. Add the total number of these buyers and how many of them are existing customers, as well as the total spend per year and how much they spend with you. This is a mix of Total Addressable Market (TAM) data, which finance will have or can buy from analysts, and company data.

Across the top of the other columns, put each of the Category Entry Points, from least to most important (as many columns as there are entry points). Bold the ones your brand was most associated with. Cut the research data by buyer type and put in each box what percentage of that buyer type said each Category Entry Point was relevant to them.

Table 14: Market segmentation

Market segmentation					
Category entry points	Least important to buyer				Most important
	[insert Category Entry Point]	[insert Category Entry Point]	[insert Category Entry Point]	[insert Category Entry Point]	[insert Category Entry Point]
Buyers group [describe] #buyers & spend #customers & spend	% buyers who said it was relevant	%	%	%	%
Repeat for each group	%	%	%	%	%

If your brand is global, it's worth filling this in for each priority country and looking at it alongside that country's brand funnel data. While these segmentations are always based on best estimates, they give you the size and shape of the market which is useful for making decisions on where to invest. Look for the segments where you already have buyers, the value is attractive and the Category Entry Points that your brand is associated with are relevant. To get going, select the best three to four Category Entry Points to prioritize in your marketing strategy.

You may be offered other segmentations by finance or sales which will look through a different lens, identifying, for example, the most profitable existing buyers or who to target for upsell. We still recommend you create this actionable market segmentation that looks through the lens of Category Entry Points.

Marketing strategy #3: Why a buyer would choose you

You have defined this in your brand strategy. Add the strategy to your marketing strategy document, but focus here on the answers to *what we do and why we do it*.

Marketing strategy #4: the priority products and services you wish to sell

Not all products and services are equal. Buyers don't have the capacity or desire to absorb all the possibilities you offer. It is unlikely you can afford to promote them all. You need to make it easy for them to find and buy what they need.

You'll have found that some of your products are best to sell first, because they are the easiest to sell, cross-sell or up sell from, or have the highest margin. This could change with the seasons, what is zeitgeist, or you may want to focus on what is new or the best sellers. Some products and services may be so quintessentially on-brand that they stand out; perhaps they're even truly different (first, unique or only – even if just in the short term).

Buyers may shop for the product/service by name, by types of products or services, or by Category Entry Points. Prioritize what you will offer them first and be able to suggest what goes with it and what the upgrade or downgrade choices are. It is usually better to sell a lesser version than lose the buyer completely. You may need to do this by country if there is variance in what you sell. Organizing your portfolio and identifying your priority products and services can take work, but it will make it easier for the buyer to navigate and stop them abandoning the process to shop elsewhere.

Watch-out #22: Making the brand easier to buy – brand architecture and naming strategy

Having prioritized what you want to sell, do you have any concerns about how easy it is for buyers to find what is right for them, what goes with what and what the natural upgrade path is? Is it clear what the product/service does? Or which products work with each other, or which services go with which products? It isn't always easy to tell from the name or visually. Offering good, better, best versions of a product/service with low, medium and high price pricing – 'Goldilocks pricing' – relies on differentiation between your own products as well as comparative pricing. Which means your portfolio has to be well organized to make what you offer easier to navigate.

If colleagues and partners are complaining about the portfolio being complicated, or hard to understand or learn you know you have a problem. If this is what you heard during your brand diagnosis, then make time now to work on your brand architecture and naming strategy. You may need to better signpost the differences and relationships between parts of your portfolio. Find a brand architecture expert to work through this with you, because it can be complicated and you need the right advice.

Grouping similar products under the same name can be helpful. HPE made its portfolio easier to buy by reducing the 29 brands it had to a handful and grouping all similar types of products and services into the right bucket: HPE ProLiant Compute, HPE Cray Supercomputing, HPE Alletra Storage, HPE Ezmeral Software, HPE Aruba Networking, HPE Services.[191] Adding a descriptor to the brand names (e.g. Software, Networking, Services), like HPE do, helps buyers easily tell what the product does, especially useful if it also has a coined (made up) name. If you offer products to very different buyers, such as consumers, governments and businesses, you may decide to allow lock ups to the logo e.g. Aviva Wealth, Aviva Private Clients.

Whatever you do, don't make it about your company's organizational structure because the buyer doesn't care. Make sure the way you organize, prioritize, name, present what you offer is easy and cohesive for the buyer to confidently know what's right for them.

Marketing strategy #5: the right pricing

Building a strong brand will also give you another lever: pricing.

When inflation and interest rates are low buyers' price sensitivity is lower and shareholders are happy to invest in innovation to produce future profit.[192] As a result, many marketers focus less on pricing. When inflation is higher or more volatile, rising costs need to be passed onto the buyer and investors shift to seeking immediate profit gains. Pricing becomes critical.

Many brands teach buyers to be price sensitive through repeated price promotions. Buyers learn to wait for the next sale, stockpile, or buy from whoever's discounting. These promotions increase sales in the short term but reduce profit margins. The overall volume of sales is unlikely to increase so really what you're doing is subsidizing the sales. Competitors quickly copy so there are even more promotions in the market, but the overall value of the market hasn't increased.[193] "Price promotions are a dangerous and addictive drug at the best of times and right now for most businesses they are sheer madness," expert on effectiveness Les Binet tells us.[194]

When you increase price, it increases revenue, but almost always decreases volume if there is no perceived added value. When you increase volume, you increase revenue and costs. Binet explains "the really big increases in profit come from brands that manage to increase both price and volume at the same time".[195] This 'price elasticity' is the amount the volume goes down by each percentage you increase the price. "Low price elasticity is key to big profits," advises Binet.[196] You can measure price elasticity with finance using econometric modelling.

Strong brands build low price elasticity by having high perceived value. Buyers will pay up to double the amount for highly relevant and differentiated brands.[197] But, "More often than not, brand spend is the first to be rationalised by finance, who can lose sight of the longer term halo that a well loved brand can have on price," CFO David Anderson tells us.[198] Professors Leonard M. Lodish and Carl F. Mela have seen the impact this has: "Companies routinely overinvest in promotions and underinvest in advertising, product development, and new forms of distribution. As a result, powerhouse brands have been weakened, often beyond recovery."[199] They go on to explain that higher sales at full price is a "quality premium" and that "brands with loyal customers face less pressure to reduce their prices and therefore enjoy a price premium. Together, quantity and price premiums reflect a brand's long-term health."[200]

Building a strong brand and reducing price promotions must be combined with sustained marketing investment in both brand and demand, as "the longer the campaign, the bigger the price effect" explains Binet. Marketing needs to reach as many buyers as possible, with creative that generates an emotional response and that builds positive associations in buyers' minds. If you target too tightly, eliminate all waste by reducing frequency or reach, market too rationally with boring creative, focus only on short-term sales activation, your brand will not be as successful.[201]

Finally, heed Binet's warning that "If pricing is wrong, other marketing efforts are futile". Work with finance to calculate your brand's current price elasticity, review your approach to price promotions and understand how brand investment and pricing choices impact demand, profitability and long-term growth. As your brand becomes stronger, work together to increase price and volume at the same time.

Marketing strategy #6: where you will be easy to buy – your place priorities

Decide the places where your products and services will be available to buy. This could be on your website, at events, in pop up or permanent shops, through intermediaries, brokers, aggregators, social media, or through third-party retailers. Oatly found a way in through Baristas; Liquid Death through tattoo parlours and bars. How can your brand show up in more places your buyers like to be?

Marketing strategy #7: all expressed as a SMART goal to focus everyone on what success looks like

A SMART goal stands for Specific, Measurable, Achievable, Relevant, Time-bound. Pull together all the marketing strategy decisions you've taken and combine that with the outcome that the business is asking marketing to achieve with the rebrand. For example, back to our brand funnel in Figure 1, we could have as the objective: 'To increase spontaneous awareness from 31% to 39% and improve familiarity from 27% to 36%, in USA and Canada, by end of the financial year.'

Marketing strategy #8: your budget

We've found it is quite usual for marketing to budget brand marketing separately from demand generation. Does that sound familiar?

Consider the buyer's perspective. They think of you as one brand and are not interested in your organizational structure. One brand enemy you face is inertia, because buyers often feel safer repeating a decision rather than making a new one. You need to build their confidence in choosing your brand. The experience they have with you has to be cohesive. This is full-funnel marketing, from brand to demand to experience.

Balancing long-term brand building versus short term demand generation is critical. Les Binet and Peter Field's initial guide of 60% long and 40% short was modified to a range for different brands, in different categories, at different stages of development, different price points, etc. Some brands may need closer to 50:50, while brands that operate primarily online may find 70:30 works well.[202] What should not be in debate is the importance of long-term brand building and the need to set aside a significant percentage of your budget for it.[203] If you're struggling to convince your leadership team to invest in this way, take a look at work from Les Binet and Peter Field, Orlando Wood, Sir John Hegarty, System1 and the course a.p.e. (advertising principles explained).

Begin by putting the brand and demand budgets together, so you have a maximum investment amount. As you define your marketing strategy and plan, you will make choices that allocate investment to where it's needed most to achieve your goals.

We are not fans of pre-allocating budget; this is often a rinse-and-repeat exercise from last year. We have never found it easy to do zero-based budgeting because it is hard to persuade leadership to allocate marketing's budget this way. Usually, they would rather invest at the same level as last year and consider adding incremental budget later to what is shown to be working. It is better to take your total budget and make your investments work harder and more cohesively. A word of caution if your budget is a percentage of revenue or profit: if sales go down your budget goes down, which means you will find it hard to build future revenue.

As a general rule, for the full funnel, we have found it effective to invest 10–20% of the budget in making ads and tactics, 10% in localization and production and 70–80% in reach and frequency. Some tactics need to be replaced more often than others. Often the tactics at the top of the funnel are more expensive than nearer purchase, so we usually find that the budget ends up being split along the lines Binet and Field recommend.

Investment consistency is the other challenge. Budgets typically get set in the last quarter for the following year, with only 12 months' commitment. Often, as the quarters progress, budgets can get cut to achieve a target margin. Leadership have 'great ideas' that eat budget that has to come from cutting somewhere else. Media always seems to be reduced first. To build demand long term you must invest consistently, so work with finance to achieve continuity.

You are ready to write your marketing plan. There are eight points to consider, which we will work through step-by-step together. These steps cater for a complex situation: multiple types of products and services, different routes to market, operating in different countries, having more than one kind of buyer, with different ways in which they might want to use what you sell. As you work through the steps you'll find your marketing plan takes the shape you need for your business.

How to write your marketing plan

Marketing plan #1: structure your marketing plan into programmes

Brand and demand are complementary. Together they help you grow. James Hurman and Rory Dolan of Tracksuit say "Put simply, more awareness = higher conversion rate."[204] We've found through experience that the more integrated the tactics, the better the overall performance.

Marketing's commitment of what it will deliver to the business (both long and short term) can be unpacked into programmes with specific objectives. These are purposeful programmes of coordinated tactics (activities) that promote your brand, products and services to the buyer. Each programme has an objective to achieve and contributes to marketing's overall commitment to the business.

Tactics will vary and can range from events, public relations and advertising to emails and content, but all cohesively do different jobs to nudge the buyer from awareness to purchase.

There are different ways to organize your programmes. Are you marketing to one or more buyer type, the same or different products?

If it is one group of buyers, Table 15 shows a way to structure your marketing efforts into programmes.

Table 15: Marketing Programmes Structure One, for one buyer type

All buyers, Programme 1, **Awareness**			
Buyer **1**, Programme 2, **Demand**, Category Entry Point (CEP) **A**	Buyer **1**, Prog 3, Demand, CEP **B**	Buyer **1**, Prog 4, Demand, CEP **C**	Buyer **1**, Prog 5, Demand, CEP **D**

Or if you have different buyers, buying the same or different products, Table 16 shows how you can approach it.

Table 16: Marketing Programmes Structure Two, for different buyer types

All buyers, Programme 1, **Awareness**							
Buyer 1, Prog 2, Demand, Category Entry Point A	Buyer 1, Prog 3, Demand, CEP B	Buyer 1, Prog 4, Demand, CEP C	Buyer 1, Prog 5, Demand, CEP D	Buyer 2, Prog 6, Demand, CEP A	Buyer 2, Prog 7, Demand, CEP B	Buyer 2, Prog 8, Demand, CEP C	Buyer 2, Prog 9, Demand, CEP D

Explore what will work best for your brand.

Marketing plan #2: Define journeys by Category Entry Points, use cases and types of products and services

Imagine that your brand is a department store, with many doors, corridors and rooms. Some buyers come to re-purchase, or find something similar, better or an alternative. They may look for a type of product/service, then consider what is available and most relevant. They may look for what they want by name or have forgotten the name but recognize it when they see it. They may come looking for something and decide to explore something else. You have to make it easy for the buyer to shop, no matter what their starting point is.

Buyers move about like they're in a game of snakes and ladders. We've seen this in data many times. This shifting up, down and across requires all the touchpoints to be cohesive to confidently nudge them on their journey. There are multiplier effects from the effectiveness of integrating your programmes end-to-end. Optimizing the balance of the full marketing mix can provide a +40% ROI according to Kantar.[205] This is why we don't worry about whether the funnel is linear or not, but focus on it being cohesive, so that the buyer can take whatever path suits them.

Structure your marketing plan to generate awareness, familiarity and favourability, to build associations and assets in each buyer's mind. Then be relevant to their Category Entry Point as they come shopping, helping them find the best fit products and services for their 'use cases'. A 'use case' means "a use to which something can be put" and is a criteria for judging whether a product or service will meet your needs.[206] If the Category Entry Point is "we're rebranding", the use case could be "as a marketer, I want to lead my first rebrand successfully", and this book *Rebrand Right* (the product) would be a helpful guide to achieving that aim.

For each of your programmes write in the Category Entry Point. Working with product marketing and sales, identify the three to five use cases that specify what the buyer is looking for. For each use case, identify which of the priority products and services is the best fit to meet those needs. Follow Steps 1–3 in Table 17, and repeat for each Category Entry Point and buyer.

Table 17: Journeys by Category Entry Point

Journey stage	Programme	What you need to do		
Aware I am aware of [brand] & **Unaware**	**All** buyers, Programme 1, **Awareness**			
Familiar I know [brand] & **Favourable** I like [brand]	e.g. Buyer **1**, Programme 2, **Demand**, Category Entry Point **A**	*Step 1: Define the Category Entry Points*		
		Step 2: Define the use cases that fit within this Category Entry Point.	*Repeat steps 2 & 3 for each use case.*	
Consider – Category Entry Point [Brand] can help me		*Step 3: Define the best fit priority products and services for each use case.*		

Not all buyers come shopping by Category Entry Point. We'll cater for buyers looking for a type of product/service and connect that into you programme structure. For now, just write down all the *types* of products and services you offer and for each identify the use cases with best fit priority product and services (see Table 18). Complete Steps 1–3 and repeat for each type of product/service you offer.

Table 18: Journeys by type of product/service

Familiar I know [brand] & **Favourable** I like [brand]	*Step 1: Define a type of product/service you offer.*			
	Step 2: Define a use case for this for this type of products and services.	*... add the next use case for this type...*		
Consider **– type of product/ service** [Brand] can help me	*Step 3: Add the priority products and services of this type that are the best fit for the use case*	*... and the priority products or services*		

Sometimes use cases fit into multiple Category Entry Points or types of products and services, sometimes priority products and services fit multiple use cases or Category Entry Points. Lack of duplication is not your aim, so don't make that the priority. Your role is to give the buyer the right information they need to move forwards.

Watch-out #23: Don't drown in the details

As we move through how to write the marketing plan, you'll see mapping the journeys gets fiddly quickly. It's a lot easier to do it on stickies on a huge virtual digital wall, so you can move and connect things as you go. There is software available that can you help you.

Marketing plan #3: Messaging that ladders

Messaging is not copy or taglines
What your brand says and how it says it is a big part of how you look, feel and sound. Messaging builds associations in the mind of the buyer using words. Messaging is not slogans or taglines or campaign lines, which are fixed, with agreed translation. Nor is it copy, which is a way of expressing a message. It is what you wish your audience to know.

You can tell when there isn't a clear approach to messaging because what is correct is subjective and so it changes all the time and isn't cohesive. Brands can also sound egotistical, always speaking from their perspective and not the buyers or quickly descending into features, functionality, pricing.

Cohesive messaging gives buyers confidence. They're more likely to trust what is being said and begin to build associations with your brand. One message can be expressed in different ways through the choice of language and use of Distinctive Brand Assets, which makes it possible to be both cohesive and fresh in your marketing. Agreed messaging gives those making the tactics the ability to crack on with making, which can be liberating.

Get the team together
It takes work to do messaging well – focus, time and commitment. No doubt teams across your business have their own messaging, but this can feel confusing to buyers. You will need to woo them into authoring one messaging approach with you, particularly the product marketing and communications teams. With the right people, it can be done in a week or two. Or you can involve everyone, take months and get thoroughly fed up. Ideally, you'd all be physically together, but you can make it work over video conferencing. You can write the messaging together or work as individuals or small groups in the morning, meeting in the afternoon to first read what has been done and then together provide constructive input for the next morning's efforts.

The messaging ladder
We have found that it's simplest to author cohesive messaging if you do it in a particular order. Building on the decisions you have already taken, do Steps 1–4 (Table 19). Then repeat Steps 3 and 4 for each use case.

Table 19: Defining messaging for journeys by Category Entry Point

Journey stage	Programme	What you need to do
Aware I am aware of [brand] & **Unaware**	**All** buyers, Programme 1, Awareness	*Start here: Step 1: Write your messaging based on your brand strategy.*
Familiar I know [brand] & **Favourable** I like [brand]	e.g. Buyer **1**, Programme 2, **Demand**, Category Entry Point A	You have defined the Category Entry Point. *Step 2: Write the message that responds to each Category Entry Point.*
		You have defined the use cases that fit within this Category Entry Point. *Step 3: Write the message that responds to this use case.*
Consider – **Category Entry Point** [Brand] can help me		You have defined the best fit priority products and services for each use case. *Step 4: Write the message that explains why this priority product/service is the best fit for the use case.*

Do one programme, then you can repeat the process for the others in your structure. Awareness remains the same for every programme and journey, so that message only needs to be written once. Read what you have written up, down, across and diagonally. If you flit between priority products and services, or use case, or type of product/service, or Category Entry Points is it still cohesive?

Write the messaging for the journeys that start by type of product/service (Table 20).

Table 20: Defining messaging for journeys by type of product/service

Familiar I know [brand] & Favourable I like [brand]	You have defined the type of product/service.			
	You have defined the use cases. *Start here: 1. Write the message that responds to each use case.*			
Consider – type of product/service [Brand] can help me	You have defined the best fit priority products and services of this type. *2. Write the message that explains why this priority product/ service is the best fit for the use case.*			

Remember we talked about all the various metaphorical doors the buyer could walk through? You now have defined what needs to be said at each stage in the buyer's journey, catering for the reasons they come shopping, or what specific use they might want to put the product/service to, as well as them looking by name or type of product/service. Every box in your table represents a possible step on the buyer's journey.

Marketing plan #4: Tactics that are integrated to work together

You now need to define the tactic(s) you will use to engage the buyer with information to nudge them forwards. These tactics, or activities, each have a specific job to do in the journey and have to work together cohesively. Too often the tactics a buyer experiences can end up feeling like random acts of marketing. Each individual tactic can be justified internally but doesn't do the job or work together with the others. This prevents you from building and reinforcing those relevant and different associations in buyer's mind that predispose them to feel you're the right choice.

For every step, look at what stage the buyer is at, which metaphorical door they have walked through (Category Entry Point, use case, etc.)

and what message you wish to communicate. What is the best way to do this? There are so many possible tactics to choose from:

- **To build awareness:** perhaps keynote speeches at conferences, exhibitions, events, pop up shops, store windows, side of pack, newsjacking (adding your brand's opinions into breaking news or trending topics), website, event invites, or influencers. Don't worry about media (advertising) yet, you'll add that later.

- **To build familiarity and favourability:** could be blogs, customer stories, films, infographics, white papers, website, thought leadership or influencers.

- **To build consideration:** maybe webinars, product demos and virtual tours, product comparisons, diagnosis tools (total cost of ownership, or which product/service is right for you, or when is best to visit), samples or hands-on product events, product reviews.

It may take more than one tactic to do the job. For example, consideration of a product may need a hands-on demo, a virtual demo and ability on your website to compare the features and functionality of the product with others you offer.

You may wish to use the same tactics for each priority product and service, because this coherence can make it easy for buyers to flit from considering one to another. Think about how you can bring the brand experience to the buyer. Consider what needs to happen before and after a tactic to make that tactic work. Every event needs an invite and follow up, for example. Work with communications to define some newsworthy tactics (keynotes, pop ups, collaborations, original research papers). If your tactic has a duration (length of a film, or voxpop, or event, or how long a pop-up shop will be open) then specify it. Do your spokespeople need new talk tracks and media training to represent the brand strategy and messaging articulately? Be specific.

Which tactics will you gate, requiring contact info to be given, like registering for an event, or for access to a whitepaper or a voucher? Put a little lock icon on the corner of that tactic's box to represent it on your drawing.

Define what you want people to do (the Call to Action) after experiencing that tactic, drawing a line from that tactic to the next step in the journey.

Marketing plan #5: Tactics made to requirements

You now have requirements for each tactic to give to those creating them: brand strategy (including brand identity and tone of voice), stage in journey, what job the tactic is doing, message, format and the duration (if relevant) and which tactic comes before and after in the journey. Every tactic you make will be made to requirements, no random acts of marketing. Kantar have calculated that this customizing for context can reward you with a +57% contribution to brand equity.[207] We have seen marketers create tactics for the wrong reasons. Not always, but not rarely either. Copious amounts of content to cover all eventualities or because a leader had a 'brilliant idea'. This new approach may present a cultural shift for your colleagues.

We're often asked how to know if the tactic is doing its job. We aren't interested in whether it can be credited with driving purchase through last touch attribution. If only life was as simple as one tactic driving sales. It's everything the buyer experiences over time that drives revenue. Remember back in chapter 1 we asked: "Imagine we gave you money to buy a new car. Which brand of car would you buy?" Which specific tactic made you want to buy that brand of car? That brand came easily to your mind, not because of one interaction, but because of all the associations that have been building over time. What matters is whether the tactic does the job as intended and whether all the tactics work together effectively.

The tactics in these always-on marketing journeys can be prepared in advance.

You can interweave into these programmes more responsive tactics that keep you relevant to what's topical. Choose tactics that are quick to make for this, such as social cards promoted organically, influencers creating and sharing content for you and public relations newsjacking.

You can also use these always-on tactics as source material for account-based marketing (ABM). Done well, account-based marketing shifts how the most valuable buyer relationships are viewed from one-time transactions to ongoing relationships, where the goal is to always provide value. Marketing, sales and service work together to speak directly to the account's needs through meaningful and joined up interactions that develop trust, loyalty and advocacy of the brand. As Alisha Lyndon, CEO of Momentum ITSMA advocates, "A strong brand is the sum of all experiences that customers have with your business. Account-based marketing and strong branding are a powerful combination that drives unparalleled business growth. ABM targets the right accounts, but it's your brand that resonates, builds trust and turns those targets into loyal customers."[208] This 'we are one' approach breaks down internal silos to orientate around the buyer. Tactics used in your marketing can be personalized to the account, which is more scalable than making everything fresh and bespoke. The continuous buyer insights from these relationships should feed your brand diagnosis, experience improvements and remarkable moments development.

Making tactics
Before you invest 10–20% of your budget in making each tactic, you will need to be savvy about what you make and what you buy-in. Some marketing departments commission everything with agencies, others do everything themselves, some do a mix. Usually, it's down to budget and appetite. There is satisfaction and usually better results in working together with subject matter experts and format specialists like amazing film makers, writers, presenters, so do as much as you realistically can yourselves and seek external expertise where you need it most.

> **Watch-out #24: Understand search intent**
>
> Before you make anything, brief a search intent specialist to look at the digital search journey. Ask them to look at all search in your category over the last year. This can be organized by Category Entry Point to understand how great the demand is for each and whether it's growing. For your priority Category Entry Points delve deeper into the language, how buyers express what they are looking for. Feed this into the people making the content, writing the copy, optimizing for search, buying ads and delivering the tactics into market.

Do an audit of what you already have against your requirements. Is there anything that can be reused or upcycled? This will make the most of your existing investments and you can get live faster. Update your tactic requirements list with what you already have.

You may have a lot of video content already that you want to keep using. It can be expensive to edit the content to be on-brand but it is usually affordable to top and tail them all in the same way. Opening and closing every film tactic with the same animated graphic component and using the same animated logo and sonic can make different executions and tactics come across as more cohesive. You can also make idents, which play with your Distinctive Brand Assets, as interstitials in films or between speeches at events. Look at the BBC's idents for inspiration.

It helps for there to be a regular way to decide how each tactic will be made that becomes habitual for all. Bring together everyone who makes tactics in marketing and talk them through the marketing strategy, plan and requirements. Give them time to go away and think about it. Then together, talk through each tactic in turn, pitching ideas to each other until you know what you want to do. As you can tell, we think about tactics as either useful or polluting. Useful doesn't need to be boring, it can be as much about an influencer using your brand in a recipe, or a gamified diagnostic quiz, as it can be playing with a Distinctive Brand Asset (think of those KFC dancing chickens). Define what each tactic's hook will be (the 'aha' or key takeaway) that makes the buyer engage. You'll use it to inform the copy for the specific ads that drive into a tactic.

Think about how you can take one idea or story and thread it through the tactics. Perhaps you have a customer partnership with a well-known brand, where they can give keynotes at the event, share their story of the use case they solved for and the products they chose. Authentic behind-the-scenes stories give buyers insight into the people, practices and values behind your brand. This could be the making of the tartan for the Dior 2024 show, designing the afternoon tea for Corinthia London, or powering the compute for a formula one team's live analytics. These collaborations that become stories act as a "forcing function across whole business to work together to deliver on the brand strategy, galvanizing everyone to deliver on the promises to deadline" points out Locus' Chief Revenue Officer, Mehul Kapadia.[209] Another approach is to pick a topical issue and theme tactics around it for a fixed period of time.

Update your journeys and give this to everyone who is making. Agree who is making what, with how much budget and the deadline. Work out how long you think it will take to make each tactic. Influencer content, blogs and articles will be much quicker than research driven tactics. Dependencies can slow you down. For example customer approvals of a case study happen at the speed of the customer. You can prevent production, localization and go-live bottlenecks by delivering in batches rather than waiting until the end and handing them over in one go. Make a schedule of what is being delivered when. Make a moment out of saying 'Go' on making each tactic – we like to say 'Commissioned' and ring a bell (yes, really!).

Check in on each tactic while it's being made to make sure it will do what's required. Get the look, feel, sound and tone on-brand. Support each other to get it right and review with legal where you need their advice. Name every file in a standard way so that you don't end up putting the wrong asset into transcreation or live. Yes, this does happen and can be disastrous – we know from bitter experience! Track approvals: who approved which file when.

Brief the marketing team on what's coming and what's live. When an opportunity to be topical comes up, it makes it easier to know if you have something already you can use, or tweak and use, or if there is a gap and you need to make something new.

Watch-out #25: Train on tone of voice

The many people involved in making will need to understand how to use the tone of voice you have defined to bring to life the *who* and the *how* from your brand strategy across a wide variety of the tactics. There are agencies and consultants that can help you define this and train people on it. If you're not able to cover this in your budget, use AI to help. For instance, you can take a selection of things written in a tone that you feel reflects your brand and use AI to define the tonal commonalities.

You may need to be flamboyant in an ad, informal in a speech and precise in a technical white paper. Provide this guidance.

A style guide will be useful. They give instructions for abbreviations, contractions, acronyms, capitalization, numbers, punctuation, names and titles, emphasizing, spelling and many more miscellaneous areas. Pick and adapt an existing one.

We always advise seeing the world from the buyer's point of view and being unconditionally inclusive. Less is more, so make the point quickly, answering the 'So what?' and be understandable without effort. Use active language, positivity, keeping sentences shorter and rhythmic, avoiding acronyms and pseudo business speak. We prefer 'Sentence case' because it is the easiest to read. Always do a final check – does it read well out loud?

Proactively support the people making your tactics to help them work out what good looks like and make sure there is a feedback loop from what works in execution.

Watch-out #26: Beware tactic burnout

Some tactics will stop performing after a while. You'll see this in your measurement. Bring the team back together and commission replacements.

You can begin marketing plan steps #6 and #7 in parallel with marketing plan #3. It is best to know what your journeys will be from the top to bottom of the funnel, the mix of tactics and what priority products and services are at the end of the journeys before working on the creative and media.

Marketing plan #6: Creative that cuts through the noise and gets attention

You need creative that cuts through the noise and generates an emotional response to help you get attention and become easy to mind. High quality creative attracts four times more profit than low quality.[210]

Les Binet tells us that: "Campaigns that consciously aim to make the brand and its marketing famous are much, much better at reducing price sensitivity and supporting premium prices than any other kind of marketing."[211]

You may already have the best answer. Before you dream of any new campaign creative ideas and advertising, what do you already have? Make popcorn and watch them all.

We stand on the shoulders of giants, inheriting the brand, chaperoning it and passing it onto our successors. We have to be market-oriented, taking decisions that work for the buyer and our brand long term. We need to look back with appreciation, understanding that the best ad may already exist. We've worked with businesses who think nothing of investing many millions in a new ad every year, without putting the media budget behind it to get it seen. The company's people, partners and Board all love the shiny new thing. Marketers enjoy the making and the kudos. The financial enemy for agencies is an effective ad they've already made. We've found this is a tough paradigm to shift, but we ask you to care more about growing revenue than being seen to launch a new ad. Effective ads rarely wear out.[212] Changing the ad every year can hurt brand building. In *The Magic of Compound Creativity*, System1 research highlights how brands that stay the course with their strategy, creative idea, campaign, agency, assets and tone of voice produce higher creative quality. They also share how brands who use these things consistently see greater 'brand effects' – higher scores on awareness, differentiation, creating brand values, building salience, fame and changing attitudes – and greater business effects – in the form of sales value gain, profit gain and market share gain.[213] When you re-watch what your brand has put in market over the last decade, is it cohesive? Does it build and strengthen those associations you want to stand for in people's minds?

Do any of the ads support your brand strategy? If one comes close, can it run as is, or be tweaked to fit? It might need a fresh voiceover, an edit, new call to action, new graphics, better use of Distinctive Brand Assets, different length edits, relicensed music or fresh sound. Do a quick calculation of how much you would need to invest in reusing or upcycling existing, versus making new. Test to understand how effective the ad is. The cost of developing new is not only money (and how much of the media reach and frequency you need to sacrifice to afford it), but also the time it takes to make because the market won't wait.

If you need new advertising, then appoint the best creative agency you can find to inject their brilliance. Agency talent works on different briefs for different types of businesses to bring compelling creative ideas to the brands they work on. Their culture hungers to create work that cuts through the noise. We've found that leadership are often more open to ideas from external experts. No matter how superb your own brand's strategists, designers and copywriters are, ideas born in-house can be challenging to get right. Why? Motivations, politics, exposure and culture. You can be too close to the brand, too conditioned by previous decisions, or unaware you're playing safe. If you ask us when to bring in external creative firepower, this is one of those moments alongside brand identity creation, creating remarkable moments and media strategy.

Brief the agency on the brand diagnosis, brand strategy and identity, marketing strategy and plan. Ask them to develop creative concepts that will work full funnel, across all tactics and media and resonate in all priority countries. Make sure you get your Distinctive Brand Assets in early and throughout. Think also about whether your ad can be recognized with sound off or with sound but no image. McDonald's has been cohesively investing in building its Distinctive Brand Assets through great creative, from the ingredients in its 'iconic stacks' posters to its 'raise your arches' eyebrows ad.[214] Aviva's 'make it click' concept is a creative device that brings the brand strategy to life.[215] If you already have strong creative you can use, then ask the agency to help make the creative idea work from brand to demand.

Testing
Testing concepts is useful, because you aren't the buyer. We've lost count of the number of times we've been asked to "just run it by…" influential voices in the business who aren't the buyer. When you take on board too many of these voices strong creative ideas can easily become diluted, words can be picked over and emotional impact reduced. Your colleagues need to feel proud, yes, but the ad has to do its job.

The findings will make your decision making more objective. Without it you are likely to enter an unpredictable world of subjective feedback and recency bias from leadership. You can test creative ideas and ads.

It can be helpful when you have a few concepts to ask buyers:

1. Do they like it? What resonates with them and why?
2. Which concept communicates the on-brand idea most clearly?
3. (If you don't put your logo on it) Which company comes to mind and why?

Predictive ad testing can be conducted in 24 hours using simple self-service platforms that gauge emotional engagement, predict long-term impact on growth, short-term sales potential and strength of brand recognition.

You can use a research provider or if you have no time or money then get 15 minutes with non-buyers or existing buyers and ask them yourself (without leading the witness!). You need to know if the core idea will work in all the countries and with the different types of buyers. We aren't keen on using focus groups for this as a few voices can sway the rest.

Focus your choice on understanding:

1. Which concept resonates the most and has the best emotive response.
2. Which concept communicates the on-brand idea most clearly.
3. Whether it is recognized as coming from you or could be recalled as another brand.
4. What localization may be necessary.

You can also test final ads in a similar way.

Share what is being tested with the media agency so they can take inspiration from the ideas for the media strategy and give you the nod that they can make the chosen concept work across different media. Share the findings with leadership and marketing colleagues, so they have the evidence for your decision on choice of concept and how well the final ads work.

You will need a construct for your ads

Every ad you make will have a job to do. Your media plan will list many lengths, sizes, formats and calls to action needed. While you're likely to work with your agency on producing the big hero ads, realistically you'll also be executing through others (agencies or colleagues in different departments or countries) or in different languages, particularly for demand. You need a construct for how to design and copywrite a demand generation ad that will be effective and easy for many people to execute cohesively and repeatedly.

It could be in a three-frame ad: frame 1 is the Category Entry Point hook; frame 2, the benefit they seek; and frame 3 the best fit product/service solution with a call to action. Or frame 1 – don't do/put up with X; frame 2 – instead have Y; frame 3 – image of it and call to action. Take a decision on the construct and work up actual ads or examples. These are ad recipes and you can tweak them as you see what works for your brand in execution.

Marketing plan #7: A media strategy that maximizes reach and frequency

You're aiming for the best media mix, reach and frequency media strategy for your goal and budget. Find the best media partner you can afford. As Izzie Rivers, CEO, Realm advises:

> *Have an honest conversation with them about what your leadership's expectations are. Spend serious time on this, your future self will thank you. This gets everyone on the same page, directs the media investment to get you the results that you want, prepares stakeholders for how to communicate goals internally and sets you up for working with analytics across media channels to measure success.*[216]

Brief them on your brand diagnosis, brand strategy, marketing strategy and plan so far. Tell them your budget. Let them know which cities you have a physical presence in and the media and publications you have understood your buyers like to consume.

Clever media strategies find ways to create fresh associations with those that know you and build new ones with those that don't. Encourage your creative and media partners to work together as magic can happen that way.

What is the right mix of media? Kantar explain that "campaigns that are well integrated and customised to respective media contribute more than 50% more impact" and that 36% of campaign effects come from media synergies.[217] As Managing Director of Magic Numbers, Dr Grace

Kite, writes, "Target audiences see different things that work together, and you get the memory and persuasiveness benefits of repetition, without getting boring. Econometrics reports a huge 35–65% more ROI. And, according to Kantar, you can more than double the effect on your brand."[218]

The media team will want to understand what you want the buyer to do after being exposed to an ad and what the next best action is. What is marketing expected to deliver for the business, are there any handovers and how will the impact be measured? How are you growing and managing your buyer data? Does your leader have any biases, like not believing in radio for their brand, that they need to address?

You need to:

- Identify the most effective combination of reach and frequency for your brand, to a maximum of 70–80% of your total budget. Reach is how many buyers will see your ads. Frequency is how often they will see them. Prioritize reach over frequency, but don't sacrifice frequency to the point it doesn't work.

- Think full-funnel – how will you reach the most future buyers and those in-market?

- Understand what would it take to do everything 'properly', compared to being more light touch or not investing in some countries.

This information will also help you build a business case for investment. Don't forget to target your colleagues with the digital advertising so they see it and feel it is real (small cost, big impact).

Make your informed choices.

Promotional (media) asset requirements

Update the journeys with the media choices. At the top, add in boxes for each channel (paid and organic) and draw a line for each to the tactic being promoted. Those ads need to land the tactic's hook, the message and right call to action.

You will need a list of all your promotional requirements and variations (format, size, weight, duration, calls to action, language, alternative copy lines or visuals). Your creative agency may make the master versions of each required ad, but it is more efficient to make variants in production.

The CMO, if that isn't you, usually wants to see every ad. CEOs like to see the most important ones. Plan for this. Show them the masters and make sure they understand that there will be variants. Once you've started localization and production it is very expensive to change anything because one master can morph into sometimes hundreds of promotional tactics (one ad, four copy variants, 11 countries, different URLs, different call to action wording, all in 10 languages, it soon adds up).

Web journeys

Do review your digital channels. If you have lots of micro sites and campaign landing pages, are they integrated or dead ends for the buyer? Have they been abandoned? Clean up, close up and archive as much as necessary. In future always drive buyers into your actual website.

Share the journeys with your digital team and UX expert to structure your website and pages to drive engagement. Make sure the website's navigation, information architecture and experience are all informed by your brand architecture and naming strategy, marketing strategy and plan. The navigation needs to cater for buyers arriving looking by Category Entry Points and by types of products and services, before moving through the journey into use cases, which connect to your product and service pages. They will also want to search by name, types of products or services, use case, Category Entry Point and so on. Aligning the navigation to the strategy can be a minor or major adjustment, so do a gap analysis with the website leader as soon as you can.

The other challenge can be that pages with a similar purpose are constructed inconsistently, so if you switch between them they don't feel easy to read. It's worth going back to wire frames, the skeletal design of the structure and functionality you want for a web page, to agree with stakeholders how a Category Entry Point, a type of product/service, a use case and a specific product/service page should be structured. As you execute your marketing plan, you will populate these pages with tactics and on page copy.

If you have updated your visual identity you will need to update the style sheets that control the layout and design of a webpage.

Connective tissue

Identify where the tactics will go and what copy is needed; from the words that sit next to them on the page, to page titles and sub-heads, the copy at the top of the page, how you word the on-page call(s) to action. B2B marketing leader Sarah Tookey calls this the "connective tissue" as it glues the journey together.[219] What do your search intent experts recommend for keywords and URLs? Commission your favourite writer(s) to write the connective tissue to these specifications or use artificial intelligence to help.

Watch-out #27: Tame social gone wild

How many social channels do you have and do you need them all? There can be an abundance of official and unofficial social channels. Less is more. Get on-brand the ones you will continue with. Carefully engage colleagues who are operating unofficial, branded social channels to close them or bring their management into line with your social media policies. There is an increased risk when a channel is perceived as speaking officially on behalf of the business but not following the governance that reduces risk. Employees talking about the brand and amplifying branded content on their own handle (@username) is brilliant and should be encouraged.

Marketing plan #8: Localized to work in each country and channel

You may agonize over how the brand expresses itself in the country it's headquartered in, but do you make sure your tactics will work just as well in all the other priority countries?

We vividly remember a global product launch, where we were on a call with Australia, UK and US marketing colleagues to look at some draft ads. The concept was all about the product being the perfect fit, and the creative featured unexpected, humorous situations that weren't the perfect fit, like surfing in the outback. We had to explain to each other what we found hilarious and why, because when one nationality laughed, the other two didn't find it funny. An ad that features an earthquake will work differently in parts of the world where they are rare, compared to where they are common and distressing. Ads with music woven into the copy won't work the same in other languages. Even speaking the same language, each country is different – Brazilian Portuguese is not identical to that spoken in Portugal. You have to consider cultural, economic, political and linguistic differences.

Localization isn't about translation. It is about transcreation – expressing the idea in a way that works in that culture to build the fame and associations you intend. That's how we solved the global launch above – executing cohesively as our buyers bought internationally, but expressing the creative idea differently in each country, to achieve the same impact. It's how Cadbury ensures that their core idea, the spirit of generosity, works in India just as well as it works in the UK.[220]

Turn each promotional master into the variants that your media plan requires. Transcreate the copy and design. Are the visuals suitable or do you need to provide alternatives? Does the design need to be flipped to work left to right, right to left, or top down? Don't forget that word length varies for different languages so make sure your design allows for that.

For the connective tissue, get the web pages into staging so you can see how it all works together with the tactics, making time for any amendments, before you transcreate the copy into multiple languages.

Brief the translators to understand the purpose and tone. Don't put live what you haven't understood, do make sure a colleague from that culture checks it first, comparing it to the original to be sure it will do the same job, and make any tweaks needed.

Increasingly, software is streamlining production by suggesting corrections, as well as originating ads or tactics, before deploying them into the chosen media channel and adding them to your digital asset management (DAM). This work involves codifying (in 'AI-ready guidelines'), each brand identity recipe with yes/no rules to guide what's on-brand for that specify execution, as well as informing the artificial intelligence on what's required for that tactic and what has previously been effective in execution. This is improving rapidly, so explore what is available early in the rebranding process.

This can improve the marketing that your brand publishes day-to-day through intelligently instructed automation, freeing up resource to invest in finding creative, emotional and fresh ways to get cut through.

Make recipes, learning how they work best before codifying them into the tools that update live executions.

Transcreate your tactics and get them into the hands of those deploying them. Tag every tactic and call to action so you can track that it's working. Search engine optimize (SEO) your pages and tactics. Don't be afraid to have your marketing go live in waves if you can't afford to do it all at once.

If you have business development reps (BDRs) and sales, give them a way of seeing the journey that buyers go on and the tactics they may engage with, so they are up to speed as the direct conversations begin, making the experience feel easy and cohesive. They are hugely influential in the sales process. Ensure they understand the brand so they can be advocates. Provide them with easy ways to tweak and share tactics with buyers themselves ('social selling').

> **Watch-out #28: Expect barriers, simplify language**
>
> Marketing has an overwhelm of jargon. Jargon can create misunderstanding and a sense of imposter syndrome. We're decades into our careers and still sit in meetings where we translate what we are hearing into normal language, to make sure we've understood what is being said.
>
> Words can also create barriers. We're straightforward about how we work, but we've experienced how saying we need to write a marketing strategy and plan can create human obstacles.
>
> Marketers may have never had to write the marketing strategy together or derive the marketing plan from it. They may think of brand and marketing, or awareness and demand, as separate. Silently or publicly, they may put barriers up. We've been in this situation many times. Rachel was once asked on a call "When will this be over so we can get back to normal?". Use language and tools that help everyone get to a shared understanding of what you mean. Help colleagues feel able to join in. If this means downplaying what it is, that's ok. There is often a lovely

> moment when a colleague rings to say they've realized this is a new marketing strategy and plan, not just a 'campaign' or a 'programme'.

How to drive brand to demand for employees

The approach to an employee marketing strategy and plan is the same. Work with HR to write and execute the plan together. The default stages in the journey are: recruiting, onboarding, thriving and departing. This can be informed and assessed with an employee brand funnel, that you can create with HR.

> **Watch-out #29: The two enemies of good marketing – boredom and blandness**
>
> We get bored of our own marketing way before it has made its impact. Feed the marketing. Don't chop and change. Don't switch it on and off. The impact builds over time. When you switch it off before it has had any long-lasting impact, you have to ramp up again when you go live again.
>
> In 'The Extraordinary Cost of Dull', a whitepaper that combined work from eatbigfish, Peter Field, the IPA and System1, the authors shared that the overwhelming emotional response to most ads in the UK and US is… nothing. Neutrality. Nothing for around 50% of most ads. It's even worse for B2B: 60% of all UK B2B ads and 54% in the US generate no emotional response.[221] We know that generating an emotional response is key to building brands; helping to get attention, build differentiation, embed associations in our minds and build that all important predisposition.
>
> There are other costs from making dull ads. "The problem of dull isn't damage. It's waste. It costs more – sometimes a lot

more – to get the same business impact with a dull ad as with an interesting one."²²² From their analysis the authors estimated that, "A brand with 5% market share airing Non-Dull ads would see annualised gains of 1.3 points of share each year. That same brand making that same high investment into Extremely Dull ads – the lowest quartile – would see only 0.1 points of share gain each year."²²³ They also warn, "The AI revolution means it's easier than ever to make an ad. Which means it's easier than ever to make a dull ad. Dodging the cost of Dull is going to be a vital imperative in an era where average is just a click away."²²⁴

Please don't get bored and don't be bland. Because both will cost you.

Final thoughts on implementation

Approaching your marketing strategy and plan in this way may sound daunting if you haven't done it before. But it works. Sotis Dramalis, CMO & SVP Marketing at SAP Asia Pacific & Japan, shares that:

> *Having tried, stress-tested and validated this brand to demand integrated marketing approach as part of marketing transformations in three major global tech brands, I managed to unify diverse geographical markets towards one common brand strategy. My teams also doubled and eventually tripled return on marketing investment measured by pipeline and revenue impact – which ultimately transitioned marketing from a sales support to a leadership function that creates tomorrow's markets.*²²⁵

You will need to tweak the approach to your brand, your buyers, your processes and the problem you're facing that has led to the rebrand in the first place. But now's the time to do the work to author your integrated, always on, brand to demand marketing strategy and plan. Rise above the noise and control the process. Drive brand to demand to revenue. Then next year's marketing strategy, marketing plan and budgeting will be so much easier!

You've moved through business strategy to brand strategy, brand identity to implementation and marketing strategy. Finally, how to know whether your rebrand is working.

Chapter 7
Measurement
and momentum

What you will know by the end of this chapter:

- The three reasons to measure
- How to listen for what's changing in the market
- How to know whether your brand CRED is improving
- How to measure the impact of your rebrand and marketing plan
- How to adjust implementation plans and keep up momentum
- How to measure *your* progress

We measure for three reasons.

Reason 1: We listen for what's changing in the market to adjust our strategy.

Reason 2: We measure the impact of our efforts on improving a brand's four CRED factors to understand how to update our plans.

Reason 3: We measure to show our efforts have impacted business growth.

You'll no doubt be asked 'Is it working?' about two seconds after everything has started to go live. By understanding the impact of your rebrand you will be able to not only answer that question, but also make adjustments.

There is an overwhelm of what can be measured. It's easy to get lost in the data and not know what to do with the information. Few marketers have the resources to measure perfectly. Be pragmatic, think like a detective to find the answers to your most critical questions and consistently measure the same way. Presenting too many measurements, or changing what they are can damage credibility with stakeholders who will start to worry that you are obfuscating. Just as finance always turn up with the same metrics, marketing must too. Take time to work out what should be on your impact dashboard and make sure you get a baseline for each of them before you rebrand, to give a point of reference.

How to listen for what's changing in the market

The market moves. The world, the category and the cultural codes your buyers are influenced by evolve. Think of the shifts to hybrid working, hybrid and electric cars, buying services in the cloud. You can tell this is happening when you actively listen for changes. Since you authored your brand diagnosis, what has changed in the market? Proactively listen to analysts, influencers, buyers and leadership to understand:

Relevance

1. Has anything changed in who your brand needs to reach and why?
2. Are the associations and relative strengths you identified in your brand strategy still important and relevant to buyers?
3. Have there been any market and cultural shifts that have influenced buyers and employees?
4. Is the value of the market growing or declining? What's your market share?

5. Have there been any changes to the Category Entry Points? Which are most important now?
6. Does the business strategy still stand?

Difference

7. Have new competitors entered? Is there a new or emerging 'brand enemy'?
8. Have there been any changes in competitors' associations and assets?

It's critical to continue to spend time with buyers. A customer buyer panel can be the most effective way to listen for what's changing from their perspective. Try to meet with them every three to six months. Read win and loss reports if you are in B2B, and look at the feedback from customers about why they stop buying from your brand. Can you hear new Category Entry Points?

Talk to the finance and sales strategy colleagues that you worked with on segmentation to update the total number of 'buyers and category spend', against total number of 'customers and spend' with your brand.

An effective approach to sustain momentum is to continue to engage and update leadership with a 30-minute call at the beginning of a new quarter to reflect on the last. Be prepared to give a few minutes update on the impact of the rebrand so that they have the latest information from you directly and can ask you questions. Ask them to update you on how the brand strategy is informing their business-as-usual decisions and behaviour, as well as how fixes, improvements and the creation of remarkable moments are improving the experience.

Mark up your brand diagnosis with what has changed and what the implications are.

How to know whether your brand CRED is improving

Having defined what rebrand meant for your business and embarked on implementation, how have everyone's efforts improved your brand CRED? Are you more cohesive, relevant, easy and different? The people you want to hear from are employees and buyers. This requires a mix of qualitative, quantitative and desk research.

Questions to explore with employees and in desk research to compare against your previous measurements include:

1. **Cohesion:** Are leaders role modelling the brand strategy? Do employees think people are behaving and taking decisions in a way that makes it real? Do they feel they are individually are being held accountable for executing the brand strategy? Are they committed to making it happen? Do they feel it makes a difference to their career progress?

2. **Cohesion:** How cohesive do employees feel you are you being across the buyer experience with your assets and associations?

3. **Cohesion:** What difference has fixing the hygiene and antithesis experiences made? Look at the journey a selection of recent buyers have experienced.

4. **Cohesion:** How cohesive is the brand across the employee journey and your HR and recruitment communications, policies and procedures?

5. **Relevance:** Would employees recommend working for the brand and why? Has your eNPS improved?

6. **Relevance:** Would employees recommend the brand to buyers and why? Has your ebNPS improved?

7. **Relevance:** How important do they believe the brand strategy is to the future of the business?

8. **Relevance:** How do employees describe the culture? How different is that from your brand strategy definition of *who we are and how we do things*?

9. **Ease:** How clear and understandable is your brand strategy? Do employees get it? Can they remember it, especially *why we exist* and *who we are and how we do things*?

10. **Ease:** How easy is it to understand and use your brand identity? How well is it being used?

11. **Ease:** Are your products and services easier to sell?

12. **Ease:** As they transition from pre-purchase to purchase, to post-purchase to repurchase, where are the friction points in the buyer experience?

13. **Difference:** What has been the impact of your remarkable moments?

Questions to explore with buyers and customers, industry analysts and influencers to compare against your previous measurements:

1. **Relevance:** Which brands come to mind easily for each Category Entry Point? Is your brand associated with more of them?

2. **Relevance:** Has your brand funnel changed? Can you see improvement?

3. **Relevance:** What is your Net Promoter Score (NPS) and why do buyers say they would or would not recommend your brand? Are they recommending or leaving your brand for the Category Entry Points that you have prioritized, or others? Look also at customer feedback and churn data.

4. **Ease:** Do buyers associate your priority products and services with your brand? When you ask buyers who sells them, do they mention your brand?

5. **Ease:** Are your products and services easy to buy?

6. **Ease:** As they transition from pre-purchase to post-purchase to repurchase, where are the friction points in the experience? If you have active customer support, always ask the buyer at the end of an interaction, 'what is the one thing we could have done better today?'. Those reasons need to be fed back to the people who can affect change quickly.

7. **Ease:** Do buyers attribute your advertising to your brand?

8. **Difference:** Are your Distinctive Brand Assets associated with your brand and becoming more recognized and attributed to your brand?

9. **Difference:** Are buyers feeling that your brand is more different than other brands in the category?

10. **Difference:** Are you perceived to be leading the category or challenging the status quo in some way?

11. **Difference and Relevance:** Are you building the associations identified in your brand strategy in people's minds? Is your brand seen to be relatively better on the areas you identified? Are those areas still important to them?
12. **Difference:** Is your brand more associated than competitors with the Category Entry Points you've been prioritizing?

When to field the employee and buyer research

We've tried fielding research annually, quarterly, even monthly. What we noticed is that results can vary from one study to another, giving false highs and lows. A lot depends on what else is going on in the world and in their business, on whether they are in market or not and how fast the category moves. It is hard to see patterns in the data if it is gathered infrequently. When rebranding, you need to be able to see if the collective efforts are making a difference in order to be able to share that to sustain commitment and momentum across the business. Our preference is to run the brand funnel research every two to three months and everything else once a year. If you can only invest in research once a year, do it during the peak sales period closest to your end of financial year so it can inform your plans. Always do the research at the same time of year from then on. To get a holistic snapshot in time, run all studies at the same time.

Update your brand diagnosis

Once you've conducted the research, you'll be able to update your brand diagnosis, comparing today against your first edition.

Complete the update to the segmentation with the latest data on Category Entry Points relevant to the different buyer groups.

Finish with:

1. What is your brand CRED rating?
2. Where do the problems and opportunities now lie?
3. What needs to improve to continue to build the brand to drive growth?

How to measure the impact of the rebrand

Whether the rebrand has had the desired impact will depend on the reasons for the rebrand, the problems you identified in your brand diagnosis and how you have implemented. For instance, for established brands seeking to stretch by entering a new market, it can be about making sure buyers now perceive the brand as a choice in that market. One example we worked on improved spontaneous awareness by over 30% and intention to purchase by more than 50% within a year and within months enjoyed a 4x increase year-on-year in the volume of opportunities and 6x increase in the value of that pipeline. For another brand who needed to grow by acting more 'as one,' we measured improvement in cross-border revenue, achieving close to a 20% increase within a year.

Case study: Aviva

B2B and B2C insurance, wealth and retirement brand Aviva also faced this growth challenge. Described in the press several years ago as "a clumsy, lumbering giant of a company formed from a series of mergers" that "struggled to establish a strong identity of its own out of the hotch-potch of brands, cultures and IT systems", it was underperforming and struggling to maximize investments.[226] Many investors felt the whole was not worth the sum of its parts. Among buyers, Aviva had very strong awareness and trust but an 'empty awareness' problem or 'likeability gap'.

People were aware of Aviva but weren't familiar or favourable. The decline in the volume of quotes, direct sales and market share was worrying.

This directed the Aviva team, led by Group Brand & Sponsorship Director Phoebe Barter and their agency adam&eveDDB, to focus their brand on something relevant that their buyers cared about – the idea that finance is complicated and Aviva makes it click. Aviva decided that improving 'affinity' (another word for likeability) would be their main thing to measure, but they saw improvements across the funnel. Spontaneous awareness was up 1 percentage point (48%) and consideration up 3 percentage points (55%), with increases across all product lines. Quotes improved 41% and sales by 14%. Unexpectedly, they saw that sales through price comparison websites did not grow but direct revenue went up 29%, with more buyers responding to the brand becoming easier to mind by buying direct. Internal engagement was also high and eNPS up 2% to 88%. After discounting price, distribution, Covid-19, category growth and other possible influencing factors, Aviva calculated that the rebrand and marketing drove £28.1m in profit.[227]

We know that knowledge of brand-building is perceived as average to poor in over 50% of boardrooms.[228] What most impedes continued attention and investment is lack of metrics that are credible to senior management.[229] And it can be hard to pull apart the impact of the rebrand not least because how people experience a brand is through everything a business does: products, services, experience and marketing.

With your finance colleagues you will be able to calculate the additional investment made for the refresh. Don't include business-as-usual investment. You can then compare that to the financial impact, just as Aviva did. The rebrand should be instrumental in improving your brand's market impact.

If leaders understand how CRED underpins brand and business growth, this will also help. You can talk to them about improvements in the brand funnel: more buyers know your brand's name, know what you do, like you emotionally, would consider or intend to purchase from you. You can show them improvements in the associations you all agreed to build in the brand strategy, in Category Entry Points and assets more recognized and attributed to your brand. Easier to grasp are positive movements in market share, margin, price elasticity, cost of acquisition, conversion and retention. They will also see the value of more talent accepting job offers, higher productivity, lower churn, more buyer and employee referrals, and find it easier to secure shareholders and investment.

How to measure the impact of your marketing plan

Before you get into the myriad micro performance indicators, first take a macro view. What shape are you expecting your funnel to be and what speed should buyers be progressing through the journey to becoming customers? If buyers are progressing slower than expected for your category, where in the journey are they getting stuck? Look at your brand funnel research, marketing and sales data with the shape and pace of the journey in mind.

James Hurman and Rory Dolan of Tracksuit advise marketers to assess the success of their efforts holistically, not independently. In their study with TikTok they found that "as brand awareness increases, performance marketing conversion rates improve significantly on TikTok. In fact, the study found that high awareness brands achieve 2.86x the conversion rate of low awareness brands. Put simply, the more familiar your brand is to all category buyers, the more efficient your performance advertising becomes."[230]

Don't forget that your horizon of measurement needs to be right. Until a full sales cycle has occurred, with enough volume, you won't be able to judge your progress. The length of the sales cycle will be how often buyers in your category come into market to shop, how long they spend researching and how long they take to buy. A full cycle will be to the point of re-purchase and whether they renew or shop with you again. This could be relatively quick in the case of a weekly food shop or slow in the case of a new air ambulance helicopter!

You see, everything can be working, yet it hasn't worked. Every indicator can look great, but buyers aren't buying, or didn't buy what you'd prioritized. This is why you have to start with the big picture and then dig into the detail. Do be wary of declaring all is well short term, because it has to be sustained to have revenue impact. And if the product and buyer experience doesn't live up to brand associations you're trying to build, you've still lost.

The more you live in the data, the more you instinctively understand what is happening and why. You see it. You feel it. You know it. Investigate your hunches. Trust them without jumping to conclusions. Partner with data scientists to find the behaviours in the data that most of us marketers aren't trained to spot.

What is the data telling you (by country, by market and rolled up)? Analyse:

1. **Are you reaching buyers?** Has awareness, familiarity and favourability improved in the brand funnel? Are you reaching enough buyers at the right frequency? Look at impressions served, TVR (television rating point is the "percentage of a base population watching a TV programme"), emails delivered and bounces.[231] Can you see an increase in share of voice? Would more employees (ebNPS) and buyers (NPS) recommend the brand?

2. **Are buyers responding?** Are buyers consuming the ads? Are they clicking on them? Is your brand's Share of Search (SoS) improving? Do you have more traffic to your website and more returning visitors? Which Category Entry Points, messages, designs, formats and search terms are driving the most traffic and engagement? Has your emailable universe declined or grown and which tactic drove the change? Check your bounce rates and understand the causes. Are more influencers recommending your brand?

3. **Are buyers engaging?** Are more buyers sharing your tactics with others, amplifying your brand? Is sentiment becoming more positive on what buyers, employees and journalists share? How does this compare to competitors? How many watch videos to the end? Are the ungated tactics being viewed and downloaded? Are more buyers using chat, what for and for what duration? For all events, physical or digital, compare registration to attendance; does location, time, topic, speakers, format make difference? What % of all visitors are engaged and does that go up or down as their journey progresses? Are website pages and tactics performing the way you intended? Look at heatmaps and actions taken, page consumption. Which tactics and content are performing, which aren't and where are they on the journey?

4. **Are buyers considering?** What's marketing's influence on leads? Are buyers transitioning through stages: from Marketing Qualified Leads (MQL) to Sales Qualified Leads (SQL) to Sales Qualified Opportunities (SQO) to customer to repurchase? Do they go from visiting to quote or basket, to purchase to repurchase? What are they buying and are those your priority products and services?

5. **What is the impact on revenue?** Is the volume and average value of sales increasing? Is the pipeline moving any faster? Are

you converting more buyers? Are more buyers repurchasing? Is the margin improving? Are buyers buying what you thought they would? Can you see changes in where they buy your products and services? Sit with finance and look at the impact so far on price elasticity (the amount the volume goes down by each percentage point you increase the price), quantity premium and quality premium (higher sales at full price), which all reflect your brand's long-term health.

How to adjust implementation plans

Bring together your colleagues to adjust the plan. Don't forget that a third of marketers are not confident in their brand-building know-how, so do take time to educate them on what is and is not working and why, in a positive manner. The more they understand how brands are strengthened the more likely they are to link brand to commercial impact.[232] Encourage everyone to go away and think, and ask them to come to a brainstorm with ideas (or send them to you beforehand if that's more comfortable). Then work through ideas for improving, testing and optimizing the plan, together. Here are some suggestions, to stimulate your thinking.

1. **Are you reaching as many buyers as possible?** Do you need to rebalance reach versus frequency? Is the media mix working as expected or do you need to adjust it?

2. **Are your Distinctive Brand Assets becoming more recognized and attributed to your brand?** If there is improvement, keep encouraging your colleagues by showing them cohesion is working. If there isn't, what do you need to do better?

3. **Have there been changes in how often buyers purchase?** If they are buying less frequently, move more budget into brand reach and frequency to strengthen consideration among future buyers. Find out why they are delaying or buying something else instead, so you can address those barriers in your messaging.

4. **Is your brand increasingly associated with the Category Entry Points you have prioritized?** If yes, great, keep going! If you aren't credible for that Category Entry Point then either identify where the problem is and fix it, or stop marketing your brand for that reason to come shopping. Make more variations on your best

performing ads using different combinations of words and visuals, layouts, calls to action.

5. **Are there Category Entry Points you would like to add to your priorities?** You want your brand to be associated with as many Category Entry Points as possible. Do you need to target new ones? Identify if you have suitable priority products and services that are relevant. If you do, can you afford to fund it full funnel? Do what you can afford and take your time to build up.

6. **Is brand funnel health improving?** Is each promotional channel behaving and performing as you think it should? Do you need to make it clearer what you do to improve familiarity or is your marketing failing to build favourability? Are buyers moving at an expected pace along the journey? What isn't cohesive and easy? If funnel health is improving, keep going. If it isn't, or if there are new leaks, fix the issues closest to purchase first (because you've invested heavily in getting buyers to that point and it is closest to sale) and work back up to awareness.

7. **Are buyers and employees recommending and amplifying your brand?** Yes, it is worth working out your Net Promoter Scores (NPS). According to SurveyMonkey's global benchmark data, which covers the NPS' of more than 150,000 organizations, the average score is +32, and the top 25% of performers have an NPS of +72 or higher.[233] But these benchmarks can vary, depending on the industry you're in – the top 25% of consumer goods and services industries have a score of 72+, whereas the top 25% of technology companies have a score of 64+. Care less about the score and more about whether it is going up or down, and why. Where are the issues? Have your remarkable moments been remarked upon? Are buyers and employees amplifying your brand across social media through content sharing?

8. **Do you have the right balance between long term brand building and short-term demand?** Do buyers attribute your campaigns to your brand and are they responding emotionally? Are you trying to pull people down the funnel too soon, when they aren't ready (you'll notice they quickly go back to consuming awareness content)? If there are broken links on the website, or sales are failing to convert, or the price is not competitive, or you're

marketing something that's out of stock, you may be creating pull-through for another brand!

9. **Are you still engaging employees in the brand?** Continue with reward and recognition. Celebrate the impact and tell the stories of decisions and behaviour that made it happen.

> ### Watch-out #30: Keep engaging employees
>
> It's easy to assume that ongoing brand-building sits with marketing. While you're improving buyer engagement and experience, keep supporting HR to improve the employee experience. Empower employees to innovate how they work and the experiences they deliver to better build the associations your brand wants to be known for.
>
> Check if you are still engaging employees in the brand. Reinforce the ideas within the brand strategy and the changes your brand is making through Internal Communications' campaigns. Explain what isn't working and engage the people in those departments to work out what to do differently.
>
> Make sure your hiring, onboarding and off-boarding are on-brand. Go deeper on learning and training around the brand strategy. Relook at working practices that don't align with *who we are and how we do things*. Consider adding new tools, rituals and remarkable moments to help share stories and feel more 'as one'. Build role-modelling of on-brand behaviours into your leadership development programs.
>
> Remember that any 'employer brand' initiative is simply an expression of the brand strategy for employees, because there is only one brand!

Keep up momentum

What next?

Definitely not a rebrand or a completely new marketing strategy!

Keep your plans and colleagues rolling. It's highly unlikely you will have tackled everything in the first year. Listen, debate, analyse, tweak, improve, optimize, adjust, nudge, encourage. Improving your brand CRED takes time, but you know this is what you need to do to keep your brand growing.

Working with marketing, sales and finance, customize your brand funnel so it goes from awareness right through to repurchase. Find the leaks in the journey that matter and work across the business to reduce them.

Your time horizon should be 18 months ahead, with more detail for the next quarter or two, and less further out. Plans may get locked for the year ahead in the run up to the new financial year, but whatever you do, don't start from scratch.

Just keep feeding your plan.

How to measure *your* progress

We covered a lot in this book. If you're new to most of it, you might feel a bit overwhelmed at this point. Believe us when we say that we know the feeling! It was overwhelming to us to try and rebrand for so many years without a clear approach. We hope it's a bit easier now you have this guide, rather than starting with a blank page. Use the advice in this book to do what you can, with the time and resources you have, to improve your brand. Do keep dipping into this book whenever you need to.

We always hope that the brands we improve will outlive us. This is not to make us feel morbid, but to remind us that we are simply caretakers on their journey. It's important to see the long term, protect the assets and associations that are strong, bring back the past when it's relevant to help brands grow into a more successful future.

Remember that we've set out an ideal. But measuring yourself against any ideal can make you feel like you're never good enough, or you're never doing enough. Please be kind to yourself. As performance coach Tim Grover suggests, keep a 'done' list, not just a 'to-do' list.[234] Do this with your team too. Each day, consider capturing three wins and identifying three wins to achieve tomorrow. You can list reading this book as one of them!

Our last piece of advice is to find people who will continue to positively challenge and support you in your career. We're not big fans of people who berate others for not knowing what they're doing. There's only the best approach you can muster at the time, with the resources and knowledge you have. This is our best approach at the time of writing but we know things will change, new data will impact how people think about brands, new tools will make older ones less useful. Keep learning and growing, but don't get bullied into thinking your opinion isn't valued or have your voice silenced by the loud egos out there.

We've both been people who want to do things 'properly' in life, hence the plea to 'rebrand right'. It has been a joy and pleasure weaving the ideas in this book together, having worked through so many rebrands for years. We're always challenging each other to be better. Find those people for you. And if you don't have those people, we're here for you! Come find us on rebrand-right.com.

We wish you much success in all your rebranding projects. We really hope you found this book useful. Thank you so much for taking the time to read it.

Rachel & Sarah

About the authors

Rachel Fairley had never heard of brand until in her first job she helped the General Counsel value the business' intangible assets. Fascinated, Rachel decided to pursue a career repositioning brands to improve their impact and drive fresh growth.

Rachel has contributed to B2B and B2C business transformations, across many industries, all over the world. Sometimes she does it by advising, sometimes by taking on the role of chief brand officer or marketing leader. All her work has come through client recommendations.

Rachel has a reputation for strategic thinking, creativity and pragmatism. Her positivity and infectious energy galvanize those around her and drive collaboration.

Rachel is partially deaf, having survived a brain tumour. Brought up in Edinburgh, she moved to London for a year in 1999; she still lives there with her husband and two sons.

Sarah Robb's career as a brand strategist began on the prestigious WPP Fellowship programme. She learnt her craft working with B2B and B2C Fortune 500 companies, and has supported clients on 57 rebrands, across the A to Z of industries.

After a decade as an agency strategist, she conducted a study of the 181 most valuable brands to get behind the jargon and to a simpler model that helps marketers better connect brands to business growth.

About the authors

This ability to bring clarity to brand strategy, think creatively and unite employees and customers through her work has won her innumerable fans.

She founded Brand Strategy Academy in 2000, an online course designed to equip strategists, designers and copywriters with the skills and tools to confidently help the brands they work with.

She lives near London with her husband and two children, speaks rusty Japanese and travels as often as she can.

> Let's keep talking!
>
> Come find us at Rebrand-Right.com.
>
> Rachel & Sarah

Authors' acknowledgements

The authors wish to thank the following for permission to reproduce copyright material:

- Kantar, for pp. 9, 16, 22, 34, 37, 41, 45, 69, 73, 100, from J. Ostler et al, 'Blueprint For Brand Growth... and how CMOs can operationalise it', *Kantar*, 2024

Every effort has been made to trace rights holders, but if any have been inadvertently overlooked the authors would be pleased to make the necessary arrangements at the first opportunity.

Thank you to Corinthia, Holly Yashi and eto for allowing us to share your brand strategies.

Thank you beta readers for taking the time to read the manuscript and give us such constructive and positive feedback: Abigail Comber, Alisha Lyndon, Amanda Jobbins, Anil Gadre, Dom Hawes, Duncan Daines, Emily Penny, Gabie Boko, Izzie Rivers, Jack Parsons, Jane Strumba, Kayci Evans, Leo McCloskey, Lucy Murphy, Marisa Kacary, Mark Baker, Mehul Kapadia, Nick Liddell, Pete Markey, Phil Randerson, Phoebe Barter, Sarah Tookey, Sue Stephenson, Shallu Behar-Sheehan, Sotiros Dramalis.

Thank you to all those who agreed to be quoted or provided information: Anil Gadre, Ben Afia, Dan White, Daryl Fielding, David Anderson, Duncan Daines, Dina Jahina and Tom Cotton at eto, Emily Jewell and

Authors' acknowledgements

Clinton Fenech at Corinthia, Emily Penny, Graham Staplehurst at Kantar, Hilton Barbour, Izzie Rivers, Leo McCloskey, Mark Choueke, Mehul Kapadia, Nick Liddell, Paul Cash, Paul Lubitz at Holly Yashi, Phoebe Barter and Sarah Poulter at Aviva, Sarah Speake, Sarah Tookey, Sean Cornell and Sotis Dramalis. Everyone in Brand Strategy Academy – thank you for your brilliant questions.

Sinead Madden, we love the cover you designed. Sean Cornell at Wonderment thanks for your creativity on the Rebrand Right brand identity and book illustrations. Catherine Gil, much appreciation for your beautiful photography. Your fresh eyes were invaluable Donovan Lambert. Chris DeAppolonio, Michael Taylor and Sanjeev Katwa thank you for supporting us with introductions. Elizabeth Hylett Clark and Rebecca Ireland, we appreciate the pragmatic advice.

Alison Jones and the entire team at Practical Inspiration Publishing, you are the publishers every author needs.

To all the brilliant people we've worked with over the years, memories of what we experienced together were flooding back to us as we wrote. Amazing clients and colleagues at wonderful companies. So many good times.

We are so thankful we met early in our careers and became good friends. Writing the book together has been a joy. To all our fabulous friends – you have kept us sane, kept us going and given us perspective and energy when it was needed most – you all rock, love you lots.

Big love to our families for your inspiration and encouragement.

Rachel & Sarah

Notes

[1] F. Cassidy et al., *The Board-Brand Rift: How Business Leaders Have Stopped Building Brands*, UK, FT, EFFWorks and IPA, 2019, https://ipa.co.uk/media/7698/the-board-brand-rift.pdf (accessed 22 July 2024), p. 22, figure 13.
[2] S. Diorio, 'Newy Global Standards For Reporting Brand Value Can Help CEOs Grow Share Price', Forbes [blog], 4 May 2018, https://www.forbes.com/sites/forbesinsights/2018/05/03/new-global-standards-for-reporting-brand-value-can-help-ceos-grow-share-price/#6175ee3812d3 (accessed 22 July 2023).
[3] B. Sharp, *How Brands Grow: What Marketers Don't Know*, Melbourne, VIC, Oxford University Press, 2010, p. 53.
[4] R. Sutherland, *Alchemy, The Magic of Original Thinking in a World of Mind-Numbing Conformity*, 2nd edn, UK, WH Allen part of Penguin Random House, 2020, p. 139.
[5] J. Ostler et al., 'Blueprint For Brand Growth… and how CMOs can operationalise it', Kantar, 2024, https://www.kantar.com/campaigns/blueprint-for-brand-growth (accessed 22 July 2024), p. 9.
[6] Sharp, p. 189.
[7] Sharp, p. 185.
[8] D. Kahneman, *Thinking, Fast and Slow*, UK, Penguin Books, 2012. Also referenced in Sharp, p. 189.
[9] 'How Brands Grow with Marketing Science (Prof. Byron Sharp)' #298, *Brand Master Podcast* [podcast], Presenter S. Houraghan, interview with Prof. Byron Sharp, 25 April 2024, https://podcasters.spotify.com/pod/show/brandmasterpodcast/episodes/298-How-Brands-Grow-With-Marketing-Science-Prof–Byron-Sharp-e2i8ojg (accessed 22 July 2024).
[10] D. Rademaker and B. Joosen, 'Brands Don't Buy Brands – People Do', *Ipsos*, 2016, https://www.ipsos.com/sites/default/files/2016-09/Brands_Don%27t_Buy_Brands.pdf (accessed 22 July 2024), p. 4.
[11] Ostler et al., pp. 16, 34, 37.
[12] Ostler et al., p. 34.
[13] Sharp, p. 193.
[14] D. L. Yohn, *What Great Brands Do: The Seven Brand-Building Principles That Separate the Best from the Rest*, California USA, Jossey-Bass, a Wiley Brand, 2014, p. 14.

Notes

[15] M. Eisner, *Work in Progress: Risking Failure, Surviving Success*, NY, USA Hyperion, 1999, p. 235.

[16] 'This Much I Learned Podcast: Boot's CMO Pete Markey on marketing leadership' episode x, *Uncensored CMO* [podcast], interview with Pete Markey, 19 December 2023, https://www.marketingweek.com/pete-markey-this-much-i-learned/ (accessed 22 July 2024).

[17] A. Gadre, personal correspondence, 8 September 2024.

[18] S. Bedbury, *A New Brand World, 8 Principles for Achieving Brand Leadership in the 21st Century*, New York USA, Penguin, 2003, p. 38.

[19] G. Creed and K. Muench, *R.E.D. Marketing: Relevance, East & Distinctiveness: The Three Ingredients of Leading Brands*, USA, HarperCollins Leadership, 2021, p. 88.

[20] D. Fielding, *The Brand Book: An Insider's Guide to Brand Building for Businesses and Organizations*, UK, Lawrence King, 2021, p. 94.

[21] 'Our vision', *Dove* [website], https://www.dove.com/uk/stories/about-dove/our-vision.html (accessed 24 July 2024).

[22] 'Brand value of Dove worldwide from 2016 to 2024', *Statista* [website], https://www.statista.com/statistics/1010915/dove-brand-value-worldwide/ (accessed 22 July 2024).

[23] S. Reames, 'I was sad to learn today of the passing of John Brown', *LinkedIn* [website], 2024, https://www.linkedin.com/posts/scott-r-1b59527_i-was-sad-to-learn-today-of-the-passing-of-activity-7172501303217049600-AOPt/?utm_source=share&utm_medium=member_desktop (accessed 22 July 2024).

[24] Reames.

[25] 'What is Nike's Mission?', *Nike.com* [website], https://www.nike.com/help/a/nikeinc-mission (accessed 22 July 2024).

[26] M. Benioff and C. Adler, *Behind the Cloud: The Untold Story of How Salesforce.Com Went from Idea to Billion-Dollar Company – and Revolutionized an Industry*, Jossey-Bass a Wiley Imprint, New Jersey USA, 2009, p. 115.

[27] M. Benioff, *Trailblazer: The Power of Business as the Greatest Platform for Change*, NY, USA, Currency, 2019.

[28] L. McGowen-Hare, 'What is a Trailblazaer', *Salesforce* [blog], 27 June 2023, https://www.salesforce.com/blog/so-what-is-a-trailblazer/ (accessed 9 September 2024).

[29] Creed and Muench, p. 75.

[30] Creed and Muench, p. 76.

[31] Ogilvy & Mather, 'IBM Smarter Planet Campaign From Ogilvy & Mather Wins Global Effie', *PR Newswire* [website], 9 June 2010, https://www.prnewswire.com/news-releases/ibm-smarter-planet-campaign-from-ogilvy–mather-wins-global-effie-95980774.html (accessed 22 July 2024).

[32] Ostler et al., p. 73.

[33] 'Market Share Masterclass: Blending Organic Growth and M&A', *Unicorny* [podcast], Presenter R. Fairley, interview with Duncan Daines, 13 June 2024, https://www.unicorny.co.uk/market-share-masterclass (accessed 22 July 2024).

[34] K. Mackay-Sinclair et al., 'Bailey's: A Radical Brand Turnaround Story With Extra Sprinkles', *IPA Effectiveness Awards* [website], https://ipaeffectivenessawards.awardsengine.com/winners/view_awards_entry.cfm?id_entry=100049 (accessed 22 July 2024).

[35] Ostler et al., p. 100.

36 Sharp, preface xiii.
37 'Identifying and Prioritising Category Entry Points. What are CEPs and why are they important?', *Ehrenberg-Bass Institute for Marketing Science* [website], https://marketingscience.info/research-services/identifying-and-prioritising-category-entry-points/ (accessed 24 July 2024).
38 J. Romaniuk, 'Category Entry Points in a Business-to-Business World', *Ehrenberg-Bass Institute for Marketing Science* [website], July 2022, https://marketingscience.info/category-entry-points-in-a-business-to-business-b2b-world/ (accessed 22 July 2024).
39 Romaniuk, 'Category Entry Points in a Business-to-Business World'.
40 Ostler et al., p. 69.
41 Ostler et al., p. 69.
42 'Gymshark partners with General Atlantic as it achieves unicorn status', *Private Equity Wire* [website], 2020, https://www.privateequitywire.co.uk/gymshark-partners-general-atlantic-it-achieves-unicorn-status/ (accessed 22 July 2024).
43 N. Liddell, 'The brand strategist's toolkit #7: Branded House and House of Brands', *LinkedIn* [website], https://www.linkedin.com/pulse/brand-strategists-toolkit-7-branded-house-brands-nick-liddell/ (accessed 22 July 2024).
44 Iain McGilchrist, *The Master and His Emissary*, 2nd edn, United States of America, Yale University Press, 2019, p. 40.
45 O. Wood, *Look Out*, UK, Institute of Practitioners in Advertising, 2021, p. 20.
46 Wood, p. 20.
47 Sage, 'Half Year 2021 Results presentation transcript', *Sage* [website], 14 May 2021, https://www.sage.com/investors/financial-information/results/ (accessed 22 July 2024).
48 'Another Dull Whitepaper: The Extraordinary Cost of Being Dull', *System1*, eatbigfish, John Evans Uncensored CMO, Peter Field, p. 9.
49 A. Smith, *No Bullsh*t Strategy: A Founder's Guide to Gaining Competitive Advantage with a Strategy that Actually Works*, UK, Matador, 2023, p. 18.
50 N. Mizik and R. Jacobson, 'Talk about Brand Strategy', *Harvard Business Review* [website], October 2005, https://hbr.org/2005/10/talk-about-brand-strategy (accessed 22 July 2024).
51 D. Boyd, 'Why Brand Difference Matters, and What You Can Do to Drive It', *IPA* [website], 13 September 2023, https://ipa.co.uk/knowledge/ipa-blog/why-brand-difference-matters-and-what-you-can-do-to-drive-it (accessed 22 July 2024).
52 G. Staplehurst and E. Thorpe, 'Imbuing Brands With a Sense of Difference', *Kantar* [blog], 18 July 2023, https://www.kantar.com/inspiration/agile-market-research/imbuing-brands-with-a-sense-of-difference (accessed 12 August 2024).
53 Liquid Death, 'About', *Liquid Death* [website], https://liquiddeath.com/en-gb/pages/manifesto (accessed 22 July 2024).
54 K. Roof, 'Liquid Death is Valued at 1.4 Bn in New Financing Round', *Bloomberg* [blog], 11 March 2024, https://www.bloomberg.com/news/articles/2024-03-11/liquid-death-is-valued-at-1-4-billion-in-new-financing-round (accessed 29 July 2024).
55 J. Teng, 'People Love Liquid Death brand. But Do They Drink It?', *Tracksuit* [blog], 18 September 2024, https://www.gotracksuit.com/au/blog/posts/liquid-death-brand-case-study (accessed 27 September July 2024).
56 Look at BrandZ, Brand Finance and Interbrand's Best Global Brands data.

Notes

57 'How Liquid Death founder, Mike Cessario, created a billion dollar water brand' episode 125, *Uncensored CMO* [podcast], Presenter J. Evans, interview with Mike Cessario, 13 March 2024, https://uncensoredcmo.com/125 (accessed 22 July 2024).
58 Benioff and Adler, pp. 29, 32.
59 Staplehurst and Thorpe.
60 'Accenture's CMO on B2B Brand Development', #237, *Renegade Thinkers Unite Podcast* [podcast], Presenter D. Neisser, interview with A. Fuller, 21 April 2021, https://renegademarketing.com/podcasts/accenture-b2b-brand-development/ (accessed 30 September 2024).
61 R. Spence Jr., *It's Not What You Sell, It's What You Stand For: Why Every Extraordinary Business is Driven By Purpose*, New York, United States of America, Portfolio, 2009, p. 45.
62 Sutherland, p. 73.
63 Model inspired by J. Romaniuk, figure 12.1 on p. 110 and Figure 12.2 on p. 112.
64 Find out more about 'The Distinctive Asset Grid' by J. Romaniuk in *Building Distinctive Brand Assets*, Melbourne, VIC, Oxford University Press, 2018, figure 11.1, p. 98.
65 Creed and Muench, p. 97. J. Romaniuk, *Better Brand Health*, Victoria, Australia, Oxford University Press, 2023, p. 86.
66 M. Ritson, 'Synthetic data is as good as real – next comes synthetic strategy', *Marketing Week* [blog], 13 June 2024, https://www.marketingweek.com/ritson-synthetic-data-strategy/ (accessed 23 August 2024).
67 C. Criado Perez, *Invisible Women*, Penguin Random House, UK, 2019.
68 M. Mace, 'Can AI replace discovery interviews. A competitive comparison', *Center for Human Insight* [blog], 24 January 2023, https://centerforhumaninsight.com/can-ai-replace-discovery-interviews/ (accessed 23 August 2024).
69 A. Daroukakis, 'Trends for 2024', https://drive.google.com/drive/folders/1EBkCM7Bt_4tYhLQlKXj7yAh98-NcqD3u (accessed 22 July 2024).
70 A. G. Lafley and R. L. Martin, *Playing to Win, How Strategy Really Works*, Massachusetts, United States of America, Harvard Business Review Press, 2013, p. 3,
71 'Accelerating the Arches: MacDonalds Growth Strategy', *MacDonald's* [website], https://corporate.mcdonalds.com/corpmcd/our-company/who-we-are/accelerating-the-arches.html (accessed 22 July 2024).
72 Dewar, S. Keller and V. Malhorta, *CEO Excellence: The Six Mindsets That Distinguish the Best Leaders from the Rest,* New York, United States of America, Scriber an imprint of Simon and Schuster, 2022, p. 24.
73 *What we do* and *why we exist*: 'Global Company Information', *SAP* [website], https://www.sap.com/about/company.html (accessed 23 July 2024). *How we look, feel and sound*: 'The best run simple', *Siegel + Gale* [website], https://www.siegelgale.com/case-study/sap/ (accessed 24 July 2024). *Who we are and how we do things*: 'Bring out your best', SAP [website], https://jobs.sap.com/job/ (accessed 23 July 2024). S. Dramalis, personal correspondence, 16 and 17 September 2024.
74 *Why we exist*: 'Our purpose and impact', *McDonald's* [website], https://corporate.mcdonalds.com/corpmcd/our-purpose-and-impact.html (accessed 23 July 2024). *What we do, who we are and how we do things*: 'Our Mission and Values', *McDonald's* [website], https://corporate.mcdonalds.com/corpmcd/our-company/who-we-are/

our-values.html (accessed 24 July 2024). *How we look, feel and sound*: 'McDonald's Brand Book', *McDonald's* [website] https://relayto.com/relayto/mcdonalds-brand-book-lh120xl13fede/paJBBAyL2 (accessed 24 July 2024).

[75] D. Jahina, personal correspondence, 20 August 2024.

[76] E. Jewell and C. Fenech at Corinthia, personal correspondence, 13 September 2024.

[77] C. Dewar, S. Keller and V. Malhorta, *CEO Excellence: The Six Mindsets That Distinguish the Best Leaders from the Rest*, New York, United States of America, Scriber an imprint of Simon and Schuster, 2022, p. 29.

[78] Extrapolated from case study in J. Stengel, *Grow: How Ideals Power Growth and Profit at the World's 50 Greatest Companies*, New York, United States of America, Ebury Publishing, 2012, pp 166–199.

[79] Extrapolated from: K. Walker, 'The bridge between hope and possibility', *Cisco* [blog], 13 November 2018, https://blogs.cisco.com/news/the-bridge-between-hope-and-possibility (accessed 27 September 2024); P. Moorhead, 'Cisco Unveils New "Bridge to Possible" Branding Campaign', *Forbes*, 15 November 2018, https://www.forbes.com/sites/patrickmoorhead/2018/11/13/cisco-unveils-new-bridge-to-possible-branding-campaign (accessed 27 September 2024).

[80] Top and bottom as expressed by Apple. *"For me, it's about products and people. Did we make the best product, and did we enrich people's lives? If you're doing both of those things – and obviously those things are incredibly connected because one leads to the other – then you have a good year."* R. Safian, Interview with Tim Cook, Why Apple Is The World's Most Innovative Company, Fast Company, 21 February 2018, https://www.fastcompany.com/40525409/why-apple-is-the-worlds-most-innovative-company (accessed 10 July 2024). *"We try to carry on the mission that he set in place, to build the best products in the world that enrich people's lives. And that hasn't changed. Lots of things change with time. But the reason for our being is the same."* R. D'Agostino and T. Cook, 'Q&A, How to Build Tomorrow', Popular Mechanics [blog], 25 August 2022, https://www.popularmechanics.com/technology/a40823584/how-to-build-tomorrow/ (accessed 5 August 2024); *"Apple's more than 100,000 employees are dedicated to making the best products on earth, and to leaving the world better than we found it."* 'Apple commits to be 100 percent carbon neutral for its supply chain and products by 2030', *Apple* [press release], 21 July 2020, https://www.apple.com/ke/newsroom/2020/07/apple-commits-to-be-100-percent-carbon-neutral-for-its-supply-chain-and-products-by-2030/ (accessed 5 August 2024). The laddering between them is our extrapolation.

[81] H. Hosterman, *Holly Yashi* [website], https://hollyyashi.com/pages/from-holly (accessed 28 July 2024).

[82] P. Lubitz, personal correspondence, 22 August 2024.

[83] 'Steve Jobs introduces "Think Different" 09/23/1997', YouTube [online video], Presenter S. Jobs, California USA, 23 September 1997, https://www.youtube.com/watch?v=FDD5G2_6hdA (accessed 23 July 2024).

[84] All of these examples are our interpretation after multiple sources online.

[85] 'Let us share our story with you. Our history', *Cadbury* [website], https://www.cadbury.com.au/our-history (accessed 23 July 2024).

[86] 'How Cadbury turned "Glass and a Half in Everyone" into one of the most effective campaign ideas in the world.' episode 136, *Uncensored CMO* [podcast],

Notes

Presenter J. Evans, interview with D. Boscawen and G Ferreira, 29 May 2024, https://uncensoredcmo.com/136 (accessed 23 July 2024).

[87] 'Brand Strategy Unpacked: Cracking the Cadbury Code', *Kantar Future Proof* [podcast], Presenter L Gorton-Lee, interview with M. Mugnai and C. Hutchinson, 27 February 2024, https://shows.acast.com/future-proof/episodes/brand-strategy-unpacked-cracking-the-cadbury-code (accessed 22 July 2024).

[88] 'Gatorade: Rehydrating an iconic beverage brand', *Prophet* [website], https://prophet.com/case-studies/gatorade/ (accessed 22 July 2024).

[89] About Amazon Staff, 'Our mission', *Amazon UK* [blog], 18 April 2018, https://www.aboutamazon.co.uk/news/job-creation-and-investment/our-mission (accessed 30 July 2024).

[90] J. P. Bezos, 'Letter to Shareholders', *Amazon*, 2015, https://s2.q4cdn.com/299287126/files/doc_financials/annual/2015-Letter-to-Shareholders.PDF (accessed 13 September 2024).

[91] E. Heyward, *Obsessed: Building a Brand People Love from Day One*, New York, Portfolio, 2020, p. 136.

[92] 'Company page', Hewlett Packard Enterprise, *LinkedIn* [website], https://www.linkedin.com/company/hewlett-packard-enterprise/ (accessed 22 July 2024).

[93] '5 steps to enhance brand purpose discussions', *IPA* [blog], 17 January 2022, https://ipa.co.uk/news/5-steps-to-enhance-brand-purpose-discussions/ (accessed 23 July 2024).

[94] 'Microsoft', *Microsoft* [website], https://www.microsoft.com/en-gb/about/ (accessed 30 September 2024).

[95] 'Our Mission', *Meta* [website], https://about.meta.com/uk/company-info/ (accessed 23 July 2024).

[96] 'At Intel, Our Values Define Us', *Intel* [website], https://www.intel.com/content/www/us/en/corporate-responsibility/our-values (accessed 23 July 2024).

[97] 'Change Powers Accenture's Biggest Brand Move in a Decade', *Accenture* [press release on website], https://newsroom.accenture.sg/asia-pacific/news/2020/change-powers-accentures-biggest-brand-move-in-decade (accessed 23 July 2024).

[98] 'Our Mission', *TikTok* [website], https://www.tiktok.com/about?lang=en (accessed 23 July 2024).

[99] 'The Walt Disney Company', *The Walt Disney Company* [website], https://thewaltdisneycompany.com/#:~:text=The%20mission%20of%20The%20Walt,the%20world's%20premier%20entertainment%20company (accessed 23 July 2024).

[100] 'Our Values', *WWF* [website], https://wwf.panda.org/discover/about_wwf/our_values/#:~:text=Our%20mission%20is%20to%20build,support%20current%20and%20future%20generations (accessed 23 July 2024).

[101] 'Impact Report 2023', *Tesla* [website], https://www.tesla.com/en_gb/impact (accessed 23 July 2024).

[102] 'Liquid Death', *Liquid Death* [website], https://liquiddeath.com/en-gb/pages/manifesto (accessed 23 July 2024).

[103] N. Asbury, *The Road To Hell: How purposeful business leads to bad marketing and a worse world. And how human creativity is the way out*, UK, The Choir Press, 2024, p. 190.

[104] 'Who we are', *EY* [website], https://www.ey.com/en_uk/about-us (accessed 30 September 2024).

[105] 'About IBM', *IBM* [website], https://www.ibm.com/uk-en/about (accessed 30 September 2024).
[106] *SAP* [website].
[107] Blackrock Investor Relations, 'L. Fink's 2019 Letter to CEOs. Purpose and Profit', *Wachtell, Lipton, Rosen & Katz* [blog], 22 May 2019, https://www.wlrk.com/docs/LarryFinksLettertoCEOsBlackRock.pdf (accessed 23 July 2024).
[108] S. Blount and P. Leinwand, 'Why are we here? If you want employees who are more engaged and productive – give them a purpose – one concretely tied to your customers and your strategy', *Northwestern University*, 1 November 2019, https://www.scholars.northwestern.edu/en/publications/why-are-we-here-if-you-want-employees-who-are-more-engaged-and-pr (accessed 25 August 2025).
[109] Mercer, 'Global Talent Trends 2018 Study', *Mercer*, 2018, https://mtshrm.org/images/downloads/2018_Compensation_Presentations/global_talent_trends__mercer.pdf
[110] N. Dhingra et al., 'Help your employees find purpose – or watch them leave', *pwc*, 5 April 2021, https://www.pwc.com/us/en/about-us/corporate-responsibility/assets/pwc-putting-purpose-to-work-purpose-survey-report.pdf (accessed 23 July 2024).
[111] 'Putting Purpose to Work: A Study of Purpose in the Workplace', *pwc*, https://www.pwc.com/us/en/purpose-workplace-study.html (accessed 23 July 2024).
[112] 'The Business Case for Purpose', *Harvard Business Review*, 2015, https://assets.ey.com/content/dam/ey-sites/ey-com/en_gl/topics/digital/ey-the-business-case-for-purpose.pdf (accessed 23 July 2024), p. 2.
[113] '2020 global Marketing Trends: Bringing authenticity to our digital age', *Deloitte*, 2020, https://www2.deloitte.com/content/dam/insights/us/articles/2020-global-marketing-trends/DI_2020%20Global%20Marketing%20Trends.pdf (accessed 23 July 2024), p. 8.
[114] 'The Business Case for Purpose', *Harvard Business Review*, 2015, https://assets.ey.com/content/dam/ey-sites/ey-com/en_gl/topics/digital/ey-the-business-case-for-purpose.pdf (accessed 23 July 2024), p. 6.
[115] N. Liddell, 'You Are a Fish. This is the Truth About Brands', *Baron Sauvage*, 2023, https://baronsauvage.com/wp-content/uploads/2023/05/You-are-a-fish.pdf (accessed 23 July 2024), p. 130.
[116] 'Why Employee Engagement is Key to Company Success', 13 May 3034, *FirstUp* [blog] https://firstup.io/uk/blog/employee-engagement-key-to-company-success/ (accessed 26 July 2024).
[117] R. Van Lee, Lisa Fabish and Nancy McGraw, 'The Value of Corporate Values', *Strategy + business a pwc publication* [blog], https://www.strategy-business.com/article/05206 (accessed 23 July 2024).
[118] P. Lencioni, 'Make Your Values Mean Something. Your Corporate Values Statement May Be Doing More Harm Than Good. Here's How to Fix It', *Harvard Business Review* [blog and magazine], July 2020, https://hbr.org/2002/07/make-your-values-mean-something (accessed 23 July 2024).
[119] 'Our Culture & Values. Fostering a Great Culture', *BMW* [website], https://www.bmwgroup.jobs/us/en/culture.html (accessed 23 July 2024).
[120] 'About Us', *Starbucks* [website], https://www.starbucks.co.uk/about-us (accessed 23 July 2024).

Notes

[121] 'Life at Airbnb', *Airbnb* [website], https://careers.airbnb.com/life-at-airbnb/ (accessed 23 July 2024).
[122] 'Connecting the World. Make Every Connection Matter.' *Meta* [website], https://www.metacareers.com/culture (accessed 23 July 2024).
[123] 'Ten Things We Know to be True', *Google* [website], https://about.google/intl/en-GB/philosophy/ (accessed 23 July 2024).
[124] 'The Toyota Way. Our Work Today is the Foundation For Tomorrow', *Toyota* [website], https://www.toyota-europe.com/about-us/toyota-vision-and-philosophy/the-toyota-way (accessed 23 July 2024).
[125] 'Conscious Culture. We Strive to Create a Culture Where All Employees Feel Safe and Can Thrive', *Cisco* [website], https://www.cisco.com/c/m/en_us/about/csr/esg-hub/people/culture.html (accessed 23 July 2024).
[126] D. Sull, Stefano Turconi and Charles Sull, 'When It Comes to Culture Does Your Company Walk the Talk?', *MIT Sloan Management Review* [blog], 21 July 2020, https://sloanreview.mit.edu/article/when-it-comes-to-culture-does-your-company-walk-the-talk/ (accessed 23 July 2024).
[127] Campaign India Team, 'Apple marketing VP: "Simplicity is not simple", *Campaign* [website] 23 June 2019, https://www.campaignasia.com/article/apple-marketing-vp-simplicity-is-not-simple/452651 (accessed 26 July 2024).
'"Our marketing ideas start with the product. Then we add a little touch of creativity" says Apple's Tor Myhren, "Simple becomes iconic. But Simplicity is not simple."' [online video], Presenter T. Myhren, *Cannes Lions International Festival of Creativity*, 9 July 2019, https://www.facebook.com/watch/?v=333107300956116 (accessed 26 July 2024).
[128] 'New Applied Now – Accenture Brand Refresh', *Graphis*, https://graphis.com/entry/492b3c22-9955-4abd-af1b-72a540d099f6 (accessed 13 September 2024).
[129] Liddell, 'You are a Fish. This is the Truth About Brands', p. 204.
[130] M. Johnson, *Branding in Five and a Half Steps*, UK, Thames & Hudson, 2016, p. 134.
[131] 'Purpose and Mission', *Mondelez International* [website], https://www.mondelezinternational.com/about-us/who-we-are/purpose-and-mission/#:~:text=people%20don't%20want%20to,of%20snacking%20around%20the%20world (accessed 23 July 2024).
[132] Mondelez International [website].
[133] Sutherland, p. 163.
[134] Sutherland, p. 121.
[135] Romaniuk, p. 14.
[136] 'Your Way, Way Better', *JonesKnowlesRichie* [website], https://jkrglobal.com/case-studies/burger-king/ (accessed 26 July 2024).
[137] 'Less is More. More or Less', *Studio Blackburn* [blog], https://studioblackburn.com/blog/less-is-more-more-or-less (accessed 12 August 2024).
[138] J. Halliday, 'Gap Scraps Logo Redesign After Protests on Facebook and Twitter', *The Guardian* [website], 12 October 2010, https://www.theguardian.com/media/2010/oct/12/gap-logo-redesign (accessed 23 July 2024).
[139] N. Zmuida, 'Tropicana Line's Sales Plunge 20% Post-Rebranding. OJ Rivals Posted Double-Digit Increases as Pure Premium Plummeted', *AdAge* [website], 2 April 2009,

https://adage.com/article/news/tropicana-line-s-sales-plunge-20-post-rebranding/135735 (accessed 23 July 2024).

[140] M. Reno, 'How Old Spice Rebranded Into An Advertising Sensation', *Brand Outlaw* [blog], 27 March 2023, https://thebrandoutlaw.com/old-spice-rebrand/ (accessed 23 July 2024).

[141] Model inspired by J. Romaniuk, figure 12.1 on p. 110 and Figure 12.2 on p. 112.

[142] 'Think Different: The DNA of breakthrough brand value growth', *Kantar* [blog], 14 July 2023, https://www.kantar.com/inspiration/advertising-media/think-different-the-dna-of-breakthrough-brand-value-growth (accessed 23 July 2024).

[143] 'Introducing Fluent Devices', *System1* [blog], 4 May 2017, https://system1group.com/blog/introducing-fluent-devices (accessed 21 September 2024).

[144] 'Findings. Distinctiveness by numbers', *JonesKnowlesRitchie* [website], https://bedistinctive.jkrglobal.com/findings#intro (accessed 30 July 2024).

[145] A. Sheridan, 'The Power of You. Why Distinctive Brand Assets are a Driving Force of Creative Effectiveness', *IPSOS*, https://www.ipsos.com/sites/default/files/ct/publication/documents/2020-02/Ipsos_Views_Power_of_You.pdf (accessed 23 July 2024), figure 5, p. 8.

[146] N. Mills, 'Formula 1 – Brand Identity', *Nick Mills* [website], https://www.nick-mills.com/formula-1-brand-identity (accessed 26 July 2024).

[147] Mills.

[148] 'Amazon's Chief Creative Officer on the power of emotional advertising, distinctive brand assets and delivering at speed', episode 123, *Uncensored CMO* [podcast], Presenter J. Evans, interview with J. Shoesmith, 28 February 2024, https://uncensoredcmo.com/123 (accessed 30 September 2024).

[149] N. Liddell, 'The brand strategist's toolkit #25: Distinctive Brand Assets and The Distinctive Brand Assets Grid', *LinkedIn* [website], https://baronsauvage.com/wp-content/uploads/2023/05/Baron-Sauvage_Toolkit_25_DBAs-and-The-DBA-Grid.pdf (accessed 26 July 2024).

[150] K. Deighton, 'Mastercard removes name from circles logo in act of digital "simplicity"', *The Drum* [blog], 7 January 2019, https://www.thedrum.com/news/2019/01/07/mastercard-removes-name-circles-logo-act-digital-simplicity (accessed 23 July 2024).

[151] 'The History of the CocaCola Contour Bottle. The Creation of a Cultural Icon', *The Coca-Cola Company* [website], https://www.coca-colacompany.com/about-us/history/the-history-of-the-coca-cola-contour-bottle (accessed 26 July 2024).

[152] T. Roach, 'A Rembrandt in the Attic: Rediscovering the Value of "Have you had your Weetabix"', *WARC* [blog], https://www.warc.com/content/paywall/article/ipa/a_rembrandt_in_the_attic_rediscovering_the_value_of_have_you_had_your_weetabix/en-GB/122398? (accessed 23 July 2024).

[153] 'Heinz Pour Perfectly', *Rethink Ideas* [blog], https://www.rethinkideas.com/work/heinz-pour-perfectly (accessed 12 August 2024); 'Heinz Ketchup Pour Perfectly, *Ads of the World* [blog], https://www.adsoftheworld.com/campaigns/heinz-ketchup-pour-perfectly (accessed 12 August 2024); 'How Heinz Reversed its Decline by Leveraging Product Truths in Amazing Ways', *On Strategy Showcase* [podcast], J. Morgan and M. Dubrick, https://www.onstrategyshowcase.com/episode/heinz (accessed 12 August 2024).

Notes

[154] 'WARC from Home: Distinctive Brand Assets – What They Are and Why They Matter', WARC [blog], 25 March 2020, ttps://www.warc.com/newsandopinion/opinion/warc-from-home-distinctive-brand-assets–what-they-are-and-why-they-matter/en-gb/3484 (accessed 23 July 2024).

[155] 'Another Dull Whitepaper: The Extraordinary Cost of Being Dull', p. 27.

[156] A. Sheridan, 'The Power Of You: Why Distinctive Band Assets are the driving force of creative excellence', *IPSOS* [blog], 19 February 2020, https://www.ipsos.com/en-uk/power-you-why-distinctive-brand-assets-are-driving-force-creative-effectiveness (accessed 23 July 2024).

[157] E. Penny, personal correspondence, 31 July 2024.

[158] 'The Economist Group Marketing communications creative guide', The Economist, 2018, https://design-system.economist.com/documents/The_Economist_Group_brand_marketing_style_guide-Dec-2018.pdf (accessed 23 July 2024).

[159] H. Bowler, 'McDonald's Scented Billboards Trigger Cravings For French Fries', *The Drum* [website], 10 April 2024, https://www.thedrum.com/news/2024/04/10/mcdonald-s-scented-billboards-trigger-cravings-french-fries (accessed 23 July 2024).

[160] Sutherland, p. 274.

[161] Sutherland, p. 296.

[162] Liddell, 'You Are a Fish. This is the Truth About Brands', p. 6.

[163] E. Ormesher, 'Smaller Images, Fewer Colors: 5 Ways to Make a Rebrand More Sustainable', *The Drum* [blog], 28 February 2023, https://www.thedrum.com/news/2023/02/28/smaller-images-fewer-colors-5-ways-make-rebrand-more-sustainable (accessed 30 July 2024).

[164] Romaniuk, p. xviii.

[165] S. Keller and B. Schaninger, *Beyond Performance 2.0, A Proven Approach to Leading Large-Scale Change*, New Jersey, USA, Wiley, 2019, p. 2.

[166] C. Dewar, S. Keller and V. Malhorta, *CEO Excellence: The Six Mindsets That Distinguish the Best Leaders from the Rest* New York, USA, Scriber an imprint of Simon and Schuster, 2022, p. 67.

[167] M. Symonds and L. Ellison, *Softwar*: an intimate portrait of Larry Ellison and Oracle / Matthew Symonds with commentary by Larry Ellison, NY USA, Simon and Schuster, 2004, p. 23.

[168] L. McCloskey, personal correspondence, 24 July 2024.

[169] R. Slater, *Saving Big Blue: Leadership Lessons & Turnaround Tactics of IBM's Lou Gerstner*, New York, McGraw-Hill, 1999, p. 93.

[170] D. Daines, personal correspondence, 8 September 2024.

[171] 'HPE The Best Part of Breaking Up', *Siegel + Gale* [blog], https://www.siegelgale.com/case-study/hpe/ (accessed 6 September 2024). M. Eagan, 'Welcome to the New Hewlett Packard Enterprise', *Siegel + Gale* [blog], https://www.siegelgale.com/welcome-to-the-new-hewlett-packard-enterprise/ (accessed 6 September 2024).

[172] J. Jackson, 'Introducing HPE's Simplified Brand Architecture', *HPE* [blog], 19 April 2023, https://www.hpe.com/us/en/newsroom/blog-post/2023/04/introducing-hpes-simplified-brand-architecture.html (accessed 6 September 2024).

[173] C. Heath and D. Heath, *The Power of Moments*, UK, Bantam Press, 2017, pp. 73–74.

[174] 'Accenture's CMO on B2B Brand Development', episode 237, *Renegade Marketing* [podcast], Presenter D. Neisser, interview with A. Fuller, 22 April 2021, https://

renegademarketing.com/podcasts/accenture-b2b-brand-development/ (accessed 20 September 2024).

[175] A. Beal, 'Issue #2: The Brand Strategy of Exchanges', *30,000 Feet* [blog], 31 January 2021, https://30000feet.substack.com/p/issue-2-the-brand-strategy-of-exchanges (accessed 26 July 2024).

[176] D. Robson, 'The Big Idea: How the "Protégé Effect" Can Help You Learn Almost Anything', *The Guardian*, 9 September 2024, https://www.theguardian.com/books/article/2024/sep/09/the-big-idea-how-the-protege-effect-can-help-you-learn-almost-anything (accessed 10 September 2024).

[177] Heath and Heath, chapters 3 and 4, pp. 45–92.

[178] Heath and Heath, p. 59.

[179] 'little hats, big difference', *innocent drinks* [website], https://www.innocentdrinks.co.uk/big-knit/about#accordion-b5fd0765e3-item-bcdd06042d (accessed 23 July 2024).

[180] A. Farnsworth, 'I Went to the Taco Bell hotel and It Was Certainly a Hotel with Taco Bell In It', Fodor's Travel [blog], 13 August 2019, https://www.fodors.com/world/north-america/usa/california/palm-springs-and-the-desert-resorts/experiences/news/i-went-to-the-taco-bell-hotel-and-it-was-certainly-a-hotel-with-taco-bell-in-it (accessed 23 July 2024).

[181] Creed and Muench, p. 122.

[182] B. Taylor, 'To Build a Strong Culture, Create Rules That Are Unique to Your Company', *Harvard Business Review* [blog], 3 December 2019, https://hbr.org/2019/12/to-build-a-strong-culture-create-rules-that-are-unique-to-your-company (accessed 23 July 2024).

[183] 'Zappos Only Hires People Who Are Weird and Lucky in Life', *Business Insider* [online video], 2011, https://www.youtube.com/watch?v=FDD5G2_6hdA (accessed 23 July 2024).

[184] B. Taylor, To Build A Strong Culture, Create Rules That Are Unique To Your Company, *Harvard Business Review* [blog] 3 December 2019, https://hbr.org/2019/12/to-build-a-strong-culture-create-rules-that-are-unique-to-your-company (accessed 30 July 2024).

[185] C. Wiley, 'What Motivates Employees According to Over 40 Years of Motivation Surveys', *International Journal of Manpower, Roosevelt University*, vol. 18, no. 3, May 1997, p. 263–280. https://www.researchgate.net/publication/235270159_What_Motivates_employees_according_to_over_40_years_of_motivation_surveys and '"The Recognition Gap" Make Sure Your Team Feels Appreciated', *Bellrock* [blog], 26 March 2018, https://bellrock.ca/learn/the-recognition-gap-make-sure-your-team-feels-appreciated/ p. 10 (accessed 28 July 2024).

[186] A. De Smet et al., 'Great Attrition or "Great Attraction"? The Choice is Yours', *McKinsey & Company* [blog], 8 September 2021, https://www.mckinsey.com/capabilities/people-and-organizational-performance/our-insights/great-attrition-or-great-attraction-the-choice-is-yours (accessed 23 July 2024).

[187] B. Sutton, 'Leaders Get the Behaviour They Display and Tolerate', Bob Sutton [blog], 2009, https://bobsutton.typepad.com/my_weblog/2009/11/leaders-get-the-behavior-they-display-and-tolerate.html (accessed 26 September 2024); H. Barbour, 'Does Your Organisation Suffer from Culture Creep?', Hilton Barbour [blog],

22 August 2021, https://www.hiltonbarbour.com/hiltonbarbourblog/2021/8/22/suffer-culture-creep (accessed 9 September 2024).

[188] D. Lee Yohn, *FUSION: How Integrating Brand and Culture Powers the World's Greatest Companies*, Massachusetts, USA, John Murray Press, 2021, p. 70.

[189] J. Dawes, 'Advertising Effectiveness and the 95–5 rule: Most B2B Buyers Are Not in the Market Right Now', *The B2B Institute on Linked In*, https://business.linkedin.com/content/dam/me/business/en-us/marketing-solutions/resources/pdfs/advertising-effectiveness-and-the-95–5-rule.pdf (accessed 23 July 2024).

[190] P. Weinberg and J. Lombardo, 'The 99:1 rule: How to Invest in a Recession', *Marketing Week* [blog], 23 January 2023, https://www.marketingweek.com/99–1-rule-invest-recession/ (accessed 23 July 2024).

[191] Jackson.

[192] Bass Model (New Product Diffusion), Number Analytics [blog], 2021, https://www.numberanalytics.com/tutorials/bass-model-new-product-diffusion (accessed 13 September 2024). 'Professor Frank Bass, *The Ehrenberg-Bass Institute for Marketing Science*, https://marketingscience.info/about-us/frank-bass/ (accessed 13 September 2024).

[193] L. M. Lodish and C.F. Mela, 'If Brands are Built over Years, Why Are They Managed over Quarters?', *Harvard Business Review*, July–August 2007, https://hbr.org/2007/07/if-brands-are-built-over-years-why-are-they-managed-over-quarters (accessed 13 September 2024).

[194] L. Binet, 'The Secret to Price Power with Les Binet', Ignite 2023 [speech/video], Kantar, YouTube, 24 April 2023, https://www.youtube.com/watch?v=zqJF7XMsLFM (accessed 13 September 2024).

[195] M. Valentine, 'Les Binet: Long-term Brand Building Plus Creative Advertising is the Key to Firmer Pricing', *Marketing Week* [blog], 21 April 2023, https://www.marketingweek.com/creativity-pays-les-binet/ (accessed 23 July 2024).

[196] L. Binet, 'The Secret to Price Power with Les Binet', Ignite 2023 [speech/video], Kantar, YouTube, 24 April 2023, https://www.youtube.com/watch?v=zqJF7XMsLFM (accessed 13 September 2024).

[197] As validated in 1,602 cases, in Ostler et al.

[198] D. Anderson, personal correspondence, 26 September 2024.

[199] Lodish and Mela.

[200] Lodish and Mela.

[201] L. Binet, 'The secret to price power with Les Binet', Ignite 2023 [speech/video], Kantar, YouTube, 24 April 2023, https://www.youtube.com/watch?v=zqJF7XMsLFM (accessed 13 September 2024).

[202] B. Carruthers, 'Beyond 60:40: putting effectiveness in context', *WARC* [blog], https://www.warc.com/content/paywall/article/event-reports/beyond-6040-putting-effectiveness-in-context/en-gb/124156? (accessed 22 July 2024). M. Valentine, 'Les Binet: Long-term brand building plus creative advertising is the key to firmer pricing', *Marketing Week* [blog], https://www.marketingweek.com/creativity-pays-les-binet/ (accessed 23 July 2024).

[203] A. Hamill, 'Les Binet on why long-term marketing matters in the age of short-termism', *WARC* [blog], 10 January 2020, https://www.warc.com/newsandopinion/

opinion/les-binet-on-why-long-term-marketing-matters-in-the-age-of-short-termism/en-gb/3307 (accessed 23 July 2024).

[204] J. Hurman and R. Dolan, 'The Awareness Advantage', *Tracksuit*, September 2024, https://www.gotracksuit.com/uk/the-awareness-advantage-report (accessed 20 September 2024), p. 7.

[205] Ostler et al., p. 22.

[206] 'use case', *Marriam-Webster dictionary* [website], https://www.merriam-webster.com/dictionary/use%20case (accessed 23 July 2024).

[207] Ostler et al., p. 22.

[208] A. Lyndon, personal correspondence, 23 September 2024.

[209] M. Kapadia, in conversation with R. Fairley and S. Behur, 20 April 2024 and personal correspondence, 10 September 2024.

[210] Average ROMI profit. Ostler et al., p. 45.

[211] M. Valentine, 'Les Binet: Long-term Brand Building Plus Creative Advertising is The Key to Firmer Pricing', *Marketing Week* [blog], 21 April 2023, https://www.marketingweek.com/creativity-pays-les-binet/ (accessed 23 July 2024).

[212] M. Jefferson, 'Study Finds Ad Effectiveness Does Nnot "Wear-out" Over Tme', *Marketing Week* [blog], 22 November 2022, https://www.marketingweek.com/study-ad-effectiveness-does-not-decline/ (accessed 23 July 2024). M. Ritson, 'Consumers Don't Get Tired of Ads, Only Marketers Do', Marketing Week [blog], 16 October 2023, https://www.marketingweek.com/consumers-tired-ads-marketers/ (accessed 23 July 2024).

[213] System 1 with IPA Effectiveness Database data, *The Magic of Compound Creativity, How consistency leads to creative quality, stronger brands and greater profits*, 2024, https://system1group.com/compound-creativity-system1-ipa (accessed 4 November 2024), pp. 9–19.

[214] A. Houston, 'Leo Burnett Reveals How it Raised Eyebrows With a Subtly Branded McDonald's Ad', *The Drum*, 19 January 2023, https://www.thedrum.com/news/2023/01/19/leo-burnett-reveals-how-it-raised-eyebrows-with-subtly-branded-mcdonald-s-ad (accessed 19 September 2024).

[215] Adam&eveDDB and Zenith Media, 'How Aviva's Advertising Built a Brand Fit for the Boardroom' for the IPA, *Aviva*, 2024.

[216] I. Rivers, personal correspondence, 20 September 2024.

[217] Kantar LIFT media effectiveness database analysis. Ostler et al., p. 41.

[218] G. Kite, 'In Brand Building it's the Little Things That Count Now', *Marketing Week*, 20 September 20204, https://www.marketingweek.com/grace-kite-brand-building-count/ (accessed 20 September 2024).

[219] S. Tookey, personal correspondence, 21 August 2024.

[220] 'How Cadbury turned "Glass and a Half in Everyone" into one of the most effective campaign ideas in the world.' episode 136, *Uncensored CMO* [podcast], Presenter J. Evans, interview with D. Boscawen and G Ferreira, 29 May 2024, https://uncensoredcmo.com/136 (accessed 23 July 2024).

[221] 'Another Dull Whitepaper: The Extraordinary Cost of Being Dull', p. 9.

[222] 'Another Dull Whitepaper: The Extraordinary Cost of Being Dull', p. 11.

[223] 'Another Dull Whitepaper: The Extraordinary Cost of Being Dull', p. 16.

[224] 'Another Dull Whitepaper: The Extraordinary Cost of Being Dull', p. 5.

Notes

[225] S. Dramalis, personal correspondence, 21 August 2024.

[226] R. Sutherland, 'Amanda Blanc interview: Insurance boss on fixing Aviva's troubles – a task that eluded a long procession of male bosses', *Daily Mail*, 21 December 2022, https://www.thisismoney.co.uk/money/markets/article-11559603/Ive-got-covered-Amanda-Blanc-fixing-Avivas-troubles.html (accessed 12 September 2024).

[227] All Aviva referenced covered in Adam&eveDDB and Zenith Media, 'How Aviva's advertising built a brand fit for the boardroom' for the IPA, *Aviva*, 2024.

[228] Cassidy et al., p. 21, figure 12.

[229] Cassidy et al., p. 18, figure 11.

[230] J. Hurman and R. Dolan, 'The Awareness Advantage', *Tracksuit*, September 2024, https://www.gotracksuit.com/uk/the-awareness-advantage-report (accessed 20 September 2024), p. 6.

[231] S. Foster, 'What is TVR', *MarketingIQ* [blog], 5 February 2024, https://www.marketingiq.co.uk/what-is-a-tvr/ (accessed 10 September 2024).

[232] Cassidy et al., p. 22, figure 13.

[233] J. Gitlin, 'What is a good Net Promoter Score? And how does it vary across industries?', *Survey Monkey* [website], https://uk.surveymonkey.com/curiosity/what-is-a-good-net-promoter-score (accessed 22 July 2024), p. 41.

[234] T. Grover and S. Lesser Wenk, *Winning: The Unforgiving Race to Greatness*, USA, Scribner, 2021, p. 48.

Index

Note: page numbers in *italic* type refer to Figures; those on **bold** type refer to Tables.

A
Abreu, Rapha 94
Accenture 43, 76, 83, 131
account-based marketing (ABM) 158–159
activation marketing *see* brand to demand
adam&eveDDB 181
Adidas 101
advertising
   boredom and dullness in 172–173
   brand diagnosis 38
   construct for 165–166
   media strategy 166–169
   promotional media assets 167–168
   reach and frequency 142, 143, 149, 163, 166–167, 185
   testing 164–165
   see also creative, marketing plan
affinity, Aviva 181–182
AI (artificial intelligence) 52, 116, 169, 170, 173
Airbnb 81
Airtel 103
Allers, Mia 113–114
Allianz 62
Altria Group 93
Amazon 17, 73, 98, 101, 135
Ambien 20
Amex 24, 71
Anderson, David 147

Andrex 102
animals, in brand identity 102
antithesis experiences (buyer experience and employee experience) 132
Apple 68, *69*, 83, 101, 103
acquisition, improving buyer 4, 182
Asbury, Nick 76
Asda 101
assets 6, 27, 38, 51 *see also* Distinctive Brand Assets
associations 6, 12, 27, 35, 38 *see also* brand strategy
attributes *see* brand identity; brand strategy (how we look, feel and sound)
Aviva 146, 164, 181–182
awards and rewards 136–137, 187
awareness
   awareness building tactics 157
   brand funnel *18*, 18–19
   Aviva 181–182

B
B2B (business-to-business) products and services 18, 20, 21, 26, 93, 100, 102, 143, 169, 172, 177, 181
B2C (business-to-consumer) products and services 18, 20, 181
Baileys 16–17
balance, and brand cohesion 10

209

Barbie 135
Barbour, Hilton 138
Barter, Phoebe 181
Bartle Bogle Hegarty 100
Bäte, Oliver 62
BAU (business-as-usual) 125, 126
behavioural science 47, 87
behaviours *see* brand strategy (who we are and how we do things)
beliefs *see* brand strategy (who we are and how we do things)
benchmarks and benchmarking 49, 54, 186
Benioff, Marc 27
Berkeley, The 88, 104, 130–131
Bezos, Jeff 73, 135
bill of materials *see* tactics
Binet, Les 147, 148, 149, 163
Birds Eye 102
Blackrock 77
BMW 80, 92
Boots 10
Booz Allen Hamilton 79
boredom, and marketing 172–173
bottom of funnel (BoFu) 18
brain lateralization 23
brand architecture 22, 145–146
brand archetype(s) 60, 83
  see also brand strategy
brand attributes 60, **67**, 80, 81, 83
  see also brand strategy (how we look, feel and sound); brand identity
brand beliefs 89, 60, **67**, 81
  see also brand strategy
brand behaviours 38, **67**, 79, 80–81, 86, **89**, 124, 187
  see also brand strategy (who we are and how we do things)
brand conviction springboard 60
  see also brand strategy
brand diagnosis 33–34, 55–56, 68, 80, 87
  analysis 54–55
  brand identity 109–110
  budgetary or time constraints 51–54
  cohesion 38–39, 40, *40*, 68
  difference 36–37, 39, *40*, 68

ease 37–38
implementation 130
leadership buy-in 55–56
marketing plan 164
rebrand remit 34–35
relevance 35–36, 39, *40*, 68
research sequencing 41–55
updating of 180
brand discriminator 60
  see also brand strategy
brand campaigns *see* brand to demand
brand codes *see* distinctive brand assets
brand driver 60, 62
  see also brand strategy
brand differentiation *see* difference (CRED factor)
brand essence 60
  see also brand strategy
brand funnel *18*, 18–19, 35, 48, 129, 139
  marketing plan 144, 148, 149, 152, 162, 164
  measurement 179, 180, 181, 182, 184, 186, 188
brand growth *see* growth
brand idea 60, 62
  see also brand strategy
brand identity 77, 91–92, 116–117
  accessibility 113
  budgetary and time constraints 116
  colour 94, 95, 97–99, 101, 107, *108*
  colour theory 98
  creative brief 110
  creative partners 110–111
  cultural issues 112–113
  dysfunctional 93
  fonts 94, 95, *108*
  getting buy-in 111–112
  guidelines 105–107
  how to change 104–107
  inclusivity 112–113
  ingredients and recipes 107–111, **108**
  legal aspects 111
  logos 95, 101, 107, *108*
  marketing plan 164
  need for change 92–95
  persona 102–103

210

Index

qualities of a good identity 95–97, *96*
risks 115
sound and sonic branding 103–104, 115
story 101–102
style guides 162
sustainability 113–114
training 138–140, 161–162
testing 114–115
trademarks 111
words 100–101
world of brand identity **50, 96**
see also Distinctive Brand Assets
brand key 60
see also brand strategy
brand ladder 60
see also brand strategy
brand onion 22, 60
see also brand strategy
brand mission 66, **67**, 75
see also brand strategy (why we exist)
brand passport 60
see also brand strategy
brand personality 27, 60, 64–94, **67, 89**, 103
  Burger King 94
  Coca-Cola 83
  Corinthia **66**
  eto **65**
  characters 102
  voice 103
  McDonald's **64**
  Salesforce 27
  see also brand identity; brand strategy (how we look, feel and sound)
brand philosophy 60
see also brand strategy
brand pillars 60, **89**
see also brand strategy
brand police 139, 106, 140
brand portfolio strategy 2
brand positioning 60, 64, 66, **67, 89**
  Corinthia **66**
  eto **64**
  IBM 16
  examples 63–66, 71–72
  see also what we do (brand strategy)

brand principles 60, 62, 66, **67**, 73, **89**
see also brand strategy
brand promise 60
see also brand strategy
brand purpose *see* purpose
brand pyramid 60, 62
see also brand strategy
brand prism 60, 62
see also brand strategy
brand salience *see* salience
brand signature 60
see also brand strategy
brand spirit 60, 66,
  see also who we are and how we do things)
brand strategy 28, 59–60, 62–63, 89–90
  brand diagnosis 38, 43
  brands beneath company brands 84–86
  connection with business strategy 61–62
  emotional response 23–24
  framework 67–84
  and implementation 124–125
  marketing plan 164
  and marketing strategy 142, 144
  outsourcing 86–87
  presentation and buy-in 87–88
  terminology 62–63
  see also how we look, feel and sound; what we do; who we are and how we do things; why we exist
brand style *50*, 60, 62, *96*, 101, 102
  animation 111
  illustrative 94–95
  photography 109
  see also brand strategy; how we look, feel and sound; brand identity
brand to demand 141–173
  for employees 172–173
  see also marketing strategy
brand truth *see* brand strategy
brand valuation studies 26, 72
brand values *see* values
brand vision *see* vision
brand voice *see* tone of voice

211

Index

branding, definition of 28
branding strategy or strategies *see* brand strategy
brandmarks, in brand identity 101
brand plan *see* brand to demand
British Airways 103
Brooks 12
budget, marketing strategy 148–150
Burberry 100, 101
Burger King 94
business development department 128
business growth *see* growth
business strategy iv, 61–62
   brand diagnosis 38, 43–44
   business growth 137, 159, 176, 182, 191
   see also growth
   marketing strategy 142
   what we are aiming for 61, *89*
   what we are focusing on 61, *89*
   where we play 61, *89*
buyer experience 132, 134
   antithesis experiences 132
   cohesion or ease improvements 133
   hygiene experiences 132
   post-purchase 132, 134
   pre-purchase 132, 134
   purchase 132, 134
   remarkable moments 123, 133, 135–137, 140, 141, 159, 164, 177, 186–187
   repurchase 132, 134
buyers
   brand diagnosis 36
   brand funnel *18*, 18–19
   brand growth 4
   decision-making 5–6, 144
   identification of 44, 143–144, **144**
   marketing plan impact measurement 184
   reason for shopping 19
   research 46–49, 52, 179–180
   search intent 159
   stealing from competitors 17
   terminology 8
   see also buyer experience

C

Cadbury 24, 71–72, 85, 98, 104, 170
   brand strategy 71, 72–73, 84, 85
campaign lines, in marketing 154
car manufacturers, scent engineering 104
case studies 13, 14, 15, 16, 23, 25, 26, 72, 181
Casper 74
campaigns *see* brand to demand
Category Entry Points (CEPs) 19–20, 185–186
   brand diagnosis 35, 37, 51, 55
   brand strategy 85
   buyer research 48–49
   marketing strategy 143–144, **144**
CEOs (chief executive officers)
   brand strategy 66–67
   implementation 124, 127, 130
   media strategy 168
celebrity spokesperson 102–103
Cessario, Mike 27
call to action 106, 108, 111, 125, 127, 131, 157, 163, 167–168, 171
change, resistance to 122
characters, in brand identity 102
channels, marketing 128, 166, 168, 169
ChatGPT 52
Cisco 68, *69*, 71, 82
Claridge's 20, 88, 104
Clear M&C Saatchi 83
clients *see* buyers
client experience *see* buyer experience
climate-conscious brand identities 113–114
CMOs (chief marketing officers) 9–10, 168
Coca Cola/Coke 72, 83, 92, 100
cohesion (CRED factor) 6–7, **8**, 9–11, **28**, **29**, 133, 178
cohesion improvements (buyer experience and employee experience) 133
   brand diagnosis 38–39, 40, *40*, 49, 68
   brand identity 94–95, 112
Colonel Sanders 102
colour, in brand identity 94, 95, 97–99, 101, 107, *108*

communications 9, 29, 83, 97, 126, 128, 150, 154, 158
Compare the Market 102
competitors, brand diagnosis 37, 38, 47, 51, 53–54, 68
Connaught, The 104
connection, Distinctive Brand Assets research 50–51
connective tissue 168–169
consideration (brand funnel) *18*, 157
consistent, consistency, consistently and inconsistent 6, 9, 79, 62, 96–97, 99, 101, 106, 112, 117, 124–125, 138–139, 150, 163, 168, 176
and investments 150
see also cohesion
consumers *see* buyers
COO (chief operating officer) 125
copyright 111
Corinthia 17, 20, **66**, 88, 94, 160
Corona 19
creative brief, brand identity 110
creative, marketing plan 162–166
CRED (**C**ohesive, **R**elevant, **E**asy and **D**ifferent) factors **8**, 9–27, **28**, **29–31**
brand identity 93–95
marketing strategy 176–180
measurement of improvements 177–180
see also cohesion (CRED factor); difference (CRED factor); ease (CRED factor); relevance (CRED factor)
Creed, Greg 12
C-suite 12, 127
brand identity 111–112, 115
cultural contexts 11, 99
brand identity 112–113
cultural and market shifts 15–16
marketing plan 169–172
culture, organizational 136, 138
cultural codes 176, 15
customer experience or journeys *see* buyer experience
Cunningham, Sheila 17

customer service 22, 128
customers *see* buyers

D
Daines, Duncan 16
Daroukakis, Amy 53
Dawes, John 143
'default male' 52
Deloitte Digital 86
demand generation *see* brand to demand
demand generation campaigns *see* brand to demand
de-merger *see* brand architecture; mergers and acquisitions
Design Council 113–114
Diagnosis *see* brand diagnosis
difference (CRED factor) 6, 7, **8**, 24–27, **28**, **31**
brand diagnosis 36–37, 39, *40*, 68, 80
brand identity 94
brand strategy 76–77
market changes 177
marketing strategy 179–180
digital channels 168
digital marketing 128, 159, 167–168, 184
digital storage, brand identity 116
digital asset management (DAM) *see* digital storage, brand identity
discounting *see* pricing
Disney 76, 100
Distinctive Brand Assets 37, 40, 47, *50,* 48, 53, 77, *96*, **108**, 185
brand identity 96–97, 101, 102, 107, 109, 110, 117
marketing plan 160, 164
research *50,* 50–51
Adidas 101
Airtel 103
Amazon 98, 101
Andrex 102
Apple 101, 103
Asda 101
Aviva 164
Berkeley, The 88, 104
Birds Eye 102

213

Index

BMW 92
British Airways 103
Burberry 100, 101
Cadbury 98, 104
Claridge's 104
Coca-Cola 92, 100
Compare The Market 102
Connaught, The 104
Corinthia 94
Disney 100
Doritos 100
Duolingo 102, 103
Economist, The 103, 104
F1, Formula 1 97, 98
Gatorade 73
Geico 102
Google 100
Headspace 102
Heinz 101–102
Hewlett Packard Enterprise 103
IKEA 101, 102
Innocent 103
Intel 103
KFC 100, 102
Lego 100
Lek Trek 102
Liquid Death 25–26
Lloyd's 102
Louis Vuitton 100
MailChimp 103
Mastercard 99–100
McDonald's 92, 99, 100, 103, 104
Mini 102
Minor Figures 102
Monzo 99
Netflix 103
Nike 11, 99, 101, 103
Oatly 103
Old Spice 95
OREO 101
Pret 103
Red Bull 102
Salesforce 26, 102
Skittles 101
Starbucks 92
Target 101

Tiffany's 98
Toblerone 100
Tony The Tiger 102
UPS 98
Viagra 99
Volvo 102
X (Twitter) 101
distinctiveness 25
 see also difference (CRED factor)
Dolan, Rory 150, 183
Doritos 15, 27, 100
Dove 13, 71, 84
Dramalis, Sotis 173
dullness, and marketing 172–173
Duolingo 102, 103

E
ease (CRED factor) 6, 7, **8**, **28**, **30–31**
 of attention to 22–24
 brand diagnosis 37–38, 49, 68
 to find, navigate and buy 20–22
 implementation 133
 ease improvements (buyer experience and employee experience) 133
 marketing strategy 148, 178–179
 to mind 19–20
 of recognition 24
 of use 22
eatbigfish 172
easy to buy 19, 21, 26, 31, 37, 142, 148, 179
easy to mind 6, 19, 24, 28, 142, 162
 see also mental availability
Echodyne Corp 122
Economist, The 103, 104
Ehrenberg-Bass Institute for Marketing Science 4, 5, 20, 24, 100, 143
Eisner, Michael 9
Ellison, Larry 122
emotions
 and attention 23–24
 brand diagnosis 37, 38
 brand strategy 68, 72
 emotive clarity 25
Employee Net Promoter Score (eNPS) 36, 178

Index

Employee Buyer Net Promoter Score (ebNPS) 36, 178, 184,
employee engagement 7, **8**, 12, **28**, 132–134, 136–137, 138–140
employee experience
  antithesis experiences 132
  cohesion or ease improvements 133
  departing stage 132, 134
  hygiene experiences 132
  onboarding stage 132, 134
  recruitment stage 132, 133
  remarkable moments 123, 133, 135–137, 140, 141, 159, 164, 177, 186–187
  reward and recognition 136–137, 187
  thriving stage 132, 134
employees
  brand diagnosis 36, 38, 39
  brand growth 7, **8**, 22, **28**
  brand relevance to 12
  brand to demand 172–173
  customer service quality 22
  implementation 132, 133–134, 136–137, 138–140
  marketing strategy 178–179, 187
  quantitative research 49–50
  reasons for quitting 136–137
  see employee experience
employer brand 10, 187
  see also brand strategy; employee engagement
eto **64–65**
EY 76, 77, 78

F

F1 *see* Formula 1
failure, reasons for 122
familiarity
  brand funnel *18*, 19
  brand identity 92, 95
  marketing plan tactics 157
Farrow & Ball 19
favicons, in brand identity 101
favourability
  brand funnel *18*, 19
  marketing plan tactics 157

field marketing colleagues 128
Field, Peter 149, 172
file naming 161
films, in brand identity 102
  see also video
finance
  and pricing 146–148
  and implementation 127
finance, and implementation 127
Fink, Larry 77
fluency 97
fonts, in brand identity 94, 95, 100, 101, *108*
Formula 1 97–98
Four Seasons 17
Franklin, Sarah 14
frameworks
  brand framework *see* brand strategy
  marketing framework *see* marketing strategy; marketing plan
freelancers, use of 116
full funnel marketing *see* marketing strategy; marketing plan
Fuller, Amy 43
funnel *see* brand funnel

G

Gadre, Anil 11
Galloway, Scott 132
Gamma Aviation 16
Gap 95
Gatorade 53, 73
Geico 102
gender data gap, synthetic research 52
Gerstner, Lou 124
Global Talent Trends Study, Mercer 78
Google 81, 100
Grover, Tim 188
growth
  attracting more buyers 4, **8**, **28**
  CRED (**C**ohesive, **R**elevant, **E**asy and **D**ifferent) factors **8**, 9–28, **28**, **29–31**
  how brands impact 3–4
  improving employee engagement, decision-making, cohesive working practices 7, **8**, **28**
  rebrand remit 7–8, **8**

stretching into new sources of revenue 4, **8**, 16–17, **28**
supporting price increases 5–7, **8**, **28**
growth marketing *see* brand to demand
growth mindset 75
Gymshark 21

H
Harvard Business Review 78
Headspace 102
Heath, Chip 130, 135, 136
Heath, Dan 130, 135, 136
Hegarty, John 149
Heinz 101–102
heuristics 4, 5, 97 *see also* easy to mind
Hewlett Packard Enterprise 74
  brand architecture and naming strategy 146
  brand identity 93, 103
  brand launch 126
  see also HP
Holly Yashi 70
Horowitz, Ben 136
Hosterman, Holly 70, *70*
how we look, feel and sound (brand strategy) 60, 63, **67**, 82–84, **89**, *103*
  Burger King 94
  Cadbury 72, 85
  Coca-Cola 83
  Corinthia **66**, 94
  Economist, The 103, 104
  eto **65**
  characters 102
  voice 103
  McDonald's **64**, 83
  Sage 94
  SAP **63–64**
  Salesforce 27
  Taco Bell 15
  HP 126
  Hewlett Packard Enterprise (HPE) 126
HR
  brand cohesion 10
  brand diagnosis 39, 44–45, 53
  brand to demand for employees 172–173

implementation 128, 133–134
policies 134
see also employee experience
humility 76
Hurman, James 150, 183
Hutchinson, Clare 72–73
hygiene experiences (buyer experience and employee experience) 132

I
IBM 16, 17, 76, 77, 79, 82, 124
icons, in brand identity 99–100
IKEA 82, 101, 102
implementation 121–123, 140–141
  brand diagnosis 130, 139
  brand identity 138–140
  brand strategy 124–125, 132–138, 139
  crucial partnerships 127–129
  employee engagement 132–134, 136–137, 138–140
  identifying success 140
  launches 129–131
  leadership engagement 42, 121, 123–125, 129
  marketing strategy 173
  objectives 123
  rewarding and recognizing on-brand impact 136–137
  setting up and leading 125–127
  timescale 125–126
  values 138
imposter syndrome xiv, 171
industry analysts 131
influencers 12, 36
Innocent 103, 135
Innovation 74, 77–78
  Eto **64**
  Hewlett Packard Enterprise (HPE) **74**
  investment in 146
  Nike 14, 71
  product innovation 75
  Salesforce 14
  Taco Bell 15
insights 34, 41, 42, 45, 46, 54, 55, 87, 128, 159

216

Institute of Practitioners in Advertising (IPA) 4, 75, 172
integrated marketing *see* marketing strategy; marketing plan
integrity, 79, 82 and brand cohesion 11
Intel 75
internal communications 133
  see employee engagement; leadership engagement
intention (brand funnel) *18*
IPSOS 6, 97, 103
IT, operations and facilities 128

J
Jackson, Jim 126
jargon xiv, 4, 22, 62, 86, 171
Jobs, Steve 71
Johnson, Michael 84

K
Kantar 3, 5, 6, 16, 17, 19, 21, 25, 27, 96, 152, 158, 166, 167
Kantar Marketplace 53
Kapadia, Mehul 160
Key Performance Indicators *see* measurement
KFC 100, 102
  see also Colonel Sanders
Kickstarter 65
Kite, Grace 166–167

L
laddering 85
  messaging ladder 154–155, **155**
  'So What?' ladders 68, *69*, 70, *70*
Lafley, A. G. 60, 61
Landor 53, 83, 93
launch *see* brand launch (implementation)
leadership xv, 12, 28–29, 34–35, 38, 41–45, 56, 62, 71, 80, 84, 87–88, 126–127, 129–130, 137–138, 149–150, 164–165, 176–177, 187
leadership engagement 42, 121, 123–124, 129
lead generation *see* brand to demand

lead generation campaigns *see* brand to demand
legal issues, brand identity 111
Lego 100
Lek Trek 102
Lencioni, Patrick 79–80
Liddell, Nick 78–79, 98, 110
likeability *see* affinity
Liquid Death 25–26, 27, 76, 148
Lloyd's 102
localization, marketing plan 169–172
Locus 160
Lodish, Leonard M. 147
logos, brand identity 95, 101, 107, *108*
[the] long and the short 10, 29, 38, 149–150, 186
Long-term marketing *see* brand to demand
lookalikes *see* brand growth
Louis Vuitton 100
loyalty, customers or buyers 4, 114, 147, 159
Lyndon, Alisha 158–159

M
Mace, Michael 52
Magic Numbers 166
MailChimp 103
Management of Change (MoC) 125
market changes 176–177
market segmentation 143–144, **144**
marketing
  boredom, blandness and dullness in 172–173
  implementation 128
marketing plan 141–142
  barriers and language 171–172
  brand to demand for employees 172–173
  Category Entry Points **152**, 152–153, **155**, 159
  creative 162–166
  cultural context and localization 169–172
  impact measurement 183–185
  media strategy 166–169

messaging that ladders 154–156, **155**, **156**
programmes structure 150, **151**
tactics 156–162, 171
Marketing Qualified Leads (MQLs) 184
marketing strategy 28, 141–142
  brand diagnosis 43
  brand to demand for employees 172–173
  budget 148–150
  buyer choice 144
  CRED (Cohesive, Relevant, Easy and Different) factors 176–180
  decisions in 143–150, **144**
  identifying buyers, market segmentation and Category Entry Points 143–144, **144**
  implementation 173, 185–187
  place/ease of buying 148
  pricing 146–148
  priority products and services 145–146
  SMART objectives (Specific, Measurable, Achievable, Relevant and Time-bound) 148
Markey, Pete 10
Martin, Roger L. 60, 61
Mastercard 9, 40, 99–100
Maybourne 104
McCloskey, Leo 122
McDonald's 10, 61, **64**, 83, 164
  brand identity 92, 99, 100, 103, 104
McGilchrist, Iain 23
McKinsey 66, 78, 122, 136–137
meaningful *see* relevance
measurement 175–176
  adjusting implementation plans 185–187
  brand CRED improvements 177–180
  impact of rebrand 181–182
  market changes 176–177
  marketing plan impact 183–185
  of your own progress 188–189
media strategy 166–169
Mela, Carl F. 147
'mental availability' 4, 19
  see also easy to mind
Mercer, Global Talent Trends Study 78
Mere Exposure Effect 92
Mergers and Acquisitions (M&A) 4, 7, 16

messaging ladder 154–155, **155**
Meta 75
  values 81
metrics *see* measurement
Microsoft 75, 84, 85
Mills, Nick 97
Mini 102
Minor Figures 102
mission 66, 75
  see also brand strategy
moments, remarkable (buyer experience and employee experience) 130, 133, 135–136
momentum 187–188
Momentum ITSMA 158
Mondelez 84, 85
monograms, in brand identity 99–100, 101
Monzo 99
Muench, Ken 12
Myhren, Tor 83

N
Nadella, Satya 75
naming strategy 101, 145–146
need states 19
  see also Category Entry Points (CEPs)
Netflix 103
Net Promoter Score (NPS) 36, 48, 49, 179, 186
neurons 33
neuroscience 4, 5, 8
  see also chapter 1
neuro testing 100
Nike 12, 13–14, 71, 82
  brand identity 99, 101, 103
  'Just Do It' slogan 11, 14
nodes, network of 6
nomenclature, in brand identity 101
  see also naming strategy
north star *see* brand strategy (what you do; why you do it)

O
Oatly 103, 148
Ogilvy 16, 87
Old Spice 95

One & Only 131, 135
Oracle 122
OREO 101
organizational culture 136, 138
outsourcing 42, 86–87

P

packaging, in brand identity 100
Pampers 68, *69*
Paris 20
partnerships with customers 160
pattern, in brand identity 100
penetration, improving market 4
  see also acquisition, improving buyer
Penny, Emily 103
perceptual leadership 25, 27, 39
performance 7, **8, 28**, 150, 183
performance marketing *see* brand to demand
P&G 95
persona 102–103
personality *see* brand personality
Phillip Morris Companies Inc. 93
'physical availability' *see* easy to buy
principles *see* brand strategy (who we are and how we do things)
pipeline 173, 181, 184
Pisani, Alfred 66
Pizza Hut 135
positioning *see* what we do (brand strategy)
post-purchase (buyer experience) 132, 134
predispose 5, 6, 25, 156
  definition 5
  see also predisposition
predisposition 4, 6, 19, 23, 25, 172
  see also predispose
pre-purchase (buyer experience) 132, 134
Pret 103
pricing
  marketing strategy 145–146, 146–148
  price increases, and brand growth 5–7, **8, 28**
products
  marketing plan **153**, 155

marketing strategy 145–146
Programme Management Office (PMO) 125, 126
Project Management Office (PMO) 56
promotion *see* advertising; communications
promotions *see* pricing
price elasticity 185, 127, 147, 148
provenance, in brand identity 102
public relations 150, 158
  see also communications
purchase (buyer experience) 132, 134
purpose 60, 62, 63, **67**, 74–79, **89**
  see also why we exist (brand strategy)
pwc 78, 84, 85

Q

qualitative research
  brand diagnosis 36
  brand identity 114–115
  buyers 46–47, 52
quantitative research
  brand diagnosis 36
  brand funnel 18
  brand identity 114
  buyers 48–49
  Distinctive Brand Asset *50,* 50–51
  employees 49–50

R

RACI (Responsible, Accountable, Consulted, Informed) 127, 133
RAG (Red Amber Green) status, brand diagnosis 39
Rahman, A. R. 103
reach and frequency 142, 143, 149, 163, 166–167, 185
Realm 166
rebranding 93
  rebranding right definition xiv
  measuring impact of 181–182
  reasons to xv, 3
  rebrand remit 7–8, **8**, 34–35
  stretch goals 81–82
  see also the whole book!
recency bias 164

recognition 24
  Distinctive Brand Assets research 50–51
recruitment experience or journey *see* employee experience
Red Bull 102
refresh xiii–xv, 3, 7, 28, 34, 41, 83, 85, 97, 113, 115, 116, 182
reinvigorate *see* refresh
rejuvenate *see* refresh
relevance (CRED factor) 6, 7, **8**, 11, **28**, **30**
  at all stages of buyer's journey 18–19
  brand diagnosis 35–36, 39, *40*, 68
  brand identity 94–95
  to buyer's reason for shopping 19
  to cultural and market shifts 15–16
  market changes 177–178
  marketing strategy 178, 179, 180
  to the right people 11–12
  stretching 16–17
  to what people care about 12–15
relative strengths *see* difference (CRED factor)
remarkable moments (buyer experience and employee experience) 123, 133, 135–137, 140, 141, 159, 164, 177, 186–187
repurchase (buyer experience) 132, 134
reputational damage, and brand identity 93
research
  buyers 46–48
  competitor audit 47, 51
  Distinctive Brand Assets *50*, 50–51
  existing research and data 46
  interviewing leaders 45–46
  outsourcing 42
  research sequencing, brand diagnosis 41–55
  researcher skill and experience 45
  sample sizes 49
  synthetic 52
  updating of brand diagnosis 180
  see also qualitative research; quantitative research
Restaurant Brands International 94
Rethink 102
revenue, impact of marketing strategy on 184–185
reward and recognition *see* awards and rewards
Rivers, Izzie 166
Robson, David 133
Romaniuk, Jenni 20, 51, 92, 96, 117
Rosewood 17

S

Sage 20, 23–24, 94
  'Boss It' campaign 23–24
sales activation 148, 171
sales department, and implementation 128, 158, 171
Sales Qualified Leads (SQLs) 184
Sales Qualified Opportunities (SQO) 184
Salesforce 14, 26, 27, 72, 102, 135
salience 4, 6, 19, 96, 163
  see also easy to mind
sample sizes, research 49
SAP 20, **63–64**, 76–77, 173
scent/smell in brand identity 104
search engine optimization (SEO) 171
search intent 159
segmentation *see* market segmentation
services
  marketing plan **153**, **155**
  marketing strategy 145–146
shapes, in brand identity 99–100, 107, *108*
Sharp, Byron 5, 6, 11, 19
short-term marketing *see* brand to demand
silos 22, 136, 159
Skittles 101
shareholder brand 10
slogans
  in brand identity 100
  in marketing 154
SMART objectives (Specific, Measurable, Achievable, Relevant and Time-bound) 126, 133
  marketing strategy 148
'So What?' ladders 68, *69*, 70, *70*
social media 169
sonic branding, in brand identity *see* sound

SoS (share of search) 36, 184
sound, in brand identity 103–104, 115
Southwest Airlines 71
Spence, Roy 47
spokespeople, in brand identity 103
stakeholders 55, 77, 111, 115, 124, 160, 168, 176
  see also crucial partnerships (implementation)
Starbucks 80, 92
stealing, of buyers from competitors 17
stop, start, continue 88, 132–133
story, in brand identity 101–102
storytelling 137, 160
straplines *see* taglines
stretching the brand 76–77, 81–82
  brand growth 4, **8**, 16–17, **28**
style guides 162
sub-brands 112
suppliers, and implementation 128, 131
SurveyMonkey 49, 186
sustainability, and brand identity 113–114
Sutherland, Rory 47, 87, 88, 104
Sutton, Bob 138
symbols, in brand identity 99–100
synthetic research 52
System 1 thinking 97
  see also easy to mind; heuristics
System1 97, 149, 163, 172

T
Taco Bell 15, 135
tactics
  burn out
  marketing plan 156–162, 171
  reusing and recycling 159–160, 163
taglines
  in brand identity 100, 103, 154
  in marketing 154
Target 101
talent experience or journey *see* employee experience
taste, in brand identity 104
TESLA 76
thought leadership xiv, 157

Tiffany's 98
TikTok 27, 76, 98, 183
Timberlake, Justin 103
Toblerone 100
tone of voice 95, 103–104, 158, 161–162, 163, 170
  training 161–162
top of funnel (ToFu) 18
Tookey, Sarah 169
Total Addressable Market (TAM) 143
touch, in brand identity 104
touchpoints 9, **29**, 122, 132, 139
  see also tactics; buyer experience; employee experience
Tony The Tiger 102
Toyota 82
Tracksuit 150, 183
training 138–140, 161–162
trademarks 111
transcreation and translation 112–113, 170
  see also localization
trends 25, 35, 41–42, 53, 78
Tropicana 95
TV advertisements, brand recognition 24
Twitter (X) 101

U
UK Government Digital Service 113–114
Unique Selling Propositions (USPs) 25
UPS 98
usage occasions 4, 11, 16, 19
  see also Category Entry Points (CEPs)
User Experience (UX) 168

V
value 79–81
  'perceived value' and rebranding 5
values 15, 36, 40, 49, 66, **67**, 79–81, 85–86, **89**, 103, 104, 124, 138, 160, 153
  Airbnb 81
  BMW 80
  Corinthia **66**
  Cadbury 72
  eto **65**
  Google 81
  McDonald's **64**

Index

Meta 122
overused 79
Starbucks 80
Zappos 136
see also brand strategy (who we are and how we do things)
'verbal brand driver' 62
VCCP 72–73
Viagra 99
video
  tactic 160
  measurement 184
vision, 60, 61, 63, 66, **89**
  SAP 63
visual identity *see* brand identity
voice, tone of 95, 103–104, 158, 161–162, 163, 170
Volvo 102

W
W hotel 135
Walmart 135
Walt Disney Company *see* Disney
WARC 4, 102
watch-outs 17, 35, 48, 49, 73, 76, 81, 84, 86, 90, 98–99, 105, 111, 115, 125, 129, 134, 138, 145, 153, 159, 161–162, 169, 171–172, 187,
web journeys 168, 170
Weetabix 100
what we do (brand strategy/business strategy) 63, **67–68**, 69, *70*, 70–74, *89*
  Baileys 16
  Casper 74
  IBM 16
  Gatorade 73
  Hewlett Packard Enterprise 73–74, 146
  Amex 71
  Apple **69**
  Aviva 81
  Cadbury 71–72
  Cisco **69**, 71
  Corinthia **66**
  Dove 13, 71
  eto **64-65**
  Mastercard 40

McDonald's **64**
Pampers **69**
Salesforce 72
SAP **63**
Southwest 71
Taco Bell 15
who we are and how we do things (brand strategy) 63, **67**, 79–82, *89*
  Airbnb 81
  Amazon 73
  BMW 80
  Cisco 82
  Corinthia **66**
  eto **64–65**
  Google 81
  IBM 82
  IKEA 82
  McDonald's **64**
  Meta 81
  Nike 82
  Salesforce 14
  SAP **63–64**
  Southwest 71
  Starbucks 92
  Toyota 82
  Zappos 136
why we exist (brand strategy) 63, **67**, 74–79, *89*
  Accenture 76
  Apple **69**
  Cisco **69**
  Corinthia **66**
  Disney 76
  eto **65**
  EY 76
  IBM 16, 76
  Intel 75
  Liquid Death 26, 76
  McDonald's **64**
  Meta 75
  Nike 14, 71
  Pampers **69**
  Sage 23
  SAP **63**
  TESLA 76
  TikTok 76

WWF 76
Wieden+Kennedy 95, 97–98
Williams, Pharrell 103
Within People 131
Wood, Orlando 23, 149
world of brand identity **50, 96**
 see also brand identity
wordmarks, in brand identity 101
Wunderman Thompson 23–24
WWF (World Wildlife Fund) 76

X
X (Twitter) 101

Y
Yohn, Denise Lee 7, 138
YouGov 53

Z
Zajonc, Robert 92
Zappos 136

A quick word from Practical Inspiration Publishing...

We hope you found this book both practical and inspiring – that's what we aim for with every book we publish.

We publish titles on topics ranging from leadership, entrepreneurship, HR and marketing to self-development and wellbeing.

Find details of all our books at: www.practicalinspiration.com

Did you know...

We can offer discounts on bulk sales of all our titles – ideal if you want to use them for training purposes, corporate giveaways or simply because you feel these ideas deserve to be shared with your network.

We can even produce bespoke versions of our books, for example with your organization's logo and/or a tailored foreword.

To discuss further, contact us on info@practicalinspiration.com.

Got an idea for a business book?

We may be able to help. Find out more about publishing in partnership with us at: bit.ly/PIpublishing.

Follow us on social media...

- @PIPTalking
- @pip_talking
- @practicalinspiration
- @piptalking
- Practical Inspiration Publishing